A WRONGFUL DEATH

A
WRONGFUL
DEATH

ONE CHILD'S FATAL ENCOUNTER WITH PUBLIC HEALTH AND PRIVATE GREED

Léon Bing

VILLARD ♜ NEW YORK

Bing, Léon.
    A wrongful death: one child's fatal encounter with public health and private greed / Léon Bing.
      p.   cm.
    ISBN 0-679-44841-1
    1. Psychiatric errors—United States—Case studies. 2. Scheck, Christy. 3. National Medical Enterprises—Corrupt practices. 4. Hospitals, Proprietary—Corrupt practices—United States. 5. Psychiatric hospitals—Corrupt practices—United States. 6. Insurance crimes—United States. 7. Teenagers—Suicidal behavior—United States—Case studies. 8. Wrongful death—United States—Case studies.   I. Title.
RC455.2.E76B53   1997
362.2—dc21   96-50338

Random House website address: http://www.randomhouse.com/
Printed in the United States of America on acid-free paper
9 8 7 6 5 4 3 2
First Edition
Book design by JoAnne Metsch

For my family,
with love and appreciation

ACKNOWLEDGMENTS

MY DEEPEST APPRECIATION is for Neil Olson, who represents my work as he sustains, supports, consoles, and guides me. Thank you, Neil, and everyone else at Donadio and Ashworth.

With similar fervor, my thanks to Ernie Villany, who is always there for me, without fanfare or fuss.

I am indebted to Craig Nelson, who has led me through the madness of three books without losing either his edge or his cool.

I'm grateful to Brian Siberell, who is always a few blocks ahead of me. CAA's gain is mine, as well.

My gratitude to Mike Seigal for his steadfast determination to represent his authors in the best possible ways. I thank him for his judgment and his smarts.

My thanks also to Tim Chen, whose indefatigable good humor soothes like lotion on a sunburn.

My appreciation to David R. Olmos, that fine journalist who dug into his own files in order to help out during those times when my spirit began to flag.

My thanks to psychiatrist James Mapps and psychoanalyst James S. Grotstein, both of whom gave unstintingly of their time and knowledge. This book would have been greatly diminished without their help.

My gratitude to Annik LaFarge, Melissa Milsten, Dan Rembert, Leta Evanthes, and Brian McLendon of Villard, who shepherded this project to completion. My thanks also to associate copy chief Beth Pearson and copy editor Margaret Wimberger for their clear thinking and endless patience.

My love and gratitude to the following dear friends, all of whom have covered my back at one time or another: Lydia and

Kevin Bartlett, Stuart Timmons, Larry Dubois, Asa Baber, Barbara Flood, Regina Scott, Sandie Wells, Shaherazad Arzani, Eric Ashworth, David Ailjanian, Paul Karlstrom, Lou N., and the great Lucy herself, Sierra Pecheur.

My appreciation for their help to FBI agents Keith Moses and Rob Hunt; Assistant Attorney General Rick Ybarra of Texas; Bill Landreth and Cindy Speight of the Department of Defense; Ed Dueñez; and Barbara Demming-Lurie.

Thanks to attorneys Douglas Campion, Rick Seltzer, Christopher Cody, and Craig Dummit. A special note of thanks to litigation paralegal Mary Back Ruiz.

My thanks to all the other kids (and their parents) who so generously shared their time and experiences with me. Tyler, Lynn, Shannon, Jack, Mike: You were great; there just weren't enough pages.

And, finally, my deepest love and appreciation to Woofie and Diz Bing, the finest dogs in the world, and to the spirit of Dexter Bing, the best cat ever.

A WRONGFUL DEATH

PREFACE

AT THE BEGINNING of the eighties I was living in the Hollywood Hills with Babe Vincenzo,* a middle-range player in American cocaine distribution. He bought in bulk: kilos of pure solids that he broke down into ounces and sold to a phalanx of dealers who, in turn, provided much of the Hollywood A list with its social necessaries.

Over the course of a few months Babe and I became friendly with the man who lived next door. Larry was a loner, an award-winning journalist who had written extensively about crime and covert government operations. He was drawn to the mix of genuine wise-guy sensibility and low-key toughness that made up Babe's personality, and he told us that Babe reminded him of a young outlaw he had interviewed for anonymous quotes in an article about smuggling. He often said that he wished we could meet him. And one evening Alex Balter* came to call. He was, at that time, free on bail as he waited for word on his appeal after a conviction on conspiracy to import and possession of a controlled substance with intent to distribute.

Alex Balter would never have been spotted as a criminal. He looked more like a junior bonds salesman or a fourth-year dentistry student. He might even have been taken for a high school senior, if his hair had not been shot through with gray. His handshake was firm and warm, his manners nearly courtly, but when Alex looked at you, it was always with cool, quiet scrutiny.

The three of us clicked, and a friendship got under way as Babe and Alex shared stories about their adventures in the drug trade.

*For reasons of privacy, I have changed the names of certain individuals; these are indicated by an asterisk at the first appearance.

Babe talked about growing up in an Italian neighborhood in Queens, New York; Alex described his childhood in a Baltimore row house with a working mother and a Hassidic grandfather who read the Talmud to him. It was when the two men talked about the product they sold that I noticed the great disparity between them. Babe had spun a romantic aura about the cocaine itself: To him it was the stuff of dreams; the bundles of cash he pulled in were secondary. Alex loved to get high, as we all did, but his focus was on the money. He maintained an icy detachment to everything but his profit line.

Babe gave away enormous sums of money ($75,000 once, in cash, to a near-stranger) to anyone with a hard-luck story. Alex had stashed just under $2 million in a numbered account in the Cayman Islands. He had a string of art galleries bringing in taxable income, and a newly purchased 240-foot freighter. The freighter, with fifty tons of prime Colombian weed in her hold, was cruising toward the Pacific Northwest coastline when a Coast Guard cutter sounded its alarm. Alex and his crew managed to jettison thirteen tons of cargo before the freighter was boarded and they were taken into custody. He learned, during his trial, that the attorney he kept on retainer to take care of business had relieved him of most of his holdings before dropping a word to the authorities.

When Alex lost his appeal, he went on the run. He was arrested three months later in South America and brought back to the United States to begin serving an eight-year sentence in a federal prison. I was placed on his visitors list and drove out to see him about six months later. By that time Babe and I were no longer together, and I had stopped using drugs.

Alex's appearance was a surprise: He was leaner, more fit than I'd expected, and his skin was deeply tanned. He looked as if he'd been away on holiday. He showed me the tennis courts where he played daily games of doubles, then walked me past the rock garden that he and another inmate had designed and planted. We talked about his Colombian wife, Maria,* and her weekly visits to the prison bringing in hampers filled with iced lobsters and

caviar, imported cheeses and biscuits. Alex seemed almost con-
tented.

He was released approximately three years later. We spoke on
the telephone from time to time, and one Friday I drove up to his
Santa Barbara estate to see him. Maria, who had two children by a
previous marriage, was newly pregnant, and the family had a long
lease on a splendidly furnished Spanish Colonial villa surrounded
by acres of terraced gardens. Alex was greatly changed: He was no
longer tanned, and he spent most of the weekend curled into a nest
of pillows he had arranged on the floor of a cedar-paneled, win-
dowless closet off one of the guest bedrooms. He kept two things
in there with him: an antique snuff bottle filled with China White
heroin, and a tiny spoon with which to snort it.

Maria called me a month later. Alex was at the point of physical and mental collapse; she needed help in finding a detox hospital where he could get clean.

I had been attending Twelve Step meetings to combat my years
of reliance not only on the cocaine itself, but on the luxe lifestyle
selling the drug provided. At one of the meetings I renewed an
acquaintance with a man I'd met a few years earlier when he was
a power player in the motion-picture industry. He was clean now,
and working as a drug counselor at one of the private psychiatric
hospitals that had begun to mushroom up around Los Angeles.
He had seen it all and done it all. He was legendary in Hollywood
for his ability to play the game. If anyone could move unerringly
through the Byzantine construction of Alex Balter's mind, it was
this guy. I called Maria with his name and the number of the
hospital.

Two days later Alex arrived at my house. He had taken a taxi
from Santa Barbara. He was disheveled and dirty. He was sodden
with drugs. And he was ready to put it all into somebody else's
hands. I loaded him into my car, and we drove in silence to the
hospital. The place looked unthreatening: a single-story sprawl
with adobe walls and a tiled roof laced with bright pink
bougainvillea. I parked in the adjoining lot and walked Alex into

the lobby, where I spoke to a woman seated at a desk behind a glass partition. Then we settled down to wait. There were no other people in the room, which was furnished with a couple of sofas and several chairs, all upholstered in fake leather. There were a few paintings, the kind you see in banks, and a spread of magazines and pamphlets laid out on a long wooden table. Alex dropped heavily into one of the chairs and closed his eyes, and we sat in silence until a door at the end of the room swung open and three staff members came to collect him. As I watched him shuffle out of the lobby, I wondered how long it would take before he checked himself out of treatment.

Alex spent nearly two months in the hospital, and it cost close to $60,000, which he paid in cash. But he got off drugs. And became a believer. The next time I saw him was at a Twelve Step meeting. He was six months clean, and it showed. He looked healthier and seemed to be happier than at any time since we'd met. He told me that Maria, her two sons, and the new baby were still living in Santa Barbara, but that he had taken a small apartment in L.A. and was now working at the same hospital in which he had been a patient. It was the best gig he'd ever had, he said, because he knew, for the first time in his life, that he was doing something that counted. He was giving back a little of what he himself had been given.

Sounded good.

I asked what kind of work he was doing. He told me that he was a "tech," short for mental-health technician, and that he functioned as a kind of unofficial counselor and all-around aide to the licensed hospital personnel. He was assigned to the adolescent unit, and he loved it. Then he said something that surprised me: He asked if I might be interested in applying for work at the same hospital.

What the hell. I needed a job.

A few days later I drove to the hospital, which was located on the other side of the Hollywood Hills on a heavily traveled street in the San Fernando Valley. I was interviewed briefly and given a cursory medical examination; my eyesight and hearing were tested and blood was drawn. Two days later I was hired as a part-time mental-health technician. It was late summer, 1985; I would be paid approximately $4.75 an hour, no benefits. My training consisted of an eight-hour tour of the adult unit, during which time I was shown how to take blood pressure and how to make notations on patients' charts. Everything else, including how to deal with the patients, seemed to be largely a matter of common sense.

About a month into the job I became friendly with one of the other techs, a young woman who had been on staff for over two years. Bridget had gotten clean while serving time for car theft; her boyfriend, a lowrider, had been the actual perpetrator, but rather than name him, Bridget had gone to prison. She was now in her mid-twenties, a smart, pretty blonde who saw the world in a clear light but managed to remain unembittered by her experiences. She filled me in about charting, explaining that it was the single most important aspect of the job as far as management was concerned. One night, over coffee in a twenty-four-hour diner near the hospital, she told me a story to illustrate the point.

An adolescent patient's mother filed suit against the hospital after she learned that her son had been placed in restraints. A patients' rights advocate had been called in, because restraints were not to be used unless it had been clearly charted that the boy was "dangerously acting out." The notation on the kid's chart made no mention of dangerous behavior.

Bridget shook her head and allowed herself a small smile before she continued. "Patients' rights really stormed in after that one. Restraints are *not* supposed to be used, but if it can be documented in the behavior log that the kid is dangerously acting out, it's okay. So writing down every little thing in the book was suddenly a real big thing." She lit another cigarette from the stub of the one she had going. "Things changed pretty radically for a while after that. But the hospital felt threatened by the loss of power, so the staff got told to 'be creative. Use your imagination.' "

She caught the expression of disbelief on my face.

"No, really. They called it 'manipulating words.' We were told to twist the new rulings so that, in effect, nothing would change. If, for example, a kid wrote on the wall, he wouldn't get punished by having to do fifty push-ups; he'd be given a writing assignment about defacing other people's property, and he'd be put on Reflection Time, sitting alone in the hall, no talking, for as many hours as his treatment team chose, with enough writing assignments to keep him busy. And, on the chart, the punishment gets changed into something that sounds therapeutic: 'Reflection Time.' "

As a part-time tech, I was to fill in the ratio of four or five techs to eighteen to twenty patients per unit. I would work on both the adult and adolescent units, wherever I was needed. Each patient was given a treatment team, which consisted of a psychiatrist, drug and mental-health counselors, outside therapists who came on an hourly basis, and the techs. My hours would be from 3:00 P.M. to 11:00 P.M., the night shift. I would be available to all treatment teams and to each patient on the unit. I made sure that patients showed up when and where they were expected. I did head counts at group meetings and during recreation periods. I'd escort patients through the locked doors of the units to the outside areas for volleyball games and general relaxation. I would go with those patients who were allowed to leave the grounds, in the hospital van, to recovery meetings. At the meetings, another tech and I would make sure that none of the patients went off unescorted. On weekends I'd go along on outings to carefully selected movies and to the zoo. During visiting hours I might be stationed to sit in the hall outside the unit, checking names on a list, buzzing the approved visitors through to the other side. I would help conduct spot searches of patients' rooms after weekend passes, or if there was a suspicion of hidden contraband. Whatever duty I pulled, I was always to be available to speak with and observe the patients. My immediate superiors were the unit managers, usually ex-techs who had been bumped up the line.

Techs were expected to go through all incoming patients' belongings in search of such items as drugs, medications, liquor, and "sharps"—razors, scissors, tweezers. Techs who sat in on group meetings were free to offer their opinions, particularly those slanted toward the belief that every patient had deeply rooted problems, the surface symptoms of which were addiction and/or alcoholism. Since most of the techs (as well as the counselors) were in recovery themselves, the language exhibited a marked conformity, with particular emphasis placed on shared beliefs about "denial" and "surrender."

The adolescent patients in particular needed convincing. Most of the kids felt a keen sense of betrayal because they had been tricked into a locked unit by their parents. Tracy* was a fifteen-year-old girl who had been told by her mother, a television producer, that she was being brought to the hospital for inoculations so that she could spend the summer in Europe with her father. Tracy was eager to get away from her mother; it seemed as if they couldn't agree about anything anymore. There were constant arguments about Tracy's friends, the music Tracy listened to in her room, her grades, her clothes, even the smell of cigarettes on her breath; her mother was convinced that Tracy was smoking pot. A few months tooling around Europe with her father sounded great—well worth the price of a couple of shots.

The afternoon she arrived, while her mom whispered to a woman sitting at a desk behind a glass partition, Tracy looked idly around the lobby of the single-story building. Her eyes slid past a door at the far end of the room, stopped, went back for a second look. The slick of light green paint couldn't mask it: This door was made of steel, and it had some serious locks in place. The small window set in at eye level was reinforced with a wire grid, and the glass was tinted for one-way viewing.

That's when it hit Tracy. She wasn't here to get any shots; this was one of those places for teenage psychos. And her mother was about to get her locked up.

Tracy bolted. She was on the other side of the heavy glass door that led to the street before her mother could turn around. She hesitated for an instant, looking right and left, then she raced toward the intersection at the end of the block. And she was almost to the corner when she heard the thud of footsteps behind her. She picked up the pace, but she was grabbed at the entrance of a Jack-in-the-Box by three male techs from the hospital. She saw a fast image of the Jack's clown head laughing down at her before she was hauled, like so much mail, back to the hospital and into a locked unit.

"Welcome to the fuckin' ding ward."

It was a boy's voice, but Tracy could tell no more than that. She knew only that about twenty kids were watching as she was bundled through a room furnished with a TV set, a Ping-Pong table, and some beat-up chairs and sofas. The chairs had been chosen for maximum weight and heft, as Tracy would learn later, when she tried to pick one up with the intention of throwing it.

She was taken past a nurses' station and into an examination cubicle, where she was handed a small booklet published by the California Department of Mental Health. The booklet spelled out the rights of minors, among them the right to an independent clinical review, the right to be heard before a judge, and the right to see a patients' rights advocate. Tracy did what many of her peers in similar positions do: She assumed the small book was a list of hospital rules, and she threw it into a corner of the room without looking at it.

Tracy's mother had been hovering at the periphery of this small procession, crying a little, speaking in short, urgent bursts to anyone who would listen. She was sorry she'd had to do this—she had no choice. She blamed Tracy's attitude, her grades, the running away, the threats. And the moods. The *moods*. Tracy shouted her mother down and salvos of angry words arced between them. Then her mother was politely hustled out of the examination room by a female tech, a nurse brushed past them on the way in, and the business of commitment got under way.

It was decided, after her mother left the hospital, that Tracy would be placed on a one-on-one. This is hospital jargon for a continuous close watch, and it carried—in 1985—an additional cost of $100 a day. A one-on-one was prescribed for any patient who exhibited disturbing behavior or who was considered to be an AWOL or suicide risk. There was a proviso: The patient's insurance had to cover the extra cost (unless, as in Alex Balter's case, it was a rare self-pay scenario). If the coverage would pay only $50 extra, the patient was placed on close observation ("close op") and checked on, usually by a tech, every fifteen minutes. If there was no coverage for such extra services, the patient at risk was observed normally, as part of the general population.

Tracy had already tried to run, she was crying uncontrollably, and her mother's insurance provided full coverage. Tracy was placed on a one-on-one and assigned to me.

I would remain at Tracy's side, at a distance of no more than arm's length, until my shift ended at eleven o'clock. If she sat on the floor in the corner of the room she'd be sharing with two other girls, I would sit with her. When it was time to eat, trays would be brought to us from the cafeteria. (As a new patient, Tracy would not be allowed off-unit for at least two days.) When she needed to use the bathroom, I would stay with her. At night I would sit next to the bed as she slept, and when I went home, another tech would take over.

When a one-on-one was ordered for an incoming patient, the assigned tech was expected to convince the patient that he or she had been brought, by whatever means, to the place where they needed to be. We were also expected to remain alert for any comments, however idle, that might lead to a dual diagnosis such as behavior disorder and depression (and, of course, always, addiction and alcoholism). A dual diagnosis was considered a sure indication of the need for long-term treatment, and in 1985 insurance companies were still lenient about lengths of stay. With adolescents, we were also to listen for any complaint that might be construed as parental abuse.

Tracy was so angry at having been tricked by her mother that she was near hysteria. This was dangerous, because if she slipped over that edge, she could easily wind up in restraints, which would have involved being carried, by as many techs as it took, to a bed with a bare mattress in an otherwise unfurnished cubicle at the far end of the unit, where she would be placed in a spread-eagle position and her wrists and ankles would be secured by padded leather straps attached to the four corners of the iron bed frame, which was bolted to the floor. This was referred to as "four-point restraint." At twenty-minute intervals a tech would look in through the small window set into the door, and in most cases the straps would be removed within an hour or so, but the patient might be kept in the room for as long as twenty-four hours. It was a frightening and demeaning procedure.

"ALL THE KIDS in the hospital with me got lied in. And sooner or later, every one of 'em ended up in restraints."

I met Jason* at a Twelve Step meeting a couple of years after he had been hospitalized, at fifteen, by his parents. He had been ditching school and running the streets, sleeping in laundromats when he was too stoned or too tired to make it home. His older brother finally cornered him at a convenience store near their house and convinced Jason to go outside and speak with their father, who was waiting in the car. Jason was so exhausted that he didn't argue when his father suggested a physical examination.

The exam was painless enough, but Jason noticed that the doctor had locked the door of his office. Still, he didn't feel threatened until the doctor suggested that they go to the patients' cafeteria. That seemed strange to Jason, but he went along with it. In the cafeteria the doctor, who was younger than Jason's father, slumped back in his chair, took off his glasses, and rubbed the bridge of his nose. Then he leaned over and, in a conversational tone, asked Jason if he was addicted to drugs. Jason looked at the doctor as if he were nuts and kept on spooning up ice cream. Then the doctor asked Jason how he felt about staying in the hospital for a few weeks. Jason told him no way. The doctor didn't say another word; he got to his feet and gestured to somebody behind Jason. That's when the kid went off. It took four people to subdue him, and he wound up in restraints.

A week later Jason convinced another boy on the locked unit to kick in a Plexiglas window while he himself made a disturbance. Both boys wriggled out the broken window, and Jason ran for a narrow passageway between two buildings. Then, with a hand and foot spanning either wall, he began to inch his way up to the roof. The other boy was unable to follow, but Jason got away.

That night he was found by private security guards in the alley behind the same convenience store and taken back to the hospital in handcuffs.

Jason made three more AWOL attempts, using a different method each time. Once he barreled into two maintenance workers as they came onto the locked unit with their cleaning carts. Another time he rotated across the court and over a fence during a volleyball game. Each time he was caught and hauled back to the hospital.

"Some of those kids I was locked up with are in jail now, and some are just regular people, but one thing's for sure: That hospital didn't do jack-shit for me. I never even got to see my so-called psychiatrist. All I ever got was an obedience course, like a dog. The staff was always into your shit there, trying to get you to cop to stuff, trying to get you to tell them shit that had happened to you, or tell them you were a junkie, or whatever. I kept fighting them for a long time, then I wised up and, every once in a while, I'd give them something to feed on. Just to keep them off me. Like, I'd say I was a thief, that I'd stolen a bunch of stuff. Well, then they'd really get on your shit: 'What did you steal? Why did you steal?' So then you'd just make up some more shit."

Two years later Jason still believed that he came out of the hospital a worse rebel than before he was taken in. "Hey, there's no way I trusted my parents after that. From then on it was all about, 'Fuck you. You want bad? I'll give you bad.' "

He went on a rampage of thieving and drug abuse that brought him to his knees. His probation officer sent him to a recovery program, and we met when he had been drug-free for nine months. He was adamant in his conviction that if he had not been tricked into a hospital he might have made an effort to take a look at his problems before they took him down.

SOME KIDS, A few, got lucky in the hospital.

Lisa had been brought in by her parents because they believed that some time spent in a controlled environment might convince their sixteen-year-old daughter—as well as themselves—that life at home didn't have to be a constant battle. Lisa had been willing enough to come to the hospital, but her attitude changed during the first week. At a group meeting, when asked by a counselor to describe her real feelings toward the hospital, Lisa said she thought "it was fucked." She was punished with a time-out, and because her insurance covered it, a one-on-one was ordered.

Adolescent patients placed on a time-out were sent into an empty room. The door was locked from the outside, and for the next hour or two, the kid simply sat on the floor. There was no furniture in a time-out room, no bed or chair, no napping or reading allowed. Kids in time-out were left to sit there, alone with whatever was going on in their head. Many kids who received this punishment went into rages—crying, screaming, kicking, hitting out with their fists—and, as a result, were placed in restraints.

I had been assigned as Lisa's one-on-one, but because this was a time-out, we were forbidden to speak to each other. She crouched, knees to chin, in one corner of the room. I sat on the other side, facing her. She refused even to look at me, and in truth, I didn't blame her. I was part of the unfairness.

We were sitting like that when there was a soft rap on the door. The sound surprised me: Nobody knocked in this place.

Lisa's head lifted as a conservatively suited young black man walked into the room. His eyes flicked past me and came to rest on the girl in the corner. She dropped her head back onto her knees and closed her eyes again. The young man introduced himself as the doctor who would be taking care of her while she was in the hospital.

No response.

He moved in closer but maintained enough distance from Lisa so that she would not feel threatened. Then he did something else that surprised me: He sat down, cross-legged, on the floor and waited. It didn't take long before her eyes opened, and only then did he speak.

"Lisa is one of my favorite names . . . maybe because it's the name of a girl in a movie I like. In this movie, Lisa is a girl about your age, and she's a patient in a hospital similar to this one."

The girl regarded him with a fixed, reptilian gaze.

"She would only speak once in a while, and when she did, it was in rhyme. Everything she said, even when she was angry, rhymed like poetry. In one scene, Lisa was sitting on the floor, drawing, and one of the attendants wanted her to get up and do her artwork at a table."

Lisa's position remained unchanged, but the lizard stare was gone. She had begun to listen.

"The attendant kept trying to get Lisa to sit at the table, but she didn't say a word. She just kept shaking her head, and she went on with her drawing. But finally, I guess she figured she had to an-swer him, so she said . . ." He paused. "Do you want to take a guess as to what it was?" He waited only long enough to see that the girl was not yet ready to speak. "She said, 'You're a bore. A big, fat bore.' "

Lisa blinked once, looked over at me, looked back at him.

"That's right. Lisa told him what she thought about him. And then she said, 'You're a bore, and I sit on the floor. I sit on the floor, but I don't watch the door.' And then she looked up at this guy, and you could see that she was hoping he'd catch on and say some-thing back in rhyme. But he didn't get it. So Lisa spoke again. This time she said, 'I sit on the floor, but I'm not a bore. Because I'm . . .' "

He paused again, looking at her.

". . . more . . ." It was only a whisper, and she turned her head away from his as soon as she spoke, but it was a beginning. He had found the way to make that initial connection.

Ten years later, when I spoke to the same psychiatrist in connection with this book, he smiled, recalling his first meeting with Lisa in the time-out room. "These days," he said, "if an insurance company heard that you were sitting on the floor, talking rhymes to a kid on a locked unit, they'd express outrage and call it fraud."

I learned, soon after I began work, that the assignment of a doctor to a particular patient pretty much depended on the luck of the draw. Although the hospital was owned by a psychiatrist, he had virtually nothing to do with the patients. His relationship was with the hospital. There were, of course, other psychiatrists on staff, like Lisa's doctor, who worked primarily with adolescents and the patients on the children's unit. There was a taciturn, sour-looking man who had appeared in a famous movie during the sixties, as a dim-witted college basketball player. His patient list at the hospital was confined to the adult unit. And there was a man in his late sixties who wore a Santa Claus beard and affected an oppressively hearty manner. He sported a button that said, DAMN, I'M GOOD!, and he urged his patients to shout out that mantra several times each day. On Halloween he came to work dressed as Merlin.

There were two or three counselors on duty during the day in both the adult and the adolescent units. One in particular, a woman named Sierra, was able to slice through the veils of self-pity and rationalization in which so many of the adult patients shrouded themselves. Sierra had traveled a hard road back from the night when she witnessed the murder of her husband by a thief who had broken into their home. She had come back from alcoholism and suicidal depression, and she knew how to share her survival skills. She was tough and fair; she earned the respect and trust of people who had, before coming into the hospital, listened only to those voices that told them exactly what they wanted to hear. Sierra shared an office and worked closely with the man who counseled Alex Balter. They made a formidable team, but their efforts were often undercut by unwitting and usually undertrained techs.

The techs were the frontline workers; they had the most consistent daily contact with the patients. Some, like Alex Balter, had been patients themselves. Others, like me, had been drafted from the ranks of newly recovering addicts and alcoholics. We were an odd mix. There was Alex, who was able to use the cunning and savvy learned on the streets and in prison to deal with kids who considered all adults to be fools. There was a young tech on the adult unit who had been in his final year of medical school when he burned out on speed. He was highly intelligent, but he lacked the capacity to empathize with people; he was efficient but lifeless. Another tech had, at one time, been an outlaw biker. He was ardent in his desire to follow a program of strict sobriety, but he looked scary and often behaved in a bullying manner. There was the thirtyish guy who had been a minor player at the fringes of the motion-picture industry until he discovered there was more money to be made in the cocaine business. He was hired about a week after I began, and he came to work wearing a doctor's coat with a stethoscope draped casually around his neck. It took the better part of a week before one of the nurses called him on it. A female tech on the adolescent unit had been a punk rocker. Her whitened hair was spiked and sprayed into points, and she was partial to black leather miniskirts. The kids loved her, and she was good at her job, but she developed a somewhat more than clinical interest in a seventeen-year-old patient, a hot-eyed little ex-hustler who had been placed in rehab by the juvenile courts. After a couple of months on the adolescent unit, he turned eighteen, was released, and moved in with the tech. It made a buzz of in-house gossip for a day or two, but in the end the front office looked the other way.

Both the adolescent and the adult units swarmed with unreleased sexual tension. Many of the so-called adult patients were in their late teens and early twenties, and as their focus slid away from getting high, they began to search out other obsessions. Flirtations flared and ebbed in a single day; notes were passed; allegiances sworn. Most of the on-unit romances remained chaste, but the techs were kept on a constant lookout for patients sneaking a few moments of forbidden privacy in linen closets and shower stalls.

The children's unit was the saddest place in the hospital. The patients here ranged in age from six to thirteen, and there were about fifteen of them. I would see them sometimes in the cafeteria, shepherded by uniformed psychiatric nurses. One afternoon I stepped into line directly behind the group. A boy who couldn't have been older than eight looked up at me and smiled. I smiled back, and he reached out to take my hand. We stood together in line like that, and I used my tray to push his along the counter. We didn't speak, we simply moved along in companionable silence. When the counter came to an end, I loosened my hold on his hand, and he turned and held up both arms for a hug before he carried his tray to a table at the far end of the room.

I didn't see the boy again for a couple of days. But the next time we were in the cafeteria at the same time, he ran up to me for another hug. A few days later I passed the group from the children's unit as they were being led outside for a play period. This time they all clamored for hugs.

The following day I was informed by one of the psychiatric nurses that hugging could prove to be counterproductive to the course of treatment prescribed for these children. When I asked for a description of the kind of treatment that precluded affection, she declined further conversation.

I would learn, years later, that the boy had been in the hospital for three years when I first saw him in the cafeteria. His pathology had mutated during the time he was kept on a locked unit: He could no longer adjust to living at home or indeed in any environment other than that provided by a psychiatric hospital.

I worked part-time at the hospital for approximately three months—long enough to learn that the length of stay prescribed for most patients depended on how much health insurance they had. And long enough to learn that too many parents, having reached a crisis point, were willing to turn their kids over to almost anybody, or any place, that had credentials. In virtually every instance, insurance paid for everything. And everything cost. The basic fee for each patient, in 1985, was $800 a day. Everything else was extra: group meetings, sessions with psychiatrists, counselors, and therapists, who were, in turn, paid a flat rate. Fully computerized tests, such as the MMPPI (Minnesota Multi-Phasic Personality Inventory), which were mandatory, went for $250 each. Biofeedback sessions, in which the patient sat back in a lounger and listened to relaxation tapes, cost $125 an hour. When one parent complained about the extra $10,000 tacked onto her bill, the response from the business office was, "Your son's alive, isn't he?"

One of the more disturbing aspects of the treatment program was a series of group meetings, conducted on a bimonthly basis, by one of the outside therapists, a psychologist whose sessions with adolescent girls inevitably dredged up recollections of parental molestation. Police cars would subsequently arrive at the facility and investigations would commence. I don't know how many of these "memories" proved out; it seemed patently clear that a wildfire of group hysteria erupted at every session.

In the end, none of it mattered very much. Once the insurance ran out, the kid was back out there, in the same environment, with the same set of problems, regardless of the stage of treatment.

My job as a tech didn't last long. I had a tendency to argue—usually from the standpoint of the kids—at staff meetings.

By the end of the eighties the hospital was closed due to lack of profit. That was the exact term used when one of the counselors called me with the news. She added that the psychiatrist/owner's "Malibu lifestyle wasn't being maintained."

According to statistics compiled by the National Institute of Mental Health, there were 450 freestanding psychiatric facilities at the beginning of this decade. That number had swelled by at least half in 1995. Charter Medical Corporation operates nearly 200 hospitals nationwide, and National Medical Enterprises (NME) ran even more than that until a federal investigation forced it to shut down its chain of psychiatric facilities, which were subsequently taken over by Charter. Both Charter and NME were listed on the major stock exchanges at the beginning of 1995. In fact, at that time fewer than two dozen investor-owned systems were operating 80 percent of all psychiatric beds.

DURING THE POSTWAR era of the 1950s, the "business of medicine" was considered to be something of an oxymoron. If you were sick, you went to the family doctor, and if you were unable to make the trip to his office, he came to you on a house call. It was still pretty much a George Bailey world back then: Every community had its own small hospital where you could go to have a baby, to get a broken bone set or a cut stitched. That small hospital also provided something of a release valve for your family if the problems you were experiencing were essentially psychiatric. The family doctor might make a diagnosis of "nervous exhaustion"— a good enough reason, in the fifties, to get you admitted to the hospital for a couple of weeks. No one looked at your records to see if hospitalization was really necessary, and it would have been unthinkable for a family member to question the decision. The doctor-patient relationship was held as sacred.

If you lived in a city, your doctor might suggest a course of treatment with a psychiatrist. In the mid-fifties, that cost about $50 for fifty minutes, and you paid for it out of pocket. Health insurance did not cover psychiatric treatment until the next decade. Some patients carved out the time and the money for daily sessions; others found that a weekly visit kept the demons at bay. For more serious problems there were hospitals like the Menninger Clinic in Topeka, Kansas, and the Scripps Clinic (now owned by Tenet Healthcare) in La Jolla, California.

It was not common practice in the fifties for psychiatrists to document their treatment. In fact, it would have been considered unethical to do so. What went on during that fifty-minute hour was between the doctor and the patient. If charting was done, it was encrypted, and each psychiatrist or psychoanalyst had his or her own shorthand, minimalist notes to remind themselves of their thinking on each case. But as insurance coverage expanded, during the sixties, to include psychiatric care, it became increasingly apparent that documentation was as significant as the treatment itself.

By the end of the fifties, conditions had begun to change for some of those family doctors. If you were enterprising, and if you had a good income stream coupled with a keen business sense, you could start up your own mini–medical industry: a hospital, a clinic, a lab. The health care system was still in its infancy, and there were no laws that restricted doctors from maintaining proprietary interest in any level of health care. By the mid-sixties you could bring a regular patient to your clinic and perform all diagnostic tests and services in your own lab, with equipment that you owned. Then you could send the patient to a pharmacy that you either owned outright or held a proprietary interest in. You could make a profit on each step of health care and still be perceived as a benevolent practitioner. You could be looked upon, without censure, as a rich man. It was all relative, of course: In rural communities defined by a main street with a single intersection, it was expected that the doctor would own the bigger house, the newer car. Things changed when the federal government decided that M.D.'s had too much power and pulled the plug with legislation; it became illegal for doctors to have proprietary interests in health care. A doctor could still own a pharmacy, a clinic, or a diagnostic service, but it was against the law for that doctor to steer a patient in that direction. With these constraints, the traditional administration of the health care system was eradicated and the path was cleared for the nonphysicians, the M.B.A.'s who looked at medical issues in terms of numbers.

By the mid-seventies, profit had become the prime concern in the health care industry. Consideration for the well-being of individuals and communities had been replaced by the only thing left: the bottom line. Nationally, there were the beginnings of a growing fear (ultimately embodied by Bill Clinton's 1992 campaign for health care reform) that the fee-for-service medical system could eventually fall into bankruptcy.

The seventies also ushered in the era of managed care, although California's Kaiser-Permanente has been around since 1945 and was the first model of a multitiered system with physicians, nurses, labs, and pharmacy under one roof. In this system, doctors are employees, willing to work for salaries with the resultant capping of overall costs for care delivered. Costs are further held down by the creation of a "gatekeeper" who stands between patients and specialists in order to screen unnecessary visits.

The mushrooming of the HMOs was really a phenomenon of the eighties and, in truth, simply paralleled what was going on in the rest of the business world. This was the era of the consolidation of more resources into fewer words. In business there were hostile takeovers and leveraged buyouts, monolithic corporations swallowing smaller companies and looting them of their assets before discarding them. In the medical industry, small practices were bought out by larger ones, patients and referral sources were taken, and the benefits provided by the smaller practice—the personal health care, the one-to-one, the accessibility of your doctor—were all discarded. Now your doctor was whomever you were put on the phone with. Chances were it would be a stranger.

The eighties provided the perfect environment in which managed care could flourish. But despite the good intentions of a more affordable and accessible medical plan, another problem arose: corporatized medical care. Profits over patients.

Statements like "We own X number of lives" began to be heard when managed-care administrators wanted to describe the breadth of their corporation. The entity with the most "lives"—corporatespeak for patients—could eat up a smaller company. To the bargaining table 300,000 lives would be brought, to be subsequently consumed, in the course of negotiations, by 1.2 million lives.

Collaterally, a psychiatrist who wanted to become a power player in health care needed to guarantee an average daily census of psychiatric beds filled in a hospital. Thirty beds, say, that would be filled 24-7-365: 24 hours a day, 7 days a week, 365 days a year.

That was the ticket in, because for many hospitals, thirty beds comprised their entire psychiatric unit. And more than a few of the smaller community hospitals had psychiatric units with as few as eight beds.

For the administrators, the name of the game was maintaining more demand than supply. It maximized profit, but it also meant that there was always somebody out there who needed a hospital bed and couldn't get it.

When psychiatric care fused with the number-of-lives game in the eighties, dramatic changes occurred. Traditionally, the relationship with the patient is the major tool a psychiatrist has to work with. When that psychiatrist begins to operate in the mode of "owning lives" and contracts with a hospital to fill beds, the doctor-patient relationship disappears, to be replaced by the relationship the psychiatrist has with the hospital.

Whether a psychiatrist becomes responsible for maintaining a census of thirty patients in a psychiatric unit or buys into a community hospital and converts it to suit the needs of a psychiatric facility, it's clear that he will not be the doctor who will be treating those patients. He won't even be familiar with the quality of their care. It becomes wheel spinning on a slot machine: Sometimes the machine comes up with a solid row of sevens and the patient hits the jackpot. Most of the time it's a blur of light and colors and the patient loses his quarter. Good show, no payoff.

Children and adolescents have always represented the biggest payday in mental-health care. As a nation, we maintain that we value our children above all else and want only what is best for them. To prove this, we are willing to pour great sums of money into their care. American children themselves are powerless because, in our nonagrarian culture, they are not part of the workforce. Without power, they are historically at risk of being imprisoned within the psychiatric system.

Before the insurance companies mutinied at the practice of paying for indefinite lengths of stay in psychiatric hospitals, children could be, and often were, kept in locked units for years. At the close of the eighties, the insurance carriers decreed that the decision to remain, or to be kept, in a hospital was between the facility and the patient's parents. Now an adolescent can be kept in a psychiatric hospital for only three weeks, and the accepted length of stay for an adult is three days. After that, unless the hospital can come up with a good enough reason (such as a dual diagnosis of depression coupled with an eating disorder or being a danger to oneself and others), the insurance runs out.

I WOULD NOT see or hear from Alex Balter for ten years after I left that small psychiatric hospital in the San Fernando Valley. Then, in 1995, I spotted his name on the front page of the *Los Angeles Times;* he was named as codefendant in a federal lawsuit based on allegations made by a major insurance company against a psychiatric-provider program he had founded. As I read the piece, I remembered an observation Alex made back when we were both techs: "This is an even better business than selling dope."

He was right.

CHAPTER ONE

IN 1992, CHRISTY SCHECK struck a blow at National Medical Enterprises, a major player in the mental-health business with more than seventy psychiatric facilities around the nation. It was a blow that would help to bring down NME.

Christy Scheck was thirteen years old.

There is a snapshot of her in her soccer uniform in the study of her parents' home. She is grinning up at her father, Bob; his face is turned toward the lens, and he is squinting in the bright sunlight. The resemblance between father and daughter is startling: the same square jaw and upturned nose, the wide-set eyes made larger by an added push of blue. Christy's face is spattered with freckles, and her hair is cut short. It sticks up in random tufts, as if she had run her hand through it, impatient with any notion of style, even for the camera.

There are dozens of photographs in this room. They crowd the bookshelves and pile up in drifts next to baseball and soccer trophies. There are formal team portraits, class pictures, and single shots of Christy frowning slightly as she winds up to pitch. A Little League jersey—number 12—has been mounted in a Lucite frame over the desk.

By the time she was four years old, it was clear to Bob Scheck that his daughter possessed extraordinary athletic ability. They played kickball in the backyard until she was six, then he taught her to play baseball. Basketball and soccer would come later. The name of the game didn't matter: Once Christy was on the playing field, all childish awkwardness would disappear, replaced by the easy, useful grace of the natural.

Bob Scheck was a career Navy enlistee when he met Merry Edwards in Detroit in 1967. She was a premed student at Wayne State; he was home on leave. By March of '68, Merry had dropped out. She married Bob soon afterward, when he was between stations, and within the month he was transferred to San Diego. Christy was born there in 1978. A second child, Molly,* was born six years later.

Both parents played vital roles in the rearing of their children. Merry read aloud, helped with homework, found games the whole family could play in the evenings. Bob concentrated on athletics, volunteering as coach or umpire whenever there was an opening on any of the school teams. He worked with Christy daily, perfecting her pitch or correcting her stance at bat. He showed up dutifully at PTA meetings and school open houses, and in turn, Merry brought Molly to all of Christy's games. Good grades were important to both parents. Christy's place as an honor student, her acceptance into the GATE (Gifted And Talented Educationally) program, and her perfect attendance record at school remain great points of pride. But it is only when Bob Scheck talks about his daughter's athletic accomplishments that his voice comes alive.

"Christy could play any position. Except shortstop." A phantom grin flickers across Bob's lips, giving the impression that this might have been a standing joke between them. "She just doesn't have the range to play shortstop. But it was pitching she loved. Anytime that girl could get someone to play catch with her, she'd be ready. If you could give her twenty-eight hours a day, she'd pitch for those twenty-eight hours. Christy didn't just have a talent for athletics. She was an athlete."

By the time Christy went into sixth grade at Horace Mann Middle School, she was playing exclusively on boys' teams.

When I ask how Christy was affected if her team suffered a loss, Bob hesitates for a moment before he replies.

"Christy takes defeat very hard. She's a gracious winner, but defeat is something she doesn't take very well." This is the second time he has referred to his older daughter in the present tense.

"One of the things I think figured in her emotional problems was not being allowed to pitch in the all-star games."

Ed Dueñez, Christy Scheck's counselor at Horace Mann, doesn't see it that way.

"I remember the first time Christy came into my office. Here was this cute little girl who was just like a little boy. Twelve years old, about, and the definitive jock. She had come in to tell me there were problems at home. She said, 'My dad's all different since he quit smoking. He used to play family games with me and my mom every night, and now he quit playing. He doesn't get involved anymore.' "

Dueñez called Merry Scheck, who came in to meet with him. Merry explained that the reason her husband had dropped out of the evening game-playing sessions was because once six-year-old Molly was included as a player, the games had been changed to accommodate her skill level, and Bob got bored.

"From then on," Ed recalled, "Christy always popped her head into my office to say hi on her way to class. She'd tell me about her weekend and talk about how she was doing at baseball, and then she'd scoot on out. We forged a little bond. There were no more problems until Christy went into eighth grade."

That was 1991, the year Christy turned thirteen, the year her father decided to take her out of boys' soccer without discussion or debate. He made his ruling, and Christy was expected to abide by it. Bob Scheck is retired from active service now. He works in a civilian capacity for the Navy, but he is still militaristic by nature. He wields a particular intensity of gaze and resonance of voice to gain the submission of others, and his tolerance for those who reason quietly is colored slightly by contempt. When Bob delivers an order, he expects it to be obeyed without argument or hesitation.

Ed Dueñez vividly recalls Christy striding into his office after she had been told that she would be playing soccer on the girls' team the following semester. "She was fuming; there was so much anger inside her. She paced up and down in front of my desk, and finally, when I asked her to sit down, she just kind of hurled her-self into a chair."

Dueñez tried to explain to her the reasoning behind her father's decision. "Your dad's only trying to protect you, Christy. He's worried you might get hurt."

"You've seen me play, Mr. Dueñez. I don't get hurt." Her tone isn't boastful; she's handing him a fact.

"Listen to me, Christy: Things are changing. You're thirteen now, and soccer is a rough game. Boys your age are growing at a different rate; they're going to be bigger than you and stronger than you. That's what's worrying your dad—he doesn't want you to get hurt. You're his daughter, Christy."

Dueñez remembers how Christy's hands tensed into fists, and the way she leaned forward in her chair.

"You just don't get it, do you, Mr. Dueñez? I'm not his daughter." She looked steadily at the counselor. "I'm his son."

CHAPTER TWO

THE SCHECK FAMILY relocated in October 1994. Their new home is located in a pleasant suburb some thirty miles southeast of San Diego. I met Bob, Merry, and Molly about three weeks after they moved in. They were not yet settled: There were pictures still to be hung and final decisions to be made about incidental pieces of furniture.

The new living room is furnished with Mission-style chairs and sofas, all of it gleaming with the singular patina of newness. The carpets are mulberry and teal, there is an upright piano stacked with classical and popular sheet music. Family portraits crowd a stone mantel: great-grandparents posing in bridal finery, Merry and Bob smiling on their wedding day, Christy and Molly at different ages. In one photograph, taken when the girls were twelve and six, Christy's arm is slung casually across Molly's shoulders and both girls seem to have been caught mid-giggle. There is a painting over the fireplace of a lighthouse surrounded by raging seas. Merry calls the painting a metaphor for her family's life.

We are seated for our initial conversation in a light-filled enclosed porch at the back of the house, a room that seems to be the catchall for everything that was too comfortable or too familiar to be thrown out when the Schecks moved. Everything in here is mismatched and well used, in contrast to the immaculate new furniture in the other rooms. This small porch bears the subtle marks of family history. Merry is sitting in one corner of a sagging sofa upholstered in a faded floral pattern. She is a tall, rather handsome woman in her early forties with short, coppery hair and green eyes shadowed by fatigue. Bob sits in a reclining chair placed at a right angle to the sofa. He has tipped the chair all the way back so that his legs are elevated. Bob Scheck is a stocky, barrel-chested man with a brush of graying hair. The most constant expression on his face is that of a man who, if not defeated, has nothing left to fear.

We have been talking about Christy's behavior at home after Bob's decision to take her out of boys' sports.

"These screaming matches would begin, often over homework, which usually ended with Bob stepping in. And then they'd get into it, too." Merry glances at her husband; he sits up in the recliner and plants both feet on the floor before speaking.

"See, Christy was the type of person, if she had a direction she was going in, she wasn't about to change it. Even with homework . . ." Bob's eyes move away for an instant, and there is a subtle softening of focus. Then he snaps back. "She didn't like my authoritarian personality over her, and I guess there were times when I was . . . inflexible." He's not talking just about homework. Merry's expression is unreadable; she's listening, that's all.

"You see, there are rules I put down for my children that are not negotiable." He holds up one finger. "You will not lip off to me or my wife." He extends a second finger. "Don't make me tell you to do some simple thing four or five times. My wife's a talker—she'll tell a child, 'No, no, no, no.' She'll try to reason. I have certain levels, and once you reach those levels, I'm going to act." Scheck hesitates. This is difficult for him. "I believe in corporal punishment."

When I ask for an example, he snaps one hand in a rapid, backward motion.

"There are times when I have done a short flip, like this, if my daughter lipped off. I mean, I wouldn't come across the room at her, but if I'm standing close to her, and she lips off, I'd flip her cheek with my fingertips. More to get her attention than to hurt her." He takes in air. "See, after the age of ten, I had a young lady on my hands, so I had to draw the line as to, you know, where do I spank? I still swatted her rear end, but I'd use something, like this small wooden breadboard we got as a gift." Bob gets to his feet, walks quickly into the kitchen, and comes back out with the breadboard. It is smaller than most, almost like a utensil for a playhouse kitchen, but regardless of its size, it is unnerving to imagine using it to strike another person.

"If I couldn't reach her, I'd use the side of my foot on her rear end." Bob demonstrates, lifting one foot to the side in a fast, jiglike movement. It is a burlesque of a kick, designed not to hurt, but to humiliate.

Christy would often retreat to her room after a confrontation. And, according to Merry Scheck, her overall moodiness increased. "Christy would stake out a place on the couch and plunk herself down, with her arms folded and headphones clamped to her ears. She'd listen to her music—mostly Christian rock—and she was all about"—Merry's voice alters as she begins to speak through tightly clenched teeth—" 'We don't want to talk to anyone. We don't want to interact. Just. Leave. Me. Alone.' " It is possible to hear, in her mother's impression of her voice, Christy's alienation from and anger toward her parents.

In early October 1991, a call came in for Merry while she was at the small contracting firm where she worked as a bookkeeper. It was the nurse at Christy's school, who told Merry that Christy had come into her office with bruises on both arms and another, larger bruise near her temple. When the nurse questioned her, Christy said that the larger bruise was the result of her father "slugging her in the head."

Merry hung up the phone and, without telling anyone, went directly to Horace Mann Middle School. As she drove, the events of the past weekend turned over in her mind. This was Monday; on Saturday the family had gone, as usual, to see Christy play soccer in one of her final games on the boys' team. At one point a wildly thrown ball struck Christy on the side of the head. The force of the blow slammed her back against the goalpost. Everyone at the game had seen it happen; there was a collective gasp around the athletic field.

Merry realized suddenly that she was thinking in terms of witnesses.

Christy was waiting in the nurse's office. She appeared relaxed, even jaunty. One leg was crossed over the other, and her foot swung back and forth in an idle motion.

Merry began talking as soon as she walked through the door. "Christy, what's going on? Why are you making these accusations?"

Christy's foot stopped moving. She stared defiantly at her mother.

"How can you say that Daddy hit you in the head?"

Christy said nothing.

"Christy!" Merry could hear the edge of shrillness in her voice.

"They're not accusations. He hit me in the head, and I'm not gonna stay in here and let you call me a liar." Christy was on her feet and out of the room before either her mother or the nurse could speak.

Merry stood there in the small, tidy office. She shook her head back and forth in a slow, almost dreamlike movement. Then she thanked the nurse and drove back to her office. She didn't know what else to do. When she got home that afternoon there was a message waiting for her. The school nurse had called to inform her that the incident would be reported to Child Protective Services.

Neither Bob nor Merry had much time to think about the CPS report: Christy didn't come home from school that afternoon. She would be gone for three days.

The Schecks called the police and reported that their daughter was missing. They called friends and friends of friends. On the third day, Merry got a call from the mother of one of Christy's classmates: Christy was alternating between her house and the house of another girl from school.

Merry smiles faintly when she arrives at this part of the story. "We had already learned that Christy was showing up at school every day. She'd heard about colleges checking out school attendance all the way back to the eighth grade."

A CPS caseworker did follow up on the nurse's report. She went to Horace Mann Middle School and interviewed both Christy and her teachers. She spoke to Molly Scheck at the elementary school.

The case was ultimately closed, but the report remained on the books.

Christy kept on running away. She would sleep over at friends' homes, always showing up at school. The Schecks were in a constant state of apprehension.

Then one evening, during dinner, Christy made a pronouncement. "We need to be in family counseling."

Both parents agreed that it wasn't a bad suggestion. Merry in particular was concerned about the kind of books Christy had been bringing home from the school library. Most of them were about parental abuse, and Christy would pore over them for hours at a time. Merry remembers one book vividly. "It was about family violence, and it was so simplistic that any kid, in any one of a hundred given moods, could read it and say, 'Oh, see? This says I've been abused.' "

The search for a therapist, however, would prove to be more difficult than Merry had imagined. Most of the people she spoke to were too busy to see new patients. A few didn't return her calls until weeks later. And Christy's disturbing behavior had accelerated alarmingly: She had begun to scratch at herself with the point of a compass.

During Christy's bouts of running away, the Schecks had been in frequent contact with the police. Now, frantic, they made an appointment with the officer in charge of police intervention. Merry talks about this woman with respect and affection.

"Officer Pitts was wonderful. She spent almost two hours with Christy and me, and she took Christy full circle through her anger with her father, her running away, everything. She made Christy see how her behavior was affecting the family. And, at the end of the meeting, Christy did something she hadn't done in weeks: She looked straight at me, and she said, 'I'm sorry, Mom'. . . " Merry's voice trails off; she has been caught off-guard by the recalled moment.

Merry Scheck is a complex woman. If her husband's judgments are harsh and immediate, Merry's decisions are restrained by circumspect curiosity and a shrewd intellect. She is slow to anger; if you look for the random spark of banked fires in her level gaze, you won't find it. Her ferocity is well hidden, like a locked and loaded rifle behind a secret door.

Things went smoothly for a couple of weeks after the meeting at the police department, and Christy's behavior improved enough to allow the Schecks to feel that a bad phase had worked itself out. They began to relax, began to believe that their lives had gotten back to normal. And, as if to underline the family's sense of well-being, Christy made the honor roll.

Everybody was in a celebratory mood. Bob and Merry took both kids out to a pizza place, Christy's favorite restaurant. She was clearly elated, teasing Molly gently, kidding around with the waitress. Her behavior toward both parents was less guarded than it had been for weeks.

It was still light when they got home. Bob okayed Christy's request to ride her bike around the neighborhood, and Merry settled down to play a board game with Molly. But some indefinable sense of unease tugged at the edges of Merry's consciousness. She remembered that her bag had been open on the floor next to the pool table when they played pool after dinner. Merry, without really knowing why, acted on impulse. She opened the bag now and took out her wallet.

The ATM card was missing.

When Christy returned she denied taking the card, denied even noticing that her mother's bag had been near the pool table. She slammed into her room, and Bob and Merry decided to let things ride until morning.

Christy was out of the house before breakfast the next day. When Merry went to the bank she found that $60 had been withdrawn from her checking account the previous evening.

Without a family counselor to consult, Merry called Ed Dueñez. He suggested that Merry meet him at school that day. She agreed readily; with an objective presence between herself and Christy, there would be less likelihood of a screaming match.

Dueñez pulled Christy out of class.

"Hiya, Mr. D. What's up?"

"Your mom's down in my office, Christy. She's pretty upset."

"What about?"

Dueñez remembers that he kept his voice at an easy, conversational pitch as they walked toward his office. "Christy, check it out: Your mom knows you took money out of her checking account."

"Huh? No way." Christy shook her head in disbelief. "Man . . ."

Dueñez remembers that Christy was wearing what he had come to think of as her uniform: shorts, long-sleeved T-shirt, backpack. He wondered if the money from the ATM was inside the backpack.

"Listen to me, Christy. There are security cameras at every ATM window. All your mom has to do is go down there and have them pull the videotape."

"They could've taken my picture anytime . . ." Her voice dropped to a mumble. They were only steps from his office now, and Dueñez stopped walking. Christy moved forward, then stopped and turned to look at him. If she was hoping to find commiseration or fearful of seeing anger in his eyes, she found neither. Years ago, in the San Diego barrio, Ed Dueñez learned to mask his responses with an impenetrable gaze.

"Okay. I did it." Then, in a rush of words, "But I had a reason, you know? This really good friend of mine needed it so he could leave home." In afterthought, she added, "He's eighteen."

"Well, you need to tell all that to your mom." Dueñez moved past her to open the door of his office.

Merry Scheck has a clear recollection of her feelings as the office door swung open and Ed Dueñez stepped aside to allow Christy to precede him into the room. There was an instant when Merry's anger evaporated and she wanted to shout at Dueñez, tell him to forget the card, forget the $60, and let the poor kid go back to class. She remembers, too, dismissing the thought as Christy spoke: "All right. I did it. So what?"

Dueñez walked around the desk and sat down. "Is there some reason you needed money so badly that you had to steal it from your mom's account?"

Christy said nothing. She stared angrily at her mother, shaking her head in the same disbelieving motion she had used in the hallway. Then she turned and walked out.

Christy refused to discuss the incident at home. She was grounded for an indefinite period, allowed only to attend school and soccer practice. Bob would accompany her to practice and back home again.

Ed Dueñez had a talk with the school nurse. They agreed that Christy was going through a classic identity crisis. "We both felt the same way about it," Dueñez says now. "When Christy's dad took her out of boys' sports, it confused her so badly she didn't know who she was supposed to be anymore. And at some point she included her mother in her anger, because Merry didn't support her desire to stay on the boys' team. Christy had been trained to be hypercompetitive, a winner among boys. She was famous for it at school. And now, just like that, she'd been told to stop."

Within days of the ATM incident, Christy began cornering people to talk about how bad things were at home. Teachers and the college students who were working as teaching interns came to Dueñez with the stories. There were no specific details. The constant refrain was simply how bad it was at home. "So now a lot of people started to worry," Dueñez says. "The behavior Christy was exhibiting made us wonder—as caretakers."

Dueñez called Merry Scheck. He told her it might be a good thing if he met with Bob. He had spoken to Bob only during open houses.

Two days later Bob Scheck came to Horace Mann Middle School. Dueñez was monitoring a couple of kids during a time-out period in the workshop room. Bob met him there.

"I could see how awkward this was for the guy," Dueñez recalls. "For the first few minutes, all he could do was look around the room and talk about the tools and the machines and how he took shop when he was in high school. Then we talked about trucks. Finally, I brought up the subject of Christy. When we got to the part about his decision to take her out of boys' sports, he blushed. And he kind of stammered"—Dueñez deepens his voice slightly, not in imitation of Bob Scheck, but to suggest that it is another person speaking—" 'Well, she's growing up now, she's not a little girl.' " Dueñez whistles softly, a single, short note. "He made that sound, and he shaped the air with his hands, like you'd show the shape of a Coke bottle. But the whistle wasn't lascivious, and neither was the gesture. This guy was just too embarrassed to talk about how his daughter was growing up. So he kind of mimed it. And I remembered that he was a Navy man, and this is how sailors sometimes describe women. He wasn't able to say the words, but that was the reason he didn't want her playing boys' sports anymore. He couldn't deal with Christy growing up." Dueñez takes a deep breath. "And Christy couldn't deal with it, either. It was a shock to her—she saw herself as a jock. Period."

After the meeting with Bob Scheck, Dueñez had Christy sign a contract stating that she would speak about "family dynamics" only with him or the school nurse. Christy not only honored the contract, she went around getting the signatures of everyone concerned. But her mood at home remained withdrawn, and she continued to run away whenever she had a disagreement with her parents.

The Schecks found a counselor by the end of October. Gary Juleen was a registered marriage, family, and child counselor (M.F.C.C.) with an office in San Diego. During the seventies Juleen had been program director of an organization that rented wings in psychiatric hospitals in order to create specialized Christian-oriented programs, blending Christian ethics with general counseling. The Scheck family were—and are—devout churchgoers. Bob, Merry, and Christy began a series of weekly and sometimes biweekly sessions with Gary Juleen.

Bob's memories of those sessions are painful. "As long as we didn't get into the 'problem area,' which was anything having to do with Christy's relationship with us, and her anger at us—me in particular—things were okay. The peace was kept. But, of course, the session would be unproductive. The minute anyone touched on that problem area, well, those were *her* problems, and she was going to take care of them by herself. She'd plant her feet and cross her arms and refuse to speak another word. Or else she'd just explode and storm out of the office." There is a short silence. "Those sessions with Gary were forewarnings of what was to come."

Gary Juleen remembers the Scheck family relationship as something "very, very strong and positive." Although his initial session with the family did not take place until two weeks after Christy told the school nurse that her father had struck her on the head, Juleen feels that Christy may have had "some conflict or agitation about that. My thinking at the time was that Christy made that statement to create some kind of spectacle, to gain attention. I don't think she realized it would actually go so far as to bring in an official from CPS." He describes that first session as "very argumentative. Very confrontational and emotional. But when Christy and I spoke alone, later, she was just beaming because her father had actually come to the session. Christy's real issue was 'bringing the family together.' "

Juleen remembers now that there were times in family sessions when Christy was able to cool her anger and simply talk. "But the majority of time she looked as though she wanted—or needed— to yell. To be able to get through to her father."

And what was Bob Scheck's response?

"At times he would argue back. At times he would just listen. Merry took a secondary role, because almost all of Christy's anger was directed at her father. Because that was the relationship she desired the most. Christy always felt, with her mother, that there was no communication problem at all. Christy's constant plea and desire was, 'I don't think my father hears me.' And, aside from sports, a great part of their communication was nonfunctional. Bob shared that he knew as Christy developed physically he was beginning to pull away from her. Her development was, in a sense, threatening to him." Juleen pauses. "I think he felt a real affection for her but couldn't verbalize it to this developing, blooming teenager. And Christy was highly intelligent, and highly intuitive. She may have felt this pulling away by her father, and she may have interpreted that as rejection. So her attempts were to at least hear things from her father that would reinforce to her that they were still, in fact, together."

And did that happen? Juleen shakes his head slowly. "At that time, early in our sessions, Bob was not able to communicate on an emotional level. He spoke factually. I said there was a part of Bob that was protected from being able to share emotionally. Not unusual in males, and Bob Scheck tends to orchestrate his life around performance, as most men do. It's about doing, as opposed to being and feeling. Christy wanted to hear *about* her father, and I don't think he could access himself enough to satisfy her."

It was agreed in one of the family sessions that the party Merry had planned for Christy's thirteenth birthday would be canceled as a result of the ATM theft. But Merry relented on the day of the birthday, November 3, and made meat loaf and macaroni and cheese, Christy's favorite meal. There were cards and a cake with candles. Christy ate without comment, glanced idly at the cards, and blew out the candles. Then, without cutting the cake, she went back to her room and closed the door.

On November 5 Christy went to traffic court to pay a jaywalking fine. Merry drove her to the courthouse, and she remembers how willingly Christy handed over some of the birthday money she had received from an aunt. That night Christy became violently ill, vomiting repeatedly. Merry's diagnosis was "stress flu." Secretly, she was worried.

CHAPTER THREE

"I THINK CHRISTY was always kind of unstable. As far back as I can remember, her favorite thing was to push the limits of what her parents would expect. She liked to see how far she could take things without getting in too much trouble. I don't know if she did stuff to get her parents mad, or if she just wanted more attention. Christy liked attention."

Ethan Penny* is only two months past his sixteenth birthday, but he looks and acts at least a couple of years older than that. His mother, Rachel,* and Merry Scheck have been close friends ever since the two women met, when Ethan and Christy were infants, aboard a westbound plane from Michigan. In the course of the flight, seated together with their babies, the women discovered that both of them were Navy wives and that they had gone to neighboring high schools in adjoining suburbs of Detroit. Both were on their way back to San Diego after trips home to show the babies to their respective families. The relationship has progressed steadily through the ensuing years.

Ethan prefers to be called Red. He got that nickname when he was small and his hair was the color of marmalade; it has since turned light blond, but the name stuck. He is coming up on six feet, and his muscles are long and fluid. He looks like someone who has put in extended hours swimming laps.

I am sitting with Red, Rachel, and Red's buddy Josh* in the Pennys' living room. It's a pleasant, pretty room, a place where kids can make themselves comfortable. The furniture is sturdy and welcoming, and there are no fussy arrangements of knickknacks to be avoided. The house is about twenty miles from downtown San Diego in the kind of neighborhood where one sees carefully maintained campers and canvas-shrouded boats in driveways. It is a neighborhood where families know one another, where carved pumpkins and paper witches decorate front porches in October and homemade cookies are exchanged at Christmas.

I've come here with Merry Scheck so that I can speak with the Penny family about Christy. We were invited for dinner: hamburgers that Red cooked on the outdoor grill. Rachel's husband, Hal,* is out of town. He is a systems analyst, working for the Defense Department, and he is also the Navy's representative to NATO for one of their communications groups. He travels often.

After dinner, Merry and Josh's mother, Nancy,* join the younger Penny kids in the den to watch a movie; the muted buzz of voices and sound effects filters through to the living room in random bursts.

"I remember the first time I thought something was wrong with Christy," Red continues. "All of us kids—my little brothers and my cousins and Christy—were in the car with my mom. It was my thirteenth birthday, and we were going to the movies. As we drove past the mall, Christy pointed at one of the stores and said, 'I'm glad we're past this place. I've got a problem with them.' And my mom said, 'No, Christy. They've got a problem with you.'"

Josh pipes up. "Hey, I was along that day, too."

Rachel, who's suffering from a cold, takes a small package of tissues from her pocket, pulls one out, and blows her nose before she speaks. "I thought it was strange that Christy would have brought that up. She'd been caught shoplifting a pair of overalls at the mall, and Merry had asked Hal and me not to tell the kids about it. But now here was Christy announcing it as if it were a badge of honor. She was clearly trying to get a rise out of the boys, like, 'Hey, I'm tough. I shoplifted.' But I shut her right down. I told her that it had caused a lot of trouble for everyone, and that it wasn't anything to brag about." She glances over at Red and Josh. "And I don't think the boys were impressed, anyway."

"No. We weren't," Josh answers with certainty. He is a soft-spoken, rather shy boy of sixteen with closely cropped dark hair and brown eyes that pin everything around him with a casually veiled intensity. Like Red and Christy, Josh is an honor student. He turns to look at Red. "Tell her what happened after that day," he says.

"Christy and Molly and their mom were over here," Red says, "and me and Josh and Christy were outside, sitting on the hood of her mom's car. I'd been talking about how I'd been kind of screwing up at school, and that I'd gotten a couple of bad grades. Christy looked at me and gave this kind of sneery laugh. Then she said, 'You think that's bad? I tried to OD on aspirin. I took a whole bunch, but all it did was make me sick.' And, like, I thought, 'Where did that come from? Why's she trying to top me?' "

"Tell her the real topper."

"Yeah. Well, she rolled back her sleeve." Red stretches out his arm and points to the area between the crook of elbow and the inner wrist. "From here to here, there were scabs and barely healed cuts. Just crisscrossing her arm."

"Both arms." Josh points to the areas on himself.

"She told us she'd go in her room when she got mad, and then she'd cut on herself. I said, 'That's really stupid, Christy.' But she pulled it off like she was this tough person 'cause she could go and cut on herself when she got mad at someone. That just freaked me out, because it came out of the blue." Red glances at his mother.

"See, kids have trouble holding secrets," he continues. "They just have to tell someone. And that's the way Christy was. She had to tell someone about the cutting and the pills. After they all left I went to my mom's room, and I told her about Christy's arms and about how she almost OD'd on aspirin. Then we called Merry. She ransacked Christy's room and came up with two empty bottles and a whole bunch of razor blades." He gives a mock shudder. "It was intense."

Rachel has been listening quietly. Now she leans forward in her chair. She is wearing an antique star-sapphire ring on her right hand, and as she speaks she begins to twist the ring in an unconscious motion. "It was pretty scary stuff, all right. And Merry needed to be told about it. At this point she was taking Christy with her on every errand, she was that afraid the kid would try to hurt herself. Or that she'd run away again." Rachel pauses. "At certain points, even though she didn't say it out loud, I think Christy would have preferred to just move in here with this family."

"That's just speculation," Red says, "but I agree with my mom."

Rachel is an elementary school teacher, but for several years she and Hal have served as foster parents. For them, gratification is to be found in a house filled with children.

"Christy used to stay over here fairly often," she volunteers, "and when she did, Hal and I were pretty tough on her. She knew we were foster parents, of course, and she had this idealized notion of a foster home. She became very friendly with one of our foster children, a girl her age named Shana King,* who had been the victim of a brutal rape." Rachel looks away, then back at me. "I firmly believe that some of the things Christy said and did were with the intent of getting involved with CPS so that she could be placed in a foster home." A hint of a smile plays at the corners of her mouth. "And I really don't know why. Hal and I were much stricter with Christy than Bob and Merry ever were. Half this neighborhood will tell you that when they think of strict parenting, they think of the Pennys." She glances over at Red, and her smile widens. "Red'll tell you. We have high expectations."

Red grins back at his mother. "Yeah. We go over to his house"—he jerks his head toward Josh—"to misbehave."

Rachel continues. "I'm very interactive with all my kids. So is Hal, when he's home. And Christy enjoyed that. She had a very good relationship with Hal, and he was strict with her, no nonsense. You don't get away with anything with Hal. He's that way with everyone, but he also gets down and does things with the kids. Like he's one of them, another kid." She gets up and reaches across the mantel to take down a framed photograph of Hal, which she hands to me. The man grinning unselfconsciously into the camera is a ringer for actor John Goodman.

"I think Christy truly adored Hal. She just hung on him all the time." Rachel takes the photograph and puts it back in place on the mantel. "Hal excels in the parenting role. It never had to be thrust upon him. I've often said that he's the better parent, the better mother and father."

Red has been listening closely, nodding from time to time. He neither agrees with his mother's last comment nor disputes it. But he does have something to add. "When we need to talk about something, we go to my dad. And when I want information, he's the one I ask. Because my mom won't tell me anything." Rachel reaches out to ruffle her son's hair. He ducks away, grabbing her hand to drop a fast kiss on the knuckles. "But if we get hurt, my mom's the one to find."

Rachel Penny seems to be greatly at ease with herself and the people around her. She is slightly overweight, but the added flesh is not unbecoming. It simply endows her with the look of someone from another place, another time. She resembles, more than anything else, a Renaissance painter's concept of Venus: all elliptic arcs and creamy skin.

She is silent for a moment before she speaks again, and when she does, there is a surprising note of something close to apology in her voice. "This is a happy home." Another brief silence. "But the Schecks had a happy home, too."

Red's voice comes quickly behind his mother's.

"Mom, Christy was never happy at home. Never."

CHAPTER FOUR

KEONDA COOPER* DOESN'T remember if they were in the first or second grade when she and Christy Scheck met. "I do remember that we were just learning to color inside the lines," she says. "And I remember that we liked each other right away, which was unusual for me because I was kind of afraid of other people. I was shy. But Christy made friends easily. Everyone liked Christy."

Keonda is seventeen now, and a high school senior. Like Christy was, she is a GATE student, and she is planning to study law. Her voice, on the telephone, is soft but confident. "Christy was just the best kind of friend, always there for me, from the day we met. She taught me to play tetherball and hopscotch. If somebody teased me or made a racial comment, she'd be there to protect me. If I felt sad about something, she was the one who could always make me laugh. Christy was a great athlete. In fourth or fifth grade we had a school Olympics, and Christy was the best one in it. I wasn't athletic at all, or only slightly, and I remember watching her play in those Olympic games and feeling so proud of her. And proud that we were friends."

Keonda's voice has thickened slightly. It is still painful for her to talk about Christy. "She used to play football with the boys at lunchtime, and she was like a boy herself, out there on the field. I guess you'd call her a tomboy, but Christy really liked being a girl. It's just that she was more comfortable doing guy things. A lot of her friends were boys—like I said, she made friends easily—but she didn't hang around with a lot of people. Christy's circle was her, and me, and another girl in our class, Luz Sanchez.* There was another girl who lived closer to Christy's house than Luz or I, and

Christy used to go over there once in a while. But she wasn't part of our circle."

I ask if Christy ever talked about using drugs.

"No, uh-uh. She wasn't into anything like that at all."

Did Christy tell Keonda when she began to cut herself with the compass point, or when she tried to overdose on aspirin?

"She never mentioned anything like that to me. And I don't think she said anything to Luz, either."

I ask if Keonda knew Christy's parents.

"Not really. I know Mr. Scheck coached baseball, and I'd see him at school sometimes. But I don't know him." She takes a breath, sighs it out slowly. "I just got to hate both of Christy's parents from stuff she said."

Such as?

"Well, I remember when we were in seventh grade. We'd both cut this one class every once in a while, and we'd walk around the hallways, and go into the girls' bathroom and talk about things. And we'd both be crying. Christy was all, 'My dad would like it better if I was a boy,' and she talked about how strict he was, and how he hit her with a wooden spoon and her mom just let him."

Why did Keonda cry?

"I cried because my friend was hurting so much."

The next time I call her, Keonda tells me that a boy who used to play baseball with Christy is at her house. She wants to know if I'd like to talk to him.

His name is Joe,* he tells me, his voice slightly hesitant. I ask him to describe Christy as a teammate.

"She was really strong on the baseball field. Very, *very* competitive. Her dad really pushed her, you know? I'd hear him yelling at her sometimes, even though he coached a different team. He was all, 'I know you can do better,' and 'You're not giving it your best,' and stuff like that. Really yelling at her. He just pushed her all the time, maybe right to the edge. Like, when we'd have a baseball raffle at school, and we'd be selling this candy because whoever sold the most would win a bike. Well, Christy's dad would just buy up all the candy, so she won a bike three different times. I'll tell you something: I don't think Christy's dad abused her. Personally, I think he just loved her a lot. I know he coached baseball because of her."

There is a pause, and when Joe speaks again, his voice is laced with an unmistakable wistfulness. "Man, that girl was one hell of a baseball player."

When Keonda comes back on the line I ask if Christy ever had a boyfriend.

"No, uh-uh. And she would've told me. 'Cause that's the only thing we ever differed about. I was really into boys, and Christy wasn't. But I do remember this one time when we were in seventh grade, and Christy came to school wearing a skirt and earrings and makeup. She never dressed like that. Ever. She always wore pretty much the same thing: boys' shorts and a T-shirt and hiking boots. And she never, ever wore makeup. But this one day she was really dressed up, and she said, 'There's this guy who likes me. Should I go for him or not?' And I said, 'Go for it! Get yourself a boyfriend.' I was really happy for her. Anyway, she told me his name, which I don't remember anymore, and said she'd point him out to me the next week." The phone is silent for a moment. "Only she wasn't there the next week."

LUZ SANCHEZ ISN'T eighteen yet, but she graduated from high school last year and is now studying at San Diego City College. Her voice is low-pitched, and she raises it from time to time to make herself heard above the sound of young children playing in the background. "I've known Christy for the longest time. Not so long as Keonda, but at least from the third grade. We didn't get close until the fifth grade." She takes a moment. "She was such a great listener. I'd go on about boys, or clothes, or whatever, and she'd just listen to me. Christy paid attention to what you were saying, and she never passed judgment like a lot of people do."

I ask what Christy talked about.

"Oh, it was usually about sports; she was very athletic. Or she might talk about schoolwork, or a book she was reading. Christy always had all her homework done, and she loved to read. Some of the boys teased her about it, but it didn't faze her. Nothing ever fazed her."

There is a seasoning to the way Luz speaks. Not exactly an accent, just a soft slide off the consonants, an elongation of certain vowels. "The thing that seemed to bother her the most was her looks. Christy was unhappy with her looks. She used to say to me, 'If only I looked like you,' or she'd say, 'If only I could be like you with people.' Because she wasn't the kind of person to go up to people, or trust them right away. She always seemed a little bit guarded, even though everyone in elementary school loved Christy. The teachers, too.

"The only place Christy was competitive was with the boys. You'd see her all the time, playing with the boys—baseball, kick-ball, four-square. She taught me to play four-square. It's played with a basketball, and I was always afraid the ball was going to hit me, but Christy said, 'So what if you get hit? As long as you win.'

"Christy was the reliable one. Always. I could count on her to be there for me no matter what. I had a lot of problems at home, because I got pregnant in the seventh grade. I was only thirteen, and I had been going out with this eighteen-year-old guy. Christy was the first one I told about him, and she just listened and nodded her head. But she never passed judgment.

"The only time I ever heard her come close to passing judgment was when I started hanging out with gang members. Christy was real concerned about that, and she kept asking me what it was I saw in them. And there was, like, this models' club—all home-girls—and Christy would say, 'You're way too pretty for that club. You look out of place with those girls.' "

I ask if Luz ever met Christy's parents. She tells me she hasn't. "Christy didn't talk much about her mom and dad. She really liked her little sister, though. She used to talk about her, how she loved her, even when she got on Christy's nerves.

"Christy started to change in the sixth and seventh grades. We weren't in the same classes anymore, but we'd see each other in the halls and at recess. She seemed a little bit withdrawn, and I know the only person she really confided in, in junior high, was Mr. Dueñez, the school counselor. She trusted him because he was like her: He didn't pass judgment on people.

"In junior high, people were really starting to tease Christy about her looks. Like, in PE, the boys, and especially the clique girls, the popular girls, would make fun of her. The girls were really rude. They'd say stuff like, 'There goes the fashion-don't.' You know, because she always wore her boys' shorts, and her backpack.

"Christy never fought back. Not once." Luz's voice, still soft, is filled with emotion. "And you know, for someone who was so aggressive on the athletic field, she wasn't at all aggressive when someone teased her about her looks. I'd get really mad and tell them to shut up, and say, 'What has she ever done to you?' But Christy would pull me back. She'd say, 'Don't worry about it. Don't get yourself in trouble over something like this. It's not important.'

"I remember this one day in the sixth grade. My boyfriend and I were walking down the hall with Christy, and some boy came up to us and said to my boyfriend, 'Hey, that girl looks just like a guy.' And I yelled at him to shut up. I'll always remember what Christy said to me: 'Don't worry about it, Luz. His time will come when he's the one who gets teased.'

"By the time we got into seventh grade, Christy wasn't happy anymore. Before the sixth or seventh grade, she was so full of energy, with her beautiful blue eyes and her rosy cheeks, but by seventh grade, she became withdrawn. Her spirit was gone, that spark she had about her was missing. I'd try to talk to her about it sometimes. I'd ask her what was going on. But Christy would always answer with the same thing: 'Nothing. Just the same old thing.' Which was Christy's way of saying she didn't want to talk about it."

Luz goes on to say that rumors about Christy began to circulate during seventh grade. When I ask Luz to be specific, she becomes vague, saying only that "a lot of people thought Christy was weird.

The girls especially were kinda mean, because Christy stuck to her own little circle of friends, and she was sort of short when she spoke to anyone else. But she was easily hurt. I remember this one day when she came to school with makeup on. She looked really pretty, but when I told her so, she looked really sad. Then she said, 'You're the first one to compliment me, Luz. Everbody else just made a joke about it.' "

Finally I ask Luz to tell me the most vivid image she has of Christy Scheck. Her reply is almost immediate. "We didn't have the same classes in junior high, but I can still see Christy walking toward me in the hall, waving at me, and saying, 'Hurry up, Luz, hurry up. You don't want to be late.' "

CHAPTER FIVE

AFTER MERRY FOUND the empty aspirin bottles and razor blades in Christy's room in November, she knew it was time to check out residential treatment centers. She was prepared only to make inquiries; actually placing Christy in a hospital was something both Bob and Merry considered to be a last resort. When Merry consulted with Gary Juleen, he recommended Southwood Psychiatric Center in Chula Vista, where he had worked in 1976 as director of a Christian-oriented psychiatric program that rented a wing at the facility. He still knew one of the staff psychiatrists there, a Dr. Arthur Quinn. Merry recalls that she and Bob were at least marginally comfortable with the idea of Southwood, even though they still hoped to avoid any kind of treatment that would take Christy away from home. But they took Juleen's suggestion seriously "because Gary still had some contact at Southwood, and because we liked the idea of having a line of communication. Of not going in cold." Merry also recalls speaking to friends who had placed their son in Southwood. "On the locked unit, on two occasions. And he was okay."

On November 12 Merry got a call from Ed Dueñez. There was a problem at school, he told her. Christy was hiding her arms.

Merry had a flash of the razor blades in Christy's room and the marks she had made on her arms with the point of the compass. The last of her hopes died. She asked Dueñez to take Christy to the nurse's office and speak to her, to tell her that she needed to be in a place where she could get help. Before Merry left her office she called Southwood to make sure they accepted Bob's military insurance: CHAMPUS.

CHAMPUS stands for Civilian Health and Medical Program of

the Uniformed Services, a federal health insurance program that covers both active and retired military personnel and their families. CHAMPUS mental-health benefits include 30 days annually of inpatient care for adults, 45 days for children, and 150 days for adolescents in residential treatment centers. Additional days are authorized when deemed necessary.

Most private insurers did not offer residential coverage. Bob Scheck was not on active duty, so his CHAMPUS benefits would cover 80 percent of Christy's hospital fees. If Scheck had been on active duty, CHAMPUS would have paid the full amount.

It must be noted that between 1980 and 1985, increases in CHAMPUS mental-health costs averaged 20 percent a year; between fiscal years 1985 and 1989, these costs increased 126 percent, reaching $613 million. In 1990 and in 1991, the year Christy Scheck was admitted to Southwood Psychiatric Center on her father's CHAMPUS plan, costs stabilized, topping out at $631 million. Inpatient mental-health care represented $500 million, or 79 percent of that total. Approximately $305 million was for treatment of children and adolescents, and about $165 million of that sum was paid to residential treatment centers.

Ed Dueñez still feels a pang of remorse when he thinks back to the day Christy went to Southwood. "I had heard about Southwood, and I knew the Schecks were considering it, but I hadn't made a personal investigation of the facility. I had the impression that there was a group home for adolescents on the premises, and I figured Christy would be going there. I went into the nurse's office, where Christy was waiting, and I talked to her. I told her, 'Christy, your folks want to send you to a group home for a while. With other kids who have the same kind of stuff going on with them that you do. And that will work for you, you'll see. This will be your time out of the house. You'll be able to sort everything out, I promise you.' "

Dueñez is silent for a long moment before he speaks again. "There was so much trust between Christy and me. But, even so, I was shocked, really shocked, at how easily she went."

Merry was surprised, too. She had expected angry resistance and a shrill argument. Instead, Christy seemed almost relieved. She was silent during the drive to Southwood, staring out the passenger window, not even bothering to turn on the radio and fiddle with the dials. Merry drove without speaking. She did not want to disturb whatever delicate balance remained between herself and her daughter.

Once Christy was inside the Southwood admittance office, her attitude was one of subdued cooperation as she answered a series of questions: Are you sexually active? Have you ever used drugs? Do you know why you're here? Merry recalls, with some indignation, that her own attitude was recorded as well. "The admissions clerk wrote that I was 'angry and bewildered.' " Her voice rings through the silent room. "Yeah. *Yeah.* I'd never placed a child in a place like that before, and it was not something I wanted to do. It was something I had to do. For Christy's safety."

Within one hour of Christy Scheck's admission to Southwood Psychiatric Center, Ed Dueñez received a telephone call. The caller spoke in an urgent whisper. "Mr. Dueñez, this isn't a group home, it's a psychiatric hospital. And, Mr. Dueñez, *I'm not crazy. . . .*"

CHAPTER SIX

WHEN MERRY SCHECK brought her thirteen-year-old daughter to Southwood Psychiatric Center in November 1991, she had no idea that it was one of a chain of seventy-six hospitals spread over twenty-four states. The chain was known as Psychiatric Institutes of America (PIA), and its corporate parent was National Medical Enterprises (NME), a $4 billion company. She was unaware that another PIA facility, Colonial Hills Hospital in San Antonio, Texas, was at the eye of a controversy that had culminated, two months earlier, with the Texas attorney general filing suit against PIA, alleging fraudulent conduct.

The case in Texas involved a fourteen-year-old boy, Jeremy Harrell, who had been picked up in front of his home and taken, in handcuffs, to Colonial Hills for a supposed drug-abuse problem. The security guards who ambushed the boy were following the instructions of a Colonial Hills psychiatrist, Dr. Mark Bowlon. Bowlon had pronounced his diagnosis of Jeremy Harrell's "problems" based solely on statements allegedly made by Jeremy's twelve-year-old brother, a patient at Colonial Hills. Bowlon had never met or spoken with Jeremy.

Jeremy Harrell was kept at Colonial Hills Hospital for five days and six nights, during which time he was not allowed to see or speak with any member of his family. He was not seen by Mark Bowlon until two days after his admission. A drug test administered at Colonial Hills proved to be negative, but at some time during the youngster's enforced hospitalization, he was induced to sign a statement that he had voluntarily committed himself for drug dependence. In addition, the Colonial Hills staff was talking about another problem: child abuse, based on a vague (and completely unfounded) statement, allegedly made, like the drug-dependency story, by the younger brother.

Initially, all of the Harrell family's efforts to gain the release of their middle son failed. Then Jeremy's older brother, eighteen-year-old Rick Harrell, got the attention of Texas state senator Frank Tejeda. Tejeda went at the situation like a buzz saw. His staff learned that Jeremy had been picked up without benefit of court order. The boy was already cuffed and locked in the backseat of the security guards' self-described "Sector One vehicle" when it pulled up at a magistrate's office so that a "warrant for emergency detention" could be signed before Jeremy was taken to Colonial Hills Hospital.

After five terrifying days on a locked unit, and in the face of endless argument and strong resistance from the Colonial Hills staff, Jeremy Harrell was released, and only after Frank Tejeda obtained a writ of habeus corpus.

Another, even more alarming fact came to light a short time after Jeremy's release: Mark Bowlon had been practicing at Colonial Hills under a temporary restricted license and with falsified credentials.

The bill for Jeremy Harrell's five-day stay at Colonial Hills came to $12,000. The Harrells' insurance provider, CHAMPUS, paid the full amount.

There were similar incidents at other PIA facilities around the country—in Florida, Alabama, Oklahoma, and New Jersey. In February 1989 the New Jersey Department of Insurance launched an undisclosed probe of NME's Fair Oaks Hospital in Summit. The investigation was based on three complaints made by former patients and hospital employees, and it was concluded during the summer of 1990. From then until May 1991, representatives of NME negotiated with the Insurance Fraud Division of the New Jersey Department of Insurance. An agreement was finally reached: NME paid out $400,000, the largest sum ever paid to the New Jersey Department of Insurance. The original penalty sought was $2 million. According to New Jersey regulations, the first settlement by an entity such as NME or PIA for insurance violations may be made without admission of guilt or criminal wrongdoing, and this "lack of finding" was a part of the negotiation. However, once the state of New Jersey reached that agreement with NME/PIA, the Insurance Department received more than three hundred additional complaints of insurance fraud by Fair Oaks, and the investigation broadened. A pivotal concern for federal and state investigators was $40 million in claims paid to Fair Oaks Hospital in 1989 by twenty-one insurance carriers. Other complaints, from other states, came from patients who accused PIA hospitals of kidnapping them or of enticing them with promotional claims as well as from patients who claimed that they were held against their will (with unnecessary treatments administered) until their insurance benefits ran out. Investigations began after charges were made that PIA was paying bounties to probation officers, teachers, and psychiatrists for referring people to PIA facilities. Alan Sidell,* a former marketing executive at Southwood Psychiatric Center, the facility to which Christy Scheck was taken, has stated that the best referral sources were licensed therapists who specialized in adolescent care, particularly those therapists with a large complement of CHAMPUS-insured patients.

Merry Scheck was not aware of any of this when she brought her daughter to NME/PIA's Southwood Psychiatric Center for treatment. She knew only that someone she trusted had recommended Southwood, and that her family's health insurer, CHAMPUS, would cover Christy's expenses.

CHAPTER SEVEN

NATIONAL MEDICAL ENTERPRISES was founded in 1968 by Richard K. Eamer, Leonard Cohen, and John C. Bedrosian, a trio of Southern California–based attorneys. (Eamer was also a CPA.) The company began as a management firm serving clients in the medical field, and one of NME's earliest allegiances was to hospitals in the maximization of reimbursements from the newly instituted government programs of Medicare and Medicaid.

Soon after its formation, NME partnered with a group of investors, buying control of several hospitals and convalescent homes. The investors, a group composed in the main of attorneys and physicians, anted up the greater portion of funding for these ventures. NME's major contribution was its expertise in the augmentation of the bottom line.

In 1969 NME went public with a stock offering of $25.5 million.

During the next decade, Richard Eamer became increasingly enamored of the business of investor-owned hospital chains. He was voluble on the subject in interviews, extolling the virtues of staffing with nonunion personnel whenever possible, to save on labor expenses. Bulk buying also cut costs, as did the hiring of M.B.A.'s to run both the hospitals and the nursing homes. Eamer, with his background in accounting, was well aware that the application of business practices was as important as the practice of good medicine.

By the mid-seventies NME was using its own construction subsidiary to build medical office complexes adjacent to many of the NME-owned hospitals. Doctors would be offered office space at subsidized rates, with the anticipated quid pro quo of patients being directed next door to the NME hospital for diagnostic and therapeutic procedures. The majority of these hospitals, such as Century City Hospital in Los Angeles, were located in upscale neighborhoods, which meant that a large percentage of the patients would be covered by private insurance. And private coverage meant that all bills would be paid in full. (Government insurance plans, which covered the majority of U.S. hospital patients in the years before the spread of HMOs, offered cost-related reimbursement rates.)

Very few NME-owned hospitals were acute-care facilities such as Cedars-Sinai Medical Center in Los Angeles, St. John's Hospital in Santa Monica, Mount Sinai in New York, or teaching hospitals like UCLA Medical Center. Acute care means high overhead: obstetrics, specialized surgery (trauma, cardiac neurosurgery, etc.), and emergency-room care are labor-intensive services; they eat into profit. Most of the NME hospitals dispensed services that did not add measurably to the overhead. NME hospitals offered radiation therapy, orthopedic surgery, and, in some facilities, psychiatric treatment.

One of the earliest NME-owned hospitals was Alvarado Community Hospital in San Diego. It was an acute-care facility sharing grounds with Alvarado Parkway Institute, a freestanding psychiatric facility and a separate corporation. When the NME brass realized that, despite the low overhead in the psychiatric unit, the charges for RBN (room, bed, and nursing) could be the same as the RBN charges for any other department in the hospital, they knew they were onto something. A further bonus was the lack of any need for specialty-department or high-maintenance equipment in the psychiatric unit. If a patient at Alvarado Parkway required treatment in an emergency room, or if an X ray or EKG was prescribed, the patient could be taken over to Alvarado Community Hospital. There would be a transportation fee (the usual amount was $120) and charges for whatever medical procedures were involved. The patient's insurance carrier would be billed. And NME would be reimbursed.

The biggest influence on profitability is payroll. At Alvarado Parkway, staffing took the biggest bite out of the overhead. Fewer people were needed to care for a larger percentage of patients. And nonunion, unlicensed workers could be hired to fill the positions of mental-health counselors and interns.

NME acquisitions increased exponentially during the seventies, with the company buying several private hospitals each year. An overseas deal with Saudi Arabia netted a $150 million, five-year hospital-management contract. (This deal was sweetened in 1980 when Richard Eamer signed for a substantial piece of a $362 million joint agreement for NME to construct, staff, and manage an extension to the hospital.) In 1979 NME completed a $47 million deal to buy the Hillhaven Corporation, a chain of nearly one hundred nursing homes. That move brought NME's revenues and profits to $723 million and $29.5 million, respectively—more than double the numbers for the previous year.

But for National Medical Enterprises, the wave of the future was in the business of mental health.

By the beginning of the eighties, NME owned 34 hospitals, located for the most part in California, and 110 nursing homes, scattered over thirty states. The corporation's bottom line was impressive: NME stock was trading at $44 per share, up by more than 50 percent from the mid-seventies. Eamer's holdings in the company, including stock options, were now worth $25 million.

In 1982 NME bought out its biggest competitor in the mental-health field: Psychiatric Institutes of America. The price was $100 million, and for that amount NME got twenty-one psychiatric hospitals, four addiction-treatment centers, and a system of treatment, called "milieu therapy," that would prove to be highly profit-enhancing. In milieu therapy, everything that comes in contact with a patient—the total environment of the facility—is considered to be a valid element of the patient's treatment. This may include anything from random conversations to games played during recreation periods. When milieu therapy is taken most literally, a food server who breaks up a fight between two patients on line in the cafeteria and then spends time reasoning with one or both patients can be considered, in that instance, a therapist—and the institution can bill the patients accordingly. It must also be stated, however, that milieu therapy has been used to great therapeutic effect at such facilities as the Menninger Clinic in Topeka, Kansas.

With the acquisition of PIA, National Medical Enterprises embarked upon an aggressive competition for patients. Most insurance carriers provided longer coverage for adolescents—sixty or ninety days, at least—than for adults, so parents were targeted in NME's advertising campaigns. Organizations like Charter Medical Corporation and CareUnit did likewise, utilizing both print ads and, in Charter's case, television commercials to put across their corporate messages.

In one full-page advertisement for Alvarado Parkway Institute, a photograph of a sullen-looking teenage girl wearing a miniskirt, boots, and a fringed jacket is in the center of the page. Over the girl's head is a legend in large, boldface letters: DISTURBING CHANGES IN APPEARANCE JUST MIGHT BE A NORMAL STAGE OF DEVELOPMENT. The copy then goes on to inform the reader of a number of alarming reasons why these changes might be emblematic of "a larger problem, which is more worrisome." The reader (and, presumably parent) is exhorted to call a given number and speak to a "professional counselor for a free assessment, which may confirm that your child is absolutely okay. If not, we'll recommend the level of treatment that will best help your child to get back on track." Parents are then offered a free growth chart, which, according to the advertising copy, "records physical growth *and* offers information about developmental changes." The ad winds up with a double-edged disclaimer: "Disturbing changes in appearance just might be a flash of individuality, but it doesn't hurt to ask."

Another Alvarado Parkway advertisement featured the photograph of a boy who looks to be about eleven. He is staring insolently into the camera. The uppercase legend above the boy's head states: DEFIANT BEHAVIOR JUST MIGHT BE A NORMAL STAGE OF DE-VELOPMENT. The copy on either side of the page delivers a list defining "defiant behavior," which includes "refusing to obey" or to clean rooms. An apprehension-lulling phrase follows, in which this behavior is provisionally explained away as "one of those developmental stages which drives parents crazy." Then the zinger: "It also may be a sign of a larger problem, and sometimes it's hard to know the difference." The rest of the copy is nearly identical to that of the other ad, with the phrase "disturbing changes" replaced by the word "defiance."

In subsequent interviews with Southwood employees, this sales pitch was referred to as the "What if . . . ?" approach. It played on parents' confusion and guilt.

By 1983 PIA accounted for nearly 45 percent of NME's total revenue. The profits of all the other NME-owned facilities—the hospitals, the nursing homes, the rehabs—paled in comparison with that of the psychiatric units.

In the June 6, 1983, issue of *Forbes* magazine, Richard K. Eamer was listed, along with nine other American CEOs, as a "Fifty-Million-Dollar Man." Eamer's yearly salary and bonus was reported to be $675,183, his benefits came to $117,436, and his stock gains added up to $2,652,099, for a grand total of $3,444,718. Eamer had joined ranks with the mandarins of American enterprise.

The same year, a new antidrug device was originated by a doctor employed at NME/PIA's Fair Oaks Hospital in Summit, New Jersey. The idea was as brilliant as it was simple: a drug hot line that would offer information, advice, and treatment referrals to cocaine users. The number was 800-COCAINE, and within three years, more than one million people would call in to talk about their problems with drugs. Those who requested referrals were given the names of nearby doctors and treatment centers. The list referred to by the hot-line operators had been compiled by the hot line itself, aided by the National Institute of Drug Abuse (NIDA), a federal agency. As lists go, this one was quite extensive: There were approximately four thousand doctors and treatment centers from which to choose. An interesting "coincidence": The centers named most frequently on the hot line were owned by PIA and NME. They included facilities like Fair Oaks; Century City Hospital in Los Angeles; Regent Hospital in New York; and Fair Oaks Hospital in Delray Beach, Florida.

By 1985 NME was listing 800-COCAINE as one of several "innovative outreach programs" in its annual shareholders' report. The hot line was credited with boosting occupancy rates in PIA facilities, but PIA president Norman Zober denied that it was merely, in his words, a "cheap referral gimmick." Zober claimed that less than 1 percent of all patients who entered PIA's substance-abuse programs had been referred there by the hot line. In fact, 800-COCAINE was garnering praise from both the medical community and the media, with radio stations across the country running free public-service announcements to raise societal awareness that help was at the other end of a telephone call.

The image of NME as corporate do-gooder was somewhat tainted, however, when NIDA, concerned about the proprietary nature of 800-COCAINE, set up its own hot line. The reason given was that the institute wanted to make sure that those who could not afford treatment in PIA facilities (the cost of which could amount to $20,000 for a twenty-eight-day stay) could still receive counseling and referral information. The director of the New York Division of Substance Abuse Services, Julio Martinez, subsequently raised the complaint that the state-subsidized hot line was being deluged with calls from people without funds or adequate insurance coverage who said they had been referred there by 800-COCAINE.

By the mid-eighties, with health insurance policies offering generous psychiatric benefits and many states deregulating the construction of new hospitals, the number of private, for-profit psychiatric hospitals rose dramatically. There had been 220 such hospitals in the United States in 1984; by 1988 that figure had reached 444. Within the same four years, the number of state and county psychiatric hospitals had gone from 277 to 285. The total number of psychiatric admissions of minors rose from 82,000 in 1980 to 112,000 in 1986. And the biggest increase was in private psychiatric hospitals: from 17,000 admissions in 1980 to 43,000 in 1986.

By 1987 NME had installed an elaborate computer system that was modeled after the nationwide Psychiatric Hospital Information System (PHIS). Composed of a systemwide tracking processor that entered all patient information into a database plugged in to PIA's corporate office in Washington, D.C., this system made it possible for NME to push a button and catch up on the insurance coverage, diagnosis, and amount spent on every patient.

In other words, Eamer and company could keep track of the dollars. They could see, for example, that a diagnosis of schizoaffective disorder brought in more than a bipolar-disorder diagnosis but not as much as full-blown schizophrenia. The system could tell them which diagnosis provided longer hospital stays and fuller reimbursement, and which hospital allowed NME to keep more of the money.

The market began to change as concern about adolescents surfaced. Studies of diagnostic criteria showed that hospitalized adolescents could not be reliably discerned from their outpatient counterparts, and that for those youngsters who were confined, lengths of stay on hospital units were too often uncorrelated to the blanket diagnosis of adjustment reaction, conduct disorder, and depression.

A greater market change was noted as employers felt the bite of rising health care costs. By the late eighties, insurance plans were limiting psychiatric-hospital stays to weeks instead of months, and new facilities found that more patients were needed to fill the same number of beds. Private psychiatric hospitals that had ridden the crest of the boom were now positioned as unwilling participants in a battle for survival from which patients would emerge as the only hostages.

First there was what PIA executives referred to as the "payor revolt." Prior to mid-1990, the greater portion of psychiatric benefits were paid on a full-indemnity basis. At that point the hospitals began to see a degradation in their net revenue. Reimbursements slipped to 80 percent, then 75, then 70 percent of monies billed.

Then the utilization review came into play. A much-used procedure in acute-care hospitals, it was relatively unheard-of in psychiatric and rehab care. The utilization review worked as a kind of one-two punch. First there was the preadmission certification, in which the patient's doctor gained permission from the insurance carrier to place the patient in the hospital by explaining the medical reasons for inpatient admission. If the admission was approved, the case underwent a concurrent review, in which the insurance carrier was apprised, on a daily or biweekly basis, of the patient's condition. The doctor was, in essence, gaining the insurance company's approval to keep the patient hospitalized.

After admission was authorized and the concurrent review had okayed the patient's continued stay, there was finally the retroactive review, which looked at the entire patient record. If there was anything in the patient's chart indicating medical treatment that could be considered unnecessary, reimbursement was adversely affected.

With the advent of the utilization review, for-profit chains were placed in the position of having to justify not only each admission, but almost every day of inpatient care.

The process of "negative charting" most likely came into use at about the same time utilization reviews began. Negative charting meant that staff members, in charting patients' affects, began to tailor their remarks in such a way as to perpetuate the need for in-hospital treatment. For example, a "bright affect" (psych-unitspeak for "a good mood") could be described as "a manic episode." Documentation for insurance companies was so important that PIA sent out a memo providing detailed instructions for writing medical charts. The cover page consisted of a mock-up of a letter from a fictitious insurance firm:

WECHEETUM INSURANCE COMPANY
1234 West Main Street
Bigtown, Pennsylvania 12345

August 9, 1991

Your Name
XXX Yourstreet Rd.
Yourcity, CA

Dear Sir/Madam:

Your Health Plan performs utilization review, and during your family member's inpatient stay, his progress has been monitored. His inpatient stay has been reviewed by physician advisors and it has been determined that further hospitalization beyond July 31, 1991, will not be a covered benefit.

The decision was based on documentation that was available to the peer reviewer on 7/29/91, and the following rationale:

> Documentation indicates that he can be
> treated at a lesser level of care by 7/31/91.

Please note that this decision does mean that he must leave the facility. His date of discharge still rests with you and his physician. You will be personally responsible for paying all hospital charges for services rendered beginning August 1, 1991.

If you or your physician do not agree with this decision, you may submit a written appeal no later than ninety (90) days from the date you receive this notice.

Sincerely,

Dan Nylklames, MD, FAPA
Medical Director

Beneath the sham letter, printed in italics, was the following note:

The wording in this letter was borrowed from an actual letter for the purpose of informing staff of the importance of accurate documentation. The in-

surance company is fictitious and it is not our intention to state or imply
anything derogatory about insurance companies or review organizations.

The letter was followed by examples stressing "the importance of good and accurate charting." The first example is a case where payment was denied for the last twenty-six days of hospitalization because "documentation in the chart indicated the patient could have been treated at a lesser level." The actual denial letter from the insurance company was reproduced:

The patient was admitted because she was manifesting numerous problems including deterioration in school performance, running away, abusing alcohol, and she was severely depressed. She had a history of two previous suicide attempts and numerous suicide threats. On May 24, there was a contradiction in the records. Her attending physician describes the patient as depressed and "continues to show poor insight." However, *the patient is described in the nursing note on the same day as manifesting brighter affect, cooperative, and writing well in a journal.*

Another example followed:

The patient in this example was admitted with the following history: suicidal ideation; depression; feeling that no one cares about or loves him; gang affiliation and possible drug/alcohol use. Less than one week later this note appears in the chart:

Bright affect. Pt. encouraged to talk more in groups. Pt. affect brighter, more open in group. Talking more about his family issue. Interacting more with peers and staff.

From this note it looks like the patient is ready to be discharged to a lower level of care. Please do not use "bright affect" as a behavior, or "brighter affect" as a response. Also, there is no indication of which family issue was discussed.

There are a couple of examples of "good documentation." In one, the patient's behavior was described as "affect flat, mood depressed, facial expression basically bland." A list followed, delineating the rules for good documentation. These included another instruction to avoid the phrase "bright affect, which usually indicates a patient is ready to go to a lower level of care." Another rule warned staff "never to mention that an incident report was written." The memo concluded with a list of "Things to Remember." For example: "Through your documentation the patient must demonstrate progress toward objectives to show benefit from hospitalization. At the same time, the patient must also have additional outstanding and unresolved problems which require an acute level of care."

And, finally: "REMEMBER, WITH ALL DOCUMENTATION YOU ARE LEAVING YOURSELF OPEN TO VAST INTERPRETATION BY INDIVIDUALS WHO DO NOT KNOW THE PATIENT OR WHAT IS HAPPENING ON THE UNIT. WHAT IS WRITTEN AND LEGIBLE IS ALL THAT COUNTS."

These memos were composed by numbers men who knew how to manipulate their target: those staff members least likely to benefit from increased reimbursements. A climate was provided for frontline workers, the people most directly involved with the patients, to inch over into practices that may not have been entirely ethical. Justification was easy: Some patients did need to be in a controlled environment. And, according to the memos, mental-health counselors, interns, and nurses were able to recognize and anticipate those patients' moods much more effectively than some yahoo from a review board. So the line was carefully drawn between health care providers and insurers.

In the wake of the insurance companies' changes in reimbursement, NME additionally implemented, in January 1991, a vast cost-reduction program. It was designed by executive vice president and CEO Ronald T. Bernstein, and it would prove to be one of the central points of the Scheck lawsuit a year and a half later.

The cost-reduction memo, sent out to PIA regional administrators, stated that "no area of expenditure is sacrosanct; if a cost cannot be justified, it should be cut." And: "Administrators, program directors and controllers are all accountable for making it happen." And: "There has been a lack of accountability to date, *e.g.,* no administrator has been placed on probation because of going over plan on expenses and not making cuts."

With the thinly veiled threats of the memo hanging over their heads, the administrators got busy. Actions were immediately taken to control salary increases, and some salaries were frozen. On many units, R.N.'s were replaced by L.V.N.'s (licensed vocational nurses), and, in turn, L.V.N.'s were replaced by psych techs. Some of the licensed personnel were replaced by paraprofessionals, as well as by interns who put in unpaid hours on the units toward a degree.

One way to cut costs was to get rid of benefited employees and high-skill workers. The full-time equivalent (FTE) calculation was a boon here. Using the FTE rule, it is not necessary for a single employee to work forty hours to reach the forty-hour (full-time staff) goal. Two part-time employees or four quarter-time workers can qualify as one FTE—and the company can reap savings by not having to provide benefits, overtime pay, and vesting in employee stock-option plans, as well as having greater flexibility in scheduling whenever the patient census drops. The downside of this scenario is most certainly a lack of continuity in patient care, treatment, and documentation.

An example of a realistic staffing ratio on any given shift would be four to five staff members to eighteen to twenty patients. In budgeting a department, eighteen FTE's might be utilized; in cost cutting, as many as thirty-six people without benefits might be on unit during three shifts: day, night, and late-night or nocturnal. Thirty-six staff workers trying to establish trusting relationships with a full unit of adolescent patients are at least eighteen people too many for any kind of stable, therapeutic connection.

According to Alan Sidell, who headed up a marketing team for child and adolescent services at Southwood, a numbers game got under way at Southwood at the beginning of the nineties. "We tried to zero in right under the legal level of four-to-one that would keep us licensed and certified, and then we would play around with the language of who went into that ratio. Which could be anyone who was physically present on a unit. Like unit clerks, whose duties are predominately secretarial, and unpaid psych interns, and bookkeepers."

Not all FTE's were paid the same hourly rate. Southwood, as a proprietary organization, did market analysis of the labor market for mental-health personnel in the San Diego area. According to Sidell, "The management at Southwood didn't want to pay out at the high end of the wage scale [$14 to $15 per hour]; the ideal design was to place Southwood at the bottom of the pay scale in the professional health community." As a result, Southwood mental-health counselors were paid between $7 and $9 an hour, and unit clerks received an hourly wage of $5 or $6.

CPR training and classes in management of assaultive behavior were compulsory for all Southwood personnel, but that training was reserved for regular employees. One of the problems at Southwood was that as cost reductions became more and more stringent, with more cutbacks of FTE hours, the units began to fill up with on-call mental-health workers who, as a rule, served a number of facilities and so were not always available to take shifts.

Sidell described another method of cost cutting on the units: "Say a kid says she feels like hurting herself. Says 'I don't feel safe.' Usually a one-on-one is ordered, and you can sit the kid near the nurses' station until that order is okayed by the program director, or by any other on-call administrator who can give the go-ahead for the 20 percent additional personnel cost a one-on-one involves. Well, rather than call in that extra staff member, Southwood management found ways to get around it: Sit the kid in the lounge, which had a glass wall, and anyone at the nurses' station can keep an eye on her. Of course, if another kid at the other end of the unit goes off . . ." Sidell shrugged. Point made.

By 1991, anecdotal reports of unnecessary hospitalizations and allegations of people locked up in PIA hospitals on the basis of hearsay were being made with some frequency. In Texas there was a forty-one-year-old carpenter from San Antonio whose story shockingly paralleled that of fourteen-year-old Jeremy Harrell: abduction by security guards to Colonial Hills Hospital; medication with tranquilizers; pressure to sign voluntary commitment papers; release secured only after an attorney produced a court order. In Boca Raton, Florida, the father of three children, aged three to nine, was accused of child molestation by his ex-wife during a custody battle. A judge deemed the woman's case to be groundless, but PIA's Fair Oaks Hospital in Delray Beach accepted the three children for commitment when the woman brought them in. The children were kept, over their father's protestations, at Fair Oaks for five weeks and returned twenty-four hours before the family's insurance benefits ran out. The bill for treatment came to more than $70,000.

Then the family of a fourteen-year-old girl in Palm Beach County, Florida, charged a PIA facility there of unethically (albeit legally) using a school-counseling program to solicit business. When the girl spoke about her sadness at a grandparent's death with a participating counselor from PIA's Lake Hospital, the counselor suggested that the girl and her mother visit that facility. They did so and, upon arrival at the hospital, were told that the counselor was recommending that the girl be admitted for a stay of ten days to two weeks. The counselor's diagnosis, they were informed, was that the girl was clearly suicidal.

The mother, alarmed by this grim pronouncement, committed her daughter. Once inside the locked unit, the girl pleaded with the hospital staff, telling them again and again that she had never, at any time, entertained the notion of killing herself. The staff members responded with lectures on denial.

It took nine days and the services of an attorney to free the fourteen-year-old from Lake Hospital. The bill for her enforced stay came to more than $12,000.

In the face of burgeoning controversy, and despite the insurance companies' decision to pare psychiatric patients' stays in hospitals to twenty-four days (six days less than in 1989), NME's psychiatric division was bringing in $1.74 billion in revenue and $320 million in operating profits. NME was the envy of the health care industry, with PIA achieving a nationwide occupancy rate of 75 percent. That was the year the company earned a net operation revenue of $3.8 billion, with profits garnered at $272 million.

In 1991 alone, the top five NME executives received compensation that added up to $35.5 million. Richard Eamer was the highest-paid executive of a California-based public company, at $19.9 million (most of that sum derived from cashing in stock options). The following year, Eamer's salary would dip to $3.8 million. Neither Eamer, nor Leonard Cohen, nor John Bedrosian, the three founders of NME, responded to requests for interviews for this book.

National Medical Enterprises was a company whose product had been widely described as "Cadillac-driven." Few people knew, in 1991, that what was being delivered might have been more aptly compared to a Ford Pinto. Certainly Bob and Merry Scheck didn't know. They knew only one thing: Their thirteen-year-old daughter needed help. And Southwood Psychiatric Center had promised to provide it.

CHAPTER EIGHT

CHRISTY REFUSED TO see either of her parents during the first ten days of her hospitalization. She refused to see Gary Juleen, the Schecks' family therapist. Refused to attend family sessions, which were monitored by Juleen, or family visits, which were less structured.

Merry called Southwood each evening. Her throat still tightens when she talks about it. "I'd speak to the charge nurse on Christy's unit. Because I couldn't get through to anyone else on the staff. And all I wanted to do was ask how Christy was feeling, what her emotional status was." An edge of defensiveness seeps into Merry's voice. "I wasn't calling to ask about what Christy was talking about in her sessions. I wasn't asking this woman to betray professional confidences. I was only asking for a clue, something that would help Bob and me to understand." She slumps against the back of the sofa for an instant, then her spine stiffens again.

"That earned her the label of 'overbearing mother.' " Bob's voice rasps after a long silence. He clears his throat softly.

Merry goes on. "We knew we had to connect with Christy again, so I finally asked the charge nurse for some kind of consequence to be implemented if Christy continued to refuse to come to the family sessions, which we felt were vital. I said, 'We need to motivate this child, because the longer she doesn't see us, the longer she won't see us. She's building a wall.'

" 'Oh, we can't do that, Mrs. Scheck.'

"Finally, I said, 'Listen, we're paying for our child to be there. We're trying to have family sessions.' "

Bob leans forward to tap the edge of the table. "You gotta realize," he says, "not only were we getting nothing from Christy, who wouldn't see us, but when we'd ask the people who were supposed to be there to help all three of us, all we'd get was, 'We can't do this, we can't do that.' Every time we asked them for information, or for—" He stops. Starts again. "Or if one of us would make a . . . suggestion on how to handle our thirteen-year-old daughter whom they'd had for maybe two weeks . . ." His voice has lifted in anger. Now he falls silent again, taking a moment before he continues. "It was always the same answer: 'Oh, we can't do that.' To this day, I don't know what their treatment was."

Under other circumstances it would not be difficult to acknowledge the feelings of frustration on both sides of the table: parents, desperate with the need to communicate with and gain understanding from the caretakers of their sick child, allowing themselves to meddle in her prescribed treatment; and hospital staff workers who must give their patients' well-being top priority. But in the case of Christy Scheck and Southwood Psychiatric Center, even the clinically correct or well-meant response from a member of the staff seems suspect.

When Christy finally agreed to attend a family session, she walked in grudgingly. Bob and Merry tried to make conversation. Gary Juleen attempted a couple of openers. Christy sat and seethed. When asked direct questions she replied in mumbled monosyllables. It seemed clear to the others that she was waiting for the moment when she could leap to her feet in a show of rage and storm out of the room. It took less than ten minutes for that to happen, and neither of her parents can recall what it was that triggered Christy's anger. She just wanted to get out of that room.

The next session mirrored the first one: painful attempts to engage Christy in conversation; Bob and Merry's sense of treading on eggs; the fear of setting off another walkout. And then the walkout.

I ask the Schecks which one of them felt targeted by Christy's rage. The response is immediate; the Schecks have put in long hours reliving the past. "Bob was specifically the target," Merry says. "Primarily, everything was aimed at Bob while Christy was on the locked unit. Her general attitude toward me was, 'You're on Dad's side.' "

But as Christy distanced herself from her parents and from Juleen in family sessions during those first weeks of her hospitalization, she poured out an inventory of conflicting reports to any staff member who would listen: She had been an active member of a notorious street gang; she had been kidnapped and raped by rival gang members; she was a hard-core drug user, everything from marijuana to crack cocaine. None of the stories produced quite the ripple Christy seemed to be after.

When Merry heard about the gang stories, she called Ed Dueñez, who verified what the Schecks knew to be the truth: All of Christy's friends at Horace Mann Middle School were either other athletes or other honor students. Red Penny confirmed this, and he went even further, saying that Christy didn't even know any gang members. That she was, in fact, contemptuous of kids who drifted into the gang lifestyle. As for drug use, the charge nurse to whom Christy boasted hadn't bought a word of the girl's story. The woman told Merry that the amount of street drugs Christy claimed she had done would have killed her the first time out. In fact, according to the nurse, Christy had no real knowledge of drugs of any kind.

But the psychiatrist in charge of Christy's treatment team, Dr. Arthur Quinn, who also carried the title of part-time director of Dual Diagnosis Services at Southwood, placed Christy in a drug-abuse group.

The Schecks had already undergone one encounter with Quinn. After their daughter's hospitalization, they met—at their insistence—with the psychiatrist. In the few minutes allotted to them, Merry described the problems she and Bob had been experiencing with Christy, focusing primarily on her unwillingness, or inability, to talk about the specifics of the emotional pain she was so clearly feeling. Wishing to explore the possibility of a chemical imbalance based on Christy's extreme mood swings, Merry requested a biological-imbalance screen. Quinn refused. When Merry questioned his decision to place Christy in the substance-abuse group, his reasoning seemed less than informed.

"Oh, I don't believe she *was* an abuser. She'll probably go once and then never go again."

"Why put her in a drug-abuse group, then?"

"It's purely educational, Mrs. Scheck."

During those last weeks of November, while Christy was on the locked unit, both Merry and Bob continued to meet with Gary Juleen. "We had to try and understand, try to work things through," Merry explains. "We needed to find out what we'd done wrong, and how Bob and I, as Christy's parents, could change to make things better."

Then Christy made a request, relayed to her parents by the charge nurse: She wanted to see her sister, Molly.

The Schecks brought Molly with them on their next visit to the hospital. A family session was already scheduled, which meant that Juleen would be in the room with them. Christy was happy to see Molly, and the younger girl, in spite of her shyness in the unfamiliar surroundings, went to hug her sister. Then she moved close to Bob again, leaning against him as if for comfort. Christy answered a couple of general queries, and, as always, a climate of forced pleasantries prevailed. Then, in describing some aspect of the hospital routine, Christy used the word "fucking" as an adjective.

It is what Bob Scheck considers "military language." And it is unacceptable in the Scheck household. He told Christy so.

Now, as Bob tells this part of the story, sitting with his wife and me in the family room of their new home, with the burnished rays of an October sun falling across his face, it is clear that he is trying very hard to keep a close rein on his emotions. "Christy let loose on me. She basically said, 'Eff you. I hate your effing guts and I want you out of my effing life.' "

Merry breaks in. "Molly grabbed Bob's fingers when Christy began to yell, and she just held on so hard . . ."

Bob holds up the index and third finger of his right hand. "She held on so hard she stopped the circulation. She was only a little kid, and she was that frightened by what was going on in that room." Bob allows his hand to drop back to the armrest of his chair. He looks down for a moment, then his head comes up again and he locks eyes with Merry. She nods her head slightly, encouraging him, returning strength to him.

"And then Christy charged out of the room," he continues. "Gary went after her, and when he opened the door, I could see Christy, standing there in the hall." Bob pauses. "She had a big grin on her face."

I ask why he thinks she might have been grinning.

"Because what she said gave her authority."

"Power." Merry's voice is very soft.

This time, when Bob looks at her, his eyes hold a challenge. "No." His voice is flat. "The authority. To abuse."

Christy's days on the locked unit of Southwood Psychiatric Center were made up of a round of therapy sessions intersected by classes. When the special-education teacher learned that Christy had been an honor student and a member of the GATE program, he asked her to tutor some of the kids in the class who were having problems at school. Christy was delighted and applied herself enthusiastically to the task.

Christy continually accused her parents of abuse in group sessions and to any counselor who would listen. She said that Merry had left her alone in the house for ten days when she was eight years old. That Bob had been at sea and that her mother had gone on a trip, leaving Christy to fend for herself. That she had been forced to drink water out of the toilet. That Merry had beaten her with pots and pans. (The time frame of the abandonment story coincided, as it happened, with Molly's birth when Christy was six, a time when Merry seldom left the house.) Christy embellished the gang/kidnapping story and told another story about being abducted from her house by a strange man who took her to a green car where another rape took place.

The Schecks spoke with several staff members, suggesting that

Christy was trying to get attention with these stories. Now, when Merry talks about it, it is with anger. "Almost from the very beginning, the inference from the Southwood staff was that whether or not any or all of the stories were true, it was still all our fault that Christy was in the hospital. That somehow, we were monsters. And I didn't feel that I could say something and that it would be held in confidence. My feeling, the whole time Christy was at Southwood, was 'Anything you say can, and will, be used against you.' "

She looks away for a moment. "It got to the point where I was beginning to question myself."

A few days after the family session with Molly, Merry went to the hospital alone. Bob was unable to get off work, and Merry didn't want to miss a family session with Christy.

"Christy behaved like the typical nasty, angry kid from the moment she walked into the room. First she complained about Bob's not being there, saying that was proof he 'didn't want to work on things.' Then, when I tried to talk with her about why she was so angry at us, she began to yell at me. And when Gary tried to intervene, she screamed at him, too: 'These are my issues, and I don't have to talk about them with you!' I knew we were going exactly nowhere. I knew I had to get through to Christy somehow. And I recall thinking, or maybe it was just feeling, that if I could get physically close to her, I could look her in the eye, and she would . . . I don't know, recognize how much I cared about her." Merry's voice has dropped to a near-whisper, and she is beginning to blink back tears. She seems determined not to cry.

"I got up out of my chair, and I came across the room toward her. Because, at this point, she had her hands up, like this." Merry crosses both forearms and holds them up in front of her face. "I knelt down in front of her, and I took hold of both her wrists, and I tried to move her arms down. I said, 'Christy, you *are* going to talk to me.' I think I said that a couple of times, because, really, I was just pleading with this girl. I could feel how she was ready to run out the door, which was her standard way of not dealing. So I got up again and went and stood in front of the door. And Christy just screamed at me." Merry's voice lifts again, approximating Christy's tone, if not the volume of her delivery. " 'These are my effing issues! Mine! And I don't effing have to talk to you about them.' "

There is another short silence. When Merry speaks again, her voice has returned to its normal pitch. "What came out of that meeting was that Christy left the session, went directly to a staff member, and said, 'My mother hit me in there.'

"Well, if I had hit her, Gary was obligated by law to report it. He charted every session, and for that one he wrote that I had tried to move Christy's arms away from her face." Merry has been holding her arms up again, briefly, in illustration of how Christy had them positioned. Now she lowers her arms, allowing both hands to drop heavily into her lap. It is a gesture that relays an ineffable weariness.

"But I don't think the staff ever bothered to read Gary's chartings. So they believed pretty much whatever Christy told them."

CHAPTER NINE

ACCORDING TO A 1994 deposition made by Nadine Peck,* associate administrator of Southwood Psychiatric Center from 1988
through 1993, the clinical staff members who worked most directly with Christy Scheck during her hospitalization at Southwood were the "line staff." Line staff was predominantly composed
of mental-health workers (also referred to, in Southwood parlance,
as counselors) and social workers. These workers were supervised
by program directors. In Christy's case, the director of the early-
adolescent program was a salaried employee (as opposed to the
mental-health counselors, who worked at an hourly rate of approximately $8) whose educational background consisted of a
master's degree in art therapy. None of the mental-health counselors in the early-adolescent program at Southwood were certified
mental-health professionals.

Bob Scheck has commented earlier on the inexperience of the
Southwood staff. Now he mentions it again. "Twenty-two-year-
old college grads, or student interns attempting to get their degrees. Inexperienced girls. That's who had the most input into my
daughter's treatment."

It would, in fact, come to light later that many of the group sessions at Southwood, including those dealing with abuse and sexual molestation, were conducted by student interns.

Gary Juleen has vivid memories of the session in which Christy
accused her mother of striking her. "That was just another attempt
on Christy's part to convince the staff that these sessions were 'horrible,' and that 'my parents are horrible.' That particular session
was conducted at the hospital, in a room off the main hallway,
with people walking by constantly. Any loud noise could be heard

by the entire wing, and Christy was just screaming. I think that was her display to the staff: a way, an attempt to bond with them."

It is difficult for Juleen to talk about Christy Scheck and her parents. He is a soft-spoken man, cautious in tone and mannerism. "I think it was all just a game to Christy, not an overt attempt to con or to be manipulative, but rather to be in control of whatever went on in her life on the unit. And one of the ways she could control it was to get the staff not to send her into family sessions. Of course, they would ask for a reason, and Christy would say, 'Because they're abusive.' Then, when she did go to family sessions, she felt guilt, keeping her head down, not wanting to speak, withdrawing. Somehow, Christy had to create an illusion for the staff that these horrible things were, in fact, happening.

"So when her mother became insistent, asking repeatedly for Christy to look at her, to speak to her, and when Christy wouldn't look up, Merry got out of her chair and tried to move Christy's arms away from her face. And that's when Christy took advantage of the situation. When her mom touched her. Christy could then go to the staff and create the illusion that her mom had abused her.

"I immediately went to the nurses' station and told the staff members who were standing there, and who in fact were looking at me in kind of a funny way, that even though they might have heard a lot of noise coming out of that room—remember, Christy was yelling at the top of her lungs—nothing of any nature of abuse had occurred."

But then why did that attitude among staff workers, the mental-health counselors in particular, continue? Juleen reflects for a moment.

"It may have been that the staff I told this to didn't clear things up with the other staff members on the unit. Didn't relay the information to offset what Christy was telling them. What's interesting to me is that after that session I went down to make sure that Christy was okay. I went into her room, and I said, 'Christy, what's going on here? Why did you do all that loud shrieking at your mom?' And Christy went off again. 'Get out of here! I hate you! I don't want to see you. Leave me alone . . .' " Juleen has not raised his voice, but the intensity of his delivery makes it possible to imagine the timbre of Christy's voice.

Then he says something truly chilling: "All the time Christy was screaming at me, the whole time she was shrieking this stuff, she was turning her head to look sideways at me. She'd smile, and then she'd go back to the screaming." He pauses. "Smiling at me, then screaming."

I ask what he thinks that meant.

"That Christy was playing a game."

To what end?

"So that the staff would rush to her room and take care of her. And that's exactly what happened. And that's when I left."

CHAPTER TEN

AS THANKSGIVING NEARED, it was decided that it would be easier for everyone if the Schecks did not insist on a family visit. Merry and Bob were delighted when Ed Dueñez called and asked if he could make a holiday visit to Christy at the hospital.

Dueñez retains an acute recollection of the day. "We sat at a table with two other kids, in the cafeteria. Another girl, and a boy, both about Christy's age." He pauses. "Well, all three of those kids began to tell horror stories about their lives at home. They sat there, one-upping each other, performing for my benefit, talking about absentee parents, wild parties, drugs at home, gangs, all of it.

"That really got to me. Christy had always been real polite, and highly articulate. Not in the least a street kid, and no way a bullshitter. Well, she was a different person that afternoon. We sat at that table and she talked the talk. And what she was doing was one-upping the other two kids."

Dueñez sighs deeply. "The other two were talking the same way, but to tell you the truth, they didn't seem to be emotionally disturbed at all, to me. They were just opposed to authority. Maybe they were a little out-of-control about it, but they weren't nuts. They were angry kids who had roamed the streets.

"But I saw right away that the hospital was where Christy had learned street-gang talk. Merry had already told me what Christy was saying about being in a gang, and getting kidnapped and raped, and now here she was, saying all that in front of me in the exact same manner as those other two kids. With the same kind of hand gestures you see on rap videos. It really was like she was another person. And she was just too fierce, and too tough for it to be real."

After the meal, Christy took Dueñez to see her room. "The instant we got to her room, Christy reverted back to being herself. Everything about her changed: her voice, her mannerisms, everything. She was real proud of her room. She showed me how, if she stood on a chair, she could see the Coronado Bridge out the window. Showed me a little gift her sister had made for her. She was Christy again."

While Dueñez and Christy were talking, a young woman stuck her head in the doorway and reminded Christy that a group meeting was scheduled. Christy invited Dueñez to attend with her.

"The meeting was held in the cafeteria, about twenty tables with four or five people to a table. There were some adults sprinkled around . . ." He pauses, thinking. "I guess *some* of them could have been visitors. But as far as I could tell, there was absolutely *no* adult supervision during that meeting. The kids vented without restraint, ragging about everything from the food to the kind of music they were allowed to listen to. Christy and I sat with the two kids I'd met earlier, and the three of them repeated and embellished all that stuff they said at lunch." He falls silent again.

"I really don't know how many staff members were in that room. All I know is nobody said a word except the kids. And the only thing out of the kids was horror stories. Maybe I should have intervened at some point, maybe I should have said something like, 'This is inappropriate.' " Dueñez's tone is shot through with the dark shadings of a long-harbored remorse. "But I was only a visitor.

"Before I left the hospital that day, I went and found the young woman who had come to Christy's room earlier. She was one of the mental-health counselors, probably twenty-two years old. I introduced myself, told her I was Christy's school counselor, and then I confronted her. I talked about Christy's lies about being kidnapped and raped, and being in a gang, and all the rest of it. I said, 'When are you people going to do some reality therapy here?'

Know what her answer was?" He does not alter his voice, does not attempt to diminish by imitation: " 'Ed, I know what you're saying. But if I cut Christy off, she's going to think I don't believe her.' "

As Dueñez relives the moment for me, anger causes his voice to lift and resonate. "And I said, 'So you're allowing her to tell all these stories, and you pretend that you believe them so that Christy gets her own credibility, and *then* you're going to yank all that away from her? Is that the treatment plan?'

"Well, this young woman, this so-called counselor, floundered. There was no intelligent answer she could give me, so she just kept trying to convince me that she knew what she was doing. In those words: 'We know what we're doing.' And I kept hitting that one point: 'You're putting Christy up against the wall by acting as if you believe these off-the-wall stories. You keep on acting like that, and she's going to believe them herself. And that's what's so crazy.' I told her that what Christy and every other kid in that group meeting needed was to be confronted with their real lives."

When Christy had been hospitalized for approximately three weeks, Merry Scheck received a call from Dr. Quinn. He informed her that Christy was "stuck" and that in order "to get her unstuck" he felt it was necessary to medicate her with antidepressants.

Reluctantly, Merry agreed. "I could see Christy getting worse, so I said okay. And at the back of my mind I was still considering that it just might be a biological problem. I thought maybe this would help."

I ask if medication had ever been prescribed for Christy before. Merry's eyes turn away for an instant, then she looks at me again. "During the first week or so that Christy was on the locked unit, she got angry about something and slammed her fist into a wall. The staff considered that kind of behavior as being 'out of control,' and so they did a takedown on her."

I remembered the term and the procedure. It is widely used in psychiatric facilities. In a takedown, the patient is pinned to the floor by as many as four, even five staff members, then lifted and carried into a room reserved for this purpose. These rooms, usually referred to as "quiet rooms," are without furniture with the exception of a bare mattress, upon which the patient is placed.

"When they did the takedown on Christy," Merry continues, "she was given Thorazine."

Thorazine is a narcoleptic, a powerful tranquilizer that has been described as a pharmacological substitute for lobotomy. It is most often used to control behavior, and I have heard it described, by psychiatric workers, as one of the "droolers," because patients often drool after the drug has been administered. (The trade names of other narcoleptics are Haldol, Melleril, and Stelazine).

Suddenly, surprisingly, Merry smiles.

"At one point they were going to put Christy in four-point restraints, and she told me later, 'Mom, the bed in that room smelled. So I calmed right down.' " The smile fades, extinguished by a surge of anger. "Now *there's* a reason to calm down: The bed smelled."

Christy was started on a daily dose of twenty-five milligrams of imipramine, a tricyclic antidepressant. When she complained of sleeplessness (a common side effect of the drug), Restoril, a mild sedative, was prescribed.

Tricyclic antidepressants have been the subject of many studies. They are lethal in overdose and, while proving to be not particularly effective against depression, they have a dulling effect on the mind. The prescribed maximum dosage of imipramine for an adolescent is 100 milligrams. By her third month at Southwood, Christy was being given 150 milligrams of imipramine a day.

Shortly after Christy was begun on daily medication, Merry commented to Gary Juleen that since all of Christy's attention-gaining accusations and outbursts had failed to deliver what Christy wanted, she expected that the next escalation would be a big one. "The next thing Christy does will be to accuse Bob of sexually molesting her."

Speaking about it now, Merry explains her reasoning. "It was just a gut feeling. But I could see it coming. Because I read that book Christy brought home from the library. That book set it all out. And I could see it coming."

CHAPTER ELEVEN

ON DECEMBER 10, 1991, Merry Scheck wrote a letter to South-wood psychiatrist Arthur Quinn stating that she was unhappy with the treatment her daughter was receiving, citing Christy's apparent deterioration and lack of progress. She also asked what the requirements were for the hospital to report any allegations of sexual abuse that Christy might make. And she asked if it was possible to work through any such allegations if they became an issue.

After mailing the letter, Merry called Quinn, requesting an appointment with him, to go over the letter point by point. Quinn told her there was no need for a meeting; they could handle the problem by telephone.

Merry waited another day. Then she placed a call to the charge nurse on the locked unit. "Remember," Merry says, "this was the same woman I'd been talking to on a regular basis, because she was the only staff member available to me. We'd spoken, in the past, about residential treatment centers and group homes, because we all knew that Christy wasn't ready to come home from the locked unit. Now we talked about alternative placements again. But making any kind of decision under these circumstances was extremely difficult."

At some point during Merry's conversation with the charge nurse, Dr. Quinn came on the line.

"Oh, you've heard," he said.

"Heard what?"

Merry remembers how Quinn sounded that day: "He was all smiles." Quinn informed Merry that Christy was to be transferred to the Southwood Residential Treatment Center. CHAMPUS had approved it.

"What? What do you mean, 'I've heard'?" Merry's voice quivers in outrage as she describes the remainder of her conversation with the psychiatrist in charge of her daughter's treatment. "Then and there I demanded a tour of the residential treatment center. I told Quinn that I wanted to speak with the intake worker and the case manager before they put her in there."

That evening Bob and Merry decided that Merry would go to the hospital the following day. "Because it was easier for me to get off work than it was for Bob. At this point, I was leaving Molly at a baby-sitter's house, and then I'd drive about forty-five minutes to get to my job. The hospital was another forty-five minutes to the south, in Chula Vista. An hour and a half, one way, from my office to the hospital."

There is no anger, no suggestion of resentment in Merry's tone; she has made a simple statement of fact. But anyone listening to her can hear how tired she is. There is a weariness at her center, and it is so profound, so deeply buried in the bone, that it will, in all likelihood, never work its way out. Merry Scheck is a woman drowned in remembrance. She and Bob Scheck are bound by it, tied together by its myriad unseen strands, each strand as strong as a filament of tensile steel. It is remembrance that whispers, How, when, what could we have done differently?

Merry's initial view of the residential treatment center, known familiarly to the Southwood staff and patients as the RTC, took place on December 13, the day after she spoke with Dr. Quinn.

Until the fall of 1991, there had been two residential treatment centers connected to Southwood Psychiatric Center. One, known as South Bay, was located about three miles from the hospital campus. South Bay ran a full-service adolescent program in three distinct units, with a total of sixty beds for patients ranging in age from six to eighteen. The other facility was a twenty-four-bed unit for adolescents on the Southwood campus itself. The two facilities were merged shortly before Christy Scheck was admitted for treatment. The official reason was that the South Bay lease was up. It is more likely that the move was precipitated by on-site inspections of both facilities made by Health Management Strategies (HMS), the reviewing arm of CHAMPUS. Numerous deficiencies were found in both locations: low staffing ratios; mental-health counselors conducting therapy sessions; unlicensed personnel heading group-therapy meetings; staff members without training or licensing in CPR. The inspection turned up other problems as well: improper and incomplete charting of patients; patients being deprived of discharge plans; improper admissions and inadequate in-service programs for trainees. Also noted were substandard safety conditions: The building in which the older adolescents were housed was found to be condemnable.

NME filed and submitted a corrective-action plan with the federal government. The plan stated, in effect, that all deficiencies would be corrected and all standards met. This was accomplished, not by the addition of more and better-trained personnel, or by the comprehensive upgrading of the adolescent housing in question, but by the more cost-effective method of shuttling the South Bay patients a few miles down the road to the Southwood facility. Finding space for the added patient load was not a problem: The original single-story Southwood hospital building was still standing; it had been replaced, in 1987, by a new, three-story structure. Although the old building was mainly in use as a storage space, it was now freshened up, and the beds were moved back, and with them, the patients from South Bay. This was an acceptable solution for HMS, and Southwood Psychiatric Center was allowed to keep federal funding for its CHAMPUS patients.

When Merry Scheck drove to Southwood on December 13 to discuss the possible transfer of her daughter to the RTC, she was sure of one thing only: She and Bob would be making this decision in a time of crisis.

Merry met with the program director of the residential treatment center and an intake worker whose name she does not recall. She did not meet the director in charge of the early-adolescent program, a woman named Lynn Skinner.* Merry recalls: "I told them that I saw Christy escalating to the point where she would make these allegations against Bob, and I asked them, 'What should we do?' Both of them were real quick with an answer. I was told, 'Kids make these allegations all the time, Mrs. Scheck. We just deal with it—you don't have to worry yourself at all.' "

Bob has been listening quietly. Now Merry looks over at him and their eyes lock for a long moment, and this time it is he who nods slightly, sending a message of support and strength to his wife. The corners of her mouth lift in a nearly imperceptible smile, then her eyes connect with mine again as she prepares to continue. "We'd talked about it until after one o'clock in the morning the night before. We'd prayed about it. And it seemed to us that if we took Christy from Southwood, the hospital, and placed her at Southwood, the residential treatment center, which was right on the same grounds, that the paperwork would carry through. Preliminary testing had been done. Why take her somewhere else? That was our thinking"—she looks down at her hands—"in that time when every decision was critical.

"So, very reluctantly, I agreed to place Christy in the Southwood RTC."

On December 13, 1991, Christy Scheck was "walked across the corridor" to the Southwood Residential Treatment Center. Merry went to the hospital for the signing-in process.

"I had been told that it would take six weeks to do another evaluation on Christy, and that she would need to be in the RTC for at least two months. Of course I wondered why another evaluation was necessary, but at that time, our only concern was getting the help Christy needed. When I got there, to sign her in, I was told that in order for Christy to be accepted on the unit, I would have to sign a bond for an additional twelve thousand dollars. And, even in the midst of all that incredible stress, the thought came to me that if I signed this bond, I would be placing my family seventeen thousand dollars in debt. I told them that I was sorry, I simply could not afford it. And I told them to get hold of Dr. Quinn. That I wanted Christy released.

"The answer I got was the one I heard most often out of Southwood employees. It was what they said whenever I asked a question they didn't have the answer to, or whenever we made a request they didn't want to fulfill." Merry takes a deep breath, holds it for an instant, then closes her eyes as she speaks. " 'Now, Mrs. Scheck . . .' " It is the tone of someone attempting to reason with a person who has just pulled out a revolver.

"I got angry. I said, 'Do you want *me* to call the doctor?' I told that woman I had another child at home to think about, that we simply could not afford a commitment for an added twelve thousand dollars. I told her we would do whatever was necessary for Christy, that we would get outside therapy. That we would do whatever it took, but that we were not going in the hole for another twelve thousand dollars. We already owed five thousand dollars to Southwood." Merry is so angry that she is having trouble keeping her voice at a conversational level. "This woman went and got somebody else from the financial office, and I was then told that if I would fill out and sign a paper stating that I could not afford to pay the additional twelve thousand dollars, that amount would be waived by Southwood."

Her voice drops. "So, knowing that Christy couldn't be home, and feeling that if she could be in treatment here, and if the insurance paid for it, and Christy would be safe, then maybe we could work things through in family sessions."

The room is silent. Nobody moves, nobody speaks. Remorse fills the air around us like the pulse of a struck gong. When Merry speaks again, her voice is a near-whisper. "I signed Christy into the Southwood RTC."

CHAPTER TWELVE

WHEN CHRISTY SCHECK was transferred from the locked unit of the Southwood acute-care hospital, she left a three-story building with the capacity to house sixty-four patients, two to a room. Adult patients were quartered on the top floor, adolescents and children on the second floor. The first floor housed administrative offices, including those of the CEO, the director of nursing, and the medical director; the intake and referral-development offices; and the hospital cafeteria and pharmacy. Marketing was done in a separate building located about a half-block from the Southwood grounds.

The unit into which Christy was moved, the early-adolescent wing of the residential treatment center, held approximately fifteen patients, two to a room, all of them between the ages of thirteen and fifteen. Next to the early-adolescent unit, and separated by a nurse's station, was the preadolescent or child unit, with a capacity for sixteen children between the ages of three and twelve. The two units formed a kind of squared U shape, with the bottom of the U formed by a corridor attaching both units to the acute-care facility. The area that housed the two units was referred to as "The Pavilion." The adolescent unit of the RTC, with patients ranging in age from fifteen to eighteen, was quartered in an adjacent building known to staff members as "The House."

The early-adolescent unit had earned a bad reputation among Southwood employees. Many staff members, particularly those who worked at the clinical level, had been vocal about it, describing a "state of tremendous chaos" and representing the unit as dangerous. These complaints were lodged during late 1990 and early 1991. There was talk of destructive patients who could not be contained, physical attacks on counselors, and progressively inadequate staffing. There had been frequent dialogues among the clinical staff about various incidents of patients threatening one another and staff workers with violence. Many workers were convinced that patients were being transferred from the acute-care hospital to the residential treatment center before their medications were stabilized and before they were able to function properly in a less structured environment.

And there was another critical area: Due to the extensive marketing push to pull customers into Southwood facilities, troubled kids from juvenile-justice systems in Nevada, Texas, New Mexico, Arkansas, and other areas of California were being admitted to Southwood. One of the out-of-state cities most inundated with Southwood marketing devices was Las Vegas. This influx of justice system juveniles into Southwood was, many employees believed, highly detrimental to other patients and staff alike. Among coworkers, the placement of these troubled adolescents into Southwood was called "dumping."

When these concerns were raised in staff meetings (comprising mental-health counselors, senior counselors, nursing and social-work staff, department heads, and psychology interns), with particular emphasis placed on the need for improved patient/staff ratios, they were met with strong resistance from the administration. Worried staff members were told to do the best they could with what was available. Further complaints seemed pointless: It was well known that marketing quotas had to be satisfied, that cost containment outweighed every other consideration. The most important thing was to keep heads in beds.

The person responsible for all bottom-line decisions at Southwood Psychiatric Center was CEO Charles E. Trojan. Trojan, who had graduated from the University of West Virginia in 1983 with a master's degree in social work and another degree in public administration, began his career as program director of a psychiatric unit in a county hospital in Freemont, Ohio. Two years later he went to work for PIA, managing the psychiatric and chemical-dependency program in a facility in Lewiston, Maine. Within a year and a half he was promoted to eastern regional director, responsible for establishing psychiatric units in general hospitals around the country and hiring managers and doctors for those units. In January 1990, at the age of thirty-six, he became CEO of PIA's Southwood Psychiatric Center.

Not everyone on the Southwood staff was able to back up Trojan's policies without feeling ethically compromised. In November 1990, the program director of the adolescent unit, George Walker, resigned. Walker had been employed at Southwood for ten years and was much admired by his fellow workers as a man of unyieldingly high moral standards. At the time Walker turned in his thirty-day notice, he is quoted as having said that he "could no longer compromise [his] values by remaining in a situation that would force [him] to watch what was once a fine organization disintegrate." Walker had been highly vocal in his criticism of budgetary constraints imposed by the Southwood administration; he was particularly concerned with the inadequacy of staff-to-patient ratios. He left Southwood without having received any other job offer.

Brenda Willis-Hughes* was a senior counselor at the South Bay RTC in 1990. She worked on all units and was responsible for overseeing the night shift, from 3:00 P.M. to 11:00 P.M. Willis-Hughes supervised the twenty-plus children, preadolescents, and adolescents in residence, as well as the mental-health counselors on that shift. She was accountable, as well, for all per-diem counselors who worked on an as-needed basis.

Willis-Hughes went on maternity leave during the summer of 1990, leaving her position as senior counselor on the early-adolescent unit. But she returned to Southwood in February 1991 as a per-diem counselor. She chose to work on the child unit because, according to her deposition in March 1994, "the early adolescent unit was dangerous. There were many destructive adolescents who the staff was having difficulty containing, and I felt, for my physical well-being . . . that it would be better for me to work on the child program."

Despite Willis-Hughes's precautionary intentions, counselors from the child unit were often called in to assist in stabilizing patients on the early-adolescent unit.

Willis-Hughes had this to say about the staffing ratios: "With the existing staffing patterns, say three or four counselors on one night, [and] twenty kids [with] two or three male adolescents acting out, being violent and destructive . . . [and] in a residential treatment center we're not allowed to use leather restraints. We can use medication, and we can manually restrain an adolescent. So there were times when ninety percent of the staff was tied up in restraining adolescent boys. That left the remainder of the adolescents without supervision. No one to do a group. No one to lead outings. No one to provide one-on-one contact."

According to Willis-Hughes, the motto of the Southwood Residential Treatment Center, with its financial and budgetary restraints, with many of its patients culled from the juvenile-justice system, was Do More with Less.

Another ethics-compromising practice at Southwood Psychiatric Center involved altering documentation of patients' medical records. This activity began just prior to the CHAMPUS/HMS review in 1991 and was undertaken in the form of "charting parties"—so named because they took place after hours, often going on until two or three in the morning, with pizza and other refreshments provided by the Southwood administration. The business of these charting parties, which began on Friday and lasted through the weekend, was to enable numerous Southwood employees (predominantly the frontline workers) to make changes on hundreds of patients' charts. The drill was as follows: The charts were spread out on two large tables located in what was known as "the gazebo area" of the Southwood campus, and the staff workers were asked by the administration to make entries, updates, and sign-offs on patient treatment plans. Included were the charts of patients with whom the employees at the charting parties had never had contact. These staff workers were requested to backdate the entries and then sign them, as if the entries, incidents, and treatment goals now being entered had, in fact, actually occurred. Charles Trojan and Dr. Arthur Quinn were both identified, along with other staff physicians, as having been present at charting parties. The employees who testified to this information under oath stated that they had also testified to the charting parties before a federal grand jury.

This was the milieu Christy Scheck walked into on December 13, 1991. It would prove to be her last place of residence.

Not surprisingly, a charting party took place just after her death in March 1992.

CHAPTER THIRTEEN

WHEN CHRISTY SCHECK moved into the early-adolescent unit of the Southwood RTC, two primary counselors were assigned to her. The first was Rebecca Boyle,* a mental-health counselor who had worked often with Christy when she was in the locked unit. Boyle received a B.A. in psychology from San Diego State in 1989 and was working toward an M.S. in counselor education at the same school. She joined Southwood in January 1991 as a full-time employee in the early-adolescent program, but her hours were gradually cut back due to budgetary restraints. As a part-time worker, she was paid approximately $8 per hour. She was not licensed in California.

The work of a primary counselor was to be available to the patient on a day-to-day basis and to speak with the patient at least once every day about whatever concerns or problems he or she was having. It was up to the primary counselor to gauge the patient's emotional state, make sure the patient got to therapy sessions and group meetings, and implement any treatments or interventions prescribed by the medical staff. At the end of a shift, it was the duty of the primary counselor to write a "pass-down note" containing all relevant information about the patient for use by the staff who would work the next shift. A primary counselor represented the patient in treatment-team meetings with the primary treating psychiatrist (Dr. Quinn, in Christy Scheck's case), nursing staff, group and individual therapists, and any social worker connected to the case. It was the duty of the primary counselor to speak with the patient's parents on a weekly basis.

In June 1994, at her deposition in the matter of *Scheck* v. *Southwood,* Rebecca Boyle was asked to describe the training provided by Southwood before she went on salary as a mental-health worker. Boyle stated that, to the best of her recollection, she received "a full day's orientation in the gazebo of the facility." She was unable to remember specifically what topics were covered in this orientation. She did recall that she spent three days "in a training situation with another mental-health counselor who was experienced on the unit."

When asked if she was provided with any written materials, any policies and procedures to review during the orientation period, she said yes, but that she was unable to remember either the contents of the material or what she did with her copy. She stated that there had been a policy and procedures manual in the counselors' office, but her memory of any specific instance in which the manual was referenced, if ever, was vague.

Rebecca Boyle's supervisor was the program director for the early-adolescent unit, Lynn Skinner, who had a master's degree in art therapy and was registered with the state of California as an art therapist. Skinner in turn reported to Nadine Peck, the RTC administrator, who had the same responsibility for the twenty-four-bed adolescent unit on the hospital grounds as the full-service, three unit, sixty-bed facility at South Bay that closed in the fall of 1991 after the CHAMPUS/HMS review. She reported directly to Southwood's CEO, Charles Trojan.

In the course of Peck's deposition in February 1994, she was asked to give the total number of counselors in the early-adolescent unit of the RTC during Christy Scheck's stay in that facility. Peck stated that she didn't know, that there were both full-time and part-time counselors. Nor could she describe the turnover in counselors on the early-adolescent unit. She did admit to recognizing, when asked, the names of two counselors who were involved with Christy Scheck during her stay in the early-adolescent unit of the residential treatment center: Rebecca Boyle and Bria Altshult,* who was assigned (with Boyle) as Christy's co–primary counselor.

Altshult began work at Southwood in either March or April of

1990 as an on-call mental-health counselor, which meant that she was called in on an as-needed basis. She worked approximately forty hours a week. She had a B.A. in communications from the University of California at San Diego and became a counselor on the early-adolescent unit of the Southwood RTC in 1991, at about the same time Christy Scheck entered the facility. In February 1992, Altshult cut her hours at Southwood when she was hired as a social worker with the San Diego Child Protective Services (CPS).

CHAPTER FOURTEEN

CHRISTY MOVED INTO the RTC on a Friday. The family-therapy session that was scheduled for Sunday was canceled by the program director, Lynn Skinner, at Dr. Quinn's suggestion in order for Christy to "become acclimated to the unit." The Schecks were told they could see Christy for a family visit that Saturday, providing she was back from an outing.

Both the outing and the visit were canceled when a takedown was performed on Christy after an explosive temper tantrum. Thorazine was prescribed, and she was placed in a quiet room with a one-on-one.

On December 23 there was a family-therapy session with Gary Juleen in attendance. Juleen requested individual therapy sessions with Christy when she was moved to the RTC, but Skinner denied the request, telling Juleen that individual sessions were "the purview of the psychiatrist." The family-therapy session was no less unpleasant than the Schecks had come to expect. Christy sulked, refusing to address either parent directly unless it was to accuse them of not caring for her or to curse at them. They rationalized that at least Christy had not stormed out of the room.

They were worried about Christmas, however. Christy was one of three patients on the early-adolescent unit who would not be going home on a holiday pass. Bob and Merry made plans to celebrate Christmas with Christy and Molly at Southwood.

"We took Christy's gifts with us," Merry recalls, "and we saved out a couple of Molly's presents so that the girls could open stuff at the same time. We'd made plans to have Christmas dinner there, in the cafeteria, and Christy was amenable to that—"Merry breaks off and glances over at her husband. "Bob was so concerned about that Christmas visit. Wasn't that when your cholesterol was up to 551?"

His shoulders lift in a small, careless gesture. "Probably." He is not a man who enjoys discussion of anything that might be construed as weakness. But he has something to say now. "You see, up to that point, Christy had either yelled at us, cussed at us, or left us. On Christmas Day I didn't know what to say, so the only thing I did was open my arms to her . . ." His voice has narrowed to a string of sound drawn painfully out of his throat. "And my daughter came over and gave me the truest hug I've ever had. And I told her I loved her. Which I did."

It is becoming increasingly difficult for Bob to speak. His eyes shine with tears, and reserve has stiffened the small muscles around his mouth.

"Actually, I love my daughter Christy more with each year." He goes quiet for a few seconds. It is clear that he is pulling in his emotions, wrapping them tightly in a web of determination. As if to cry at this moment for all that has been lost would risk awakening some slumbering core of agony. "And that day, on Christmas, Christy said to me, 'I love you, too, Dad.' "

Merry has been watching him closely, alert for that break in his recitation where she can slide in smoothly—not to interrupt, but to relieve. "We had another session on the twenty-seventh of December," Merry says. "Now, I must tell you, that all through these times, Gary Juleen was doing his best to pull the family together, to create a climate of communication." She is looking at Bob as she speaks. His eyes are closed. "And in that session, two days after Christmas, it was like neither Gary nor I were in the room."

Bob's eyes have opened so quickly that the motion of the lids was undetectable, and when he speaks, his voice is strong again. "He called it a 'transparency.' Meaning we got through to each other, got rid of all the crap that didn't mean anything." He sits up straight in the chair, planting both feet on the floor. "For one hour my daughter and I sat, eye to eye, without arguing, without cussing, without getting up and running. She threw her best shots, and I answered them. I told her there were some things I would be willing to renegotiate. Some I would be willing to change. And, even then, in that place, some things I was not going to change. But Christy never took her eyes off me. And Christy is very much like I am: If she gets in a position of either being cornered or doing something wrong, or if she gets in a position that makes her uneasy, she won't look at you, eye to eye." Remembering this moment that, if not happy, at least does not intensify his pain, Bob once more speaks about his daughter in the present tense. In this moment, for her father, Christy is still alive.

"For one hour we sat like that, looking straight into each other's eyes. And that was the only time I felt a real glimmer of hope." Bob places both hands on the chair arms and gets heavily to his feet. Then he moves around the table and walks into the kitchen. The lace on one of his sneakers has come untied; I can hear the light ticking sound it makes as it strikes the vinyl flooring.

Merry's voice breaks the silence. "Christy left that session, and she didn't notice that Gary was doing some stuff in the charting room. She didn't know he was in there, and she stood just outside the doorway, with one of the mental-health counselors, and she started telling this girl about the horrendous family session she'd just gone through. She proceeded to give the details of who said what, and how bad it was, and what her father said, and so on . . ." Merry's voice drifts off on a note of uneasy frustration. "Gary spoke to the counselor after Christy left, and he said, 'Wait a minute. That's not what went on in there at all.' "

Merry sighs deeply and shakes her head. Bob has come back into the room and is standing now at the bank of windows that extends across the wall behind the sofa. He looks out over a small pond surrounded by carefully tended shrubs and clusters of bamboo. The entire area is shaded by an elm tree. Merry told me earlier that she plans to put a wooden bench out there, so that she can sit under the tree in warm weather and write poetry.

Now, without turning away from the window, Bob speaks again. "Of course, by this time, the Southwood staff was deter-

mined that Gary Juleen was biased in favor of 'the parents.' "
Merry nods in agreement. "And so, of course, Gary's word couldn't
be trusted."

Juleen's memory of that afternoon is that after Christy described the session to a staff member as "horrendous," the staff
member sent Christy to her room "so that she could calm down.
The staff seemed a little bit shocked when I contradicted Christy,
and I didn't pursue it. Then the woman told me that Christy
wanted to talk to me in her room.

"The conversation I had with Christy in her room was entirely
different than what she had said to the staff person. It was nothing
but positive. She said how wonderful the session had been, and
how she felt that things were beginning to happen between her
and her family. And I didn't confront her because I felt she generally knew what really happened in our sessions, and that was what
was important."

Merry recalls that this was about the time that one of Christy's
counselors called the Schecks at home. "She just reamed me up one
side and down the other for my 'lack of parenting skills,' and for
the terrible person that I was. This girl demanded to know why I
wasn't taking some parenting classes if I didn't know any better
than to act the way I did. And I said, 'Excuse me, would you like
to see the certificate for the two years of child development that I
took?' I asked this girl—who could not have been older than
twenty-two—what it was she thought she knew about me. I told
her that all she knew was what my daughter told her, that she had
no idea what I was really like. But she proceeded to tell me off."
Merry closes her eyes for an instant. "She was just . . . yelling. And
it absolutely devastated me. The things Christy was saying about
me, the accusations"—her voice has plunged into a tone so soft it
is difficult to hear the words—"tore into me like pieces of shrap-
nel. That's why I fought so hard." Her strength floods back now as
she speaks, sparked by the wellspring of anger that wages battle
for dominion over the constant pain.

"And all the time, I'm trying to get some information about my

daughter. I kept on thinking that I was dealing with professionals." She smiles suddenly. "They accused me of trying to find out
the nitty-gritty details of what was going on in Christy's therapy
sessions. And that wasn't my point at all." Her voice has lifted
until it rings through the room. "I was trying to learn how I could
help my daughter. I was trying to find out if Christy was giving us
clues as to *what really were her issues.*"

Bob has turned away from the window and is standing just behind his wife. Now he grips her shoulders with both hands and
squeezes gently. Merry's right hand comes up to clasp his as she
continues to speak. "We had another family session on the fifth of
January, and it was completely superficial. Just small talk. But
that evening Christy had another takedown, and this time they
gave her three increasing doses of Thorazine. On that one evening
she got twenty-five milligrams, forty milligrams, and fifty milligrams in succession.

"Now, I'd been reading the *PDR* [*Physicians' Desk Reference*], and
nurses' drug handbooks. I'd gotten copies of literature given to
M.D.'s about meds, and that seemed to me an excessive and po-
tentially dangerous amount of medication. But . . ." Her lips curve
into a sour little smirk. " 'Now, Mrs. Scheck . . .' " It is becoming
a familiar and macabre one-liner.

"The next day, January sixth, they increased Christy's dosage of
imipramine by another twenty-five milligrams, bringing her up
to a hundred and twenty-five milligrams a day. On the evening of
the sixth, in a journal entry, Christy wrote that the Thorazine was
making her groggy. And the last billing notice I had from Dr.
Quinn was dated the sixth of January, 1992."

Merry takes in a deep breath and allows it to escape in a long,
slow hiss. "On the seventh of January, Christy made the accusation
of molestation against Bob."

CHAPTER FIFTEEN

"THAT WHOLE MOLESTATION story was a lie. A complete lie."

Rachel Penny's voice cuts across her living room. "Christy was just so angry at Bob. And not just about being taken out of boys' sports, either. We talked about that, Merry and I. But I couldn't talk to Bob about it. It was a closed subject as far as he was concerned. But I did talk to Christy about it. I told her that if she continued to play in boys' sports, she'd eventually come up against a muscleman who would outdo her. Told her if she went into girls' sports, it would allow her to stand out, to be the star. And that it would give her more opportunities for college scholarships.

"It would also be an opportunity for her to meet other girls her age who were also athletic and had a love of sports the way Christy did. Because I think that when Christy turned twelve or thirteen, she wanted more girlfriends. Especially at school. She wanted that sense of belonging."

Rachel leans forward in her chair, elbows propped on knees, hands dangling loosely. "Christy's anger ran pretty deep, though, and being taken out of boys' sports was only a part of it. You see, all the way growing up, the primary focus of that father-daughter relationship was sports. That's how Bob and Christy related." She pauses. "Well, as Christy began to develop into a young woman, I noticed that it was hard for Bob to relate to her *as* a young woman. As she began to develop breasts, and when her periods started, Bob began to retreat from her. He simply didn't know how to relate to her anymore. He could only relate through the sports. You see, previously, he could wrestle with Christy, and he could goof off with her, and they could do other things besides sports. But when Christy began to develop, he just couldn't handle it. He didn't feel comfortable wrestling with her anymore, so he stopped. But he didn't tell Christy why. He didn't give her a reason—he just backed away from her."

Red and Josh have just rejoined us in the living room and have been listening quietly. Now Red speaks up. "You know, about that wrestling stuff? Well, me and Christy were wrestling one day, just about the time all this started to happen, and I landed flat on top of her. She started yelling, 'Get off me! We shouldn't wrestle anymore.'"

Rachel nods slowly and says, "I sat down with her, because, you have to remember, these kids grew up together. We have pictures of them in the bathtub together, when they were one, and two, and three years old. Christy, and Red, and our younger son, Jason.* Then, when Christy and Red got to be five and six, we decided that the boys could bathe together, but that Christy would then bathe alone. And she didn't like it; she didn't understand why they were being separated. I explained to her that now, at a certain age, she couldn't sleep in the bed with them, or change clothes with them anymore. And that was real hard for Christy to accept. She had a hard time with the whole issue of accepting her body as a girl."

Red cuts in. "Also, she had a guy's haircut. And she always wore these clothes that could go either way."

"Yes," Rachel agrees. "She did look androgynous. From the back, you really couldn't tell if Christy was a girl or a boy."

"And that ticked her off." There is an edge of anger in Red's voice.

Rachel's voice has lowered, softened. "She was so pretty, too. She would have looked beautiful in girls' clothes. She had that perfect skin, no blemishes at all. And those sky-blue eyes." She smiles. "And she had a nice little figure."

Red shakes his head. "Not little. Nothing about Christy was ever little. She was always real . . ." He hesitates, searching for the word he wants. "She was always real . . . burlesque."

Rachel and I exchange a glance. Then we both smile.

"Do you mean burly?" Rachel asks.

"*Yeah*. She was burly. Like"—he hesitates again—"a Russian woman."

I mention that Merry had shown me some pages from the journal Christy kept while she was at Southwood. The entry described how Merry hit Christy with pots and pans when she got angry.

Red is talking before his mother can reply. "No. Not the mother. Her dad, I could believe. Because he was always real physical with her. Whenever they were over here, and Christy did something that annoyed him, he'd reach over and smack her. It was 'a couple of guys' thing between the two of them. He'd smack her on the upper arm, the way guys do with each other, and he'd say, 'Knock that off.' He never smacked her hard enough to leave a mark or anything, but it was just . . . the shock of, you know . . . being hit by a parent. It's not so much the pain, it's the realization that you've just made your parent mad enough to hit you. And Christy would kind of cringe." Red is silent for a moment. "But her mom?" He shakes his head again. "No way would Christy's mom hit her."

Rachel agrees, and adds, "Neither Bob nor Merry were ever, or seldom ever, physical with their kids. If anything, they were the kind of parents who'd say, 'Christy, don't do that.' " Her voice changes slightly. " 'Christy, don't *do* that.' "

Rachel moves through a litany of hollow parental edicts:

" 'Christy, I said not to do that.'

" 'Christy, if you do that one more time, I'm going to get up and spank you.'

" 'Christy, I'm getting angry now.'

" 'Christy, you heard me—stop that!'

"And finally it would get to the point of, 'Okay, Christy, you've got yourself a time-out. Go sit on the couch.' "

Rachel has modified her tone with each progression. Now her voice slides back to its normal pitch. "What Bob and Merry would usually end up doing was to look at Hal and me in complete exasperation, like, 'Well, she pushed all our buttons. Now what?' And, at that point, Hal or I would just look at Christy and tell her to get her butt on that couch and keep it there for five, or even ten minutes." Rachel allows herself a slice of smile. "And she'd do it for us, because the first time she'd misbehave is when we'd punish her. No second or third or fourth—or one-hundredth attempt. Our kids'll tell you, you get one warning. That's it."

Red nods. "That's it," he says. "I think Bob saw the rein my dad has over us. And my folks constantly told him that he had to be more affirmative with Christy. They told him he needed to bear down on her. But he never really hurt her. I'd never say Bob Scheck hit Christy hard enough to hurt."

Rachel slides in smoothly. "But, you know, that was only the past few years, when Bob was trying to exert some control. Which I think Christy resented. Because, up to then, it was Christy who controlled her parents. She was the undisputed queen of that house."

Spoiled?

Red glances at his mother, then shrugs. "A little. The first time I ever heard some kind of discourse between Christy and her family was when we were pretty young. We got in an argument over who had the worst family, and Christy said she had too many chores around the house, and"—his voice assumes a singsong cadence—"her father was too mean, and he never let her do anything. Like that. It was the first time I'd ever heard anything like that coming from Christy. Because she was always so hyper, and she got away with so much. Way more than me."

I ask Rachel if Molly's birth could have created some resentment, some sense of having been deposed, for Christy. Rachel thinks about it for a moment.

"Oh, I suppose there could have been some resentment, but I don't think that was a big factor. But, two children now, and both of them hyperactive, ADD [attention deficit disorder] kids. I remember you couldn't give Christy chocolate. Or sugar. And after a certain time in the evening"—she holds up both hands, palms up—"oh, boy. There was just a whole list of things you didn't dare feed her or you'd be peeling her off the wall. And Molly was the same way."

I ask about the medication given to Christy at Southwood. A sudden spurt of anger darkens Rachel's expression. "*Three* times the normal dose of imipramine? I asked my kids' doctor about it, and that was his answer. He was reluctant to say anything, but I pushed. And, of course, the other meds: the Thorazine and the Restoril." There is a beat of silence. "And then there was the PMS. Christy went through real changes when she began her period at twelve; she began to have these terrible mood swings. Both Merry and I noticed, the closer she got to her period, the moodier she became."

Red breaks in. "She'd come over here with her earphones on, and her cassettes, and she'd just sit on the sofa and listen to her music. We all used to say, 'Christy's got *major* PMS.'"

But surely PMS wouldn't have been enough to create a climate for the kind of allegations Christy made against her parents?

Rachel permits herself a small sound of annoyance. "That's not what I'm saying. I'm saying that it should have at least been considered as a causal effect in some of Christy's problems."

Rachel takes off her glasses and places them on the small table next to her chair. Then, using the heels of both hands, she rubs the area around her eyes. She leans her head against the back of the chair and sits quietly, both eyes closed, for a moment. Then she puts on the glasses again and looks at me.

"Whatever the causes, Christy was angry. And the particular focus of that anger was her father. Let me tell you something: We had a child here for foster care who was the victim of a terrible attack. This girl, Shana, was eight years old when she was taken from her bedroom in her parents' home one night and brutally raped and sodomized. She told the doctor who examined her that a strange man had come into her room through the window, that he had taken her into a green car, where he attacked her. But the police were suspicious of Shana's father, and even though he kept insisting that he was innocent, and there was no physical evidence that he had molested his child, both parents were charged with child neglect. For *allowing* the molestation to take place. Well, they pleaded guilty, because their attorney told them they could be separated from Shana for a year if the case went to trial.

"That guilty plea was all the authorities had to hear. Shana was placed into foster care and a private therapist was hired by the county to see her twice a week. And after about a year of having it suggested to her that it was her father who had raped her, Shana gave in and identified him as her attacker.

"The father was accused of two counts of felony child abuse, and a trial date was set. But this time he had a different attorney, who saw to it that Shana's clothes were reexamined. A DNA test proved that the semen found did not match that of Shana's father. The charges against him were dropped, but it took over two years. And in a later court appearance, Shana told the judge that she 'just got sick of hearing the therapist say my dad did it every time I went there.' "

Rachel has been speaking in a quietly intense tone. Now her voice lifts. "Christy and Shana used to talk together all the time when Shana was living here with us. They talked about every detail of Shana's molestation, and Christy simply took those details and borrowed them, repeating them almost verbatim, at the hospital. The kidnapping, the rape, even the green car. And she knew the ramifications of what would happen to her own parents if those accusations were leveled. She knew exactly what was going to happen when she said that Bob molested her." She sighs deeply. "I honestly believe that Christy felt she could control and manipulate the situation—to her advantage—somewhere along the road. But it all got away from her."

Red has been making small sounds in his throat as his mother speaks. When I ask if he agrees with her assessment, he thinks about it for a moment before he replies. "I don't know. But I'd give anything to know what Christy was thinking about when she was in that hospital."

CHAPTER SIXTEEN

THE SCHECKS WERE informed of Christy's allegations against Bob on January 8, 1992. As it happened, Merry had an appointment to meet with a social worker from Child Protective Services as a result of another allegation Christy had made, this one involving Molly. Christy told one of the Southwood counselors that Bob had struck Molly on the head, leaving a bruise. Christy said that Molly had told her about it at the last family meeting, on December 27.

"Well," Merry explains, "Christy didn't see Molly on the twenty-seventh, because we didn't bring Molly to that meeting. And she wasn't at the 'transparency session' the next day, either, when Christy and Bob connected. I explained that to the social worker, and I told her that I'd spoken with both of Molly's babysitters to ask if either of them had seen anything on Molly. Just . . . perchance." Merry's voice, although soft, is tinged with anger. "But the main thing was that *Christy had not seen Molly*.

"When I got to the social worker's office, she told me that she'd already been to Molly's school. To see Molly. And not only did Molly *not* know what the woman was talking about, there were no bruises anywhere on the child.

"At that point, I told the social worker that I saw all of this coming." Merry's voice flattens out now, as if she were reciting a list. "I said, 'I believe this is a ploy for attention. This never happened. Christy is in a psychiatric unit, she's a child on heavy medication.' I asked this woman to please take that into consideration."

After Merry left the CPS offices, she called Rachel Penny. Rachel urged her to have Christy examined by a doctor as soon as possible. Merry called Kaiser Medical Center as soon as she got off the phone and made an appointment with a pediatrician there. Then she called Southwood and told the disembodied voice on the other end that she was requesting that a member of the Southwood staff take Christy to the medical center for an examination.

"My daughter has made an allegation of sexual molestation against her father. She also says that she was kidnapped and raped. Let's find out."

The voice on the other end assumed a waspish tone. "Well, you know, Mrs. Scheck, we're understaffed."

"Take my daughter to Kaiser. If you won't, I'll pick her up myself."

"Now, Mrs. Scheck . . ."

"I don't want to hear it."

One of the Southwood mental-health counselors, whom Merry describes as "a young bodyguard," brought Christy to Kaiser Medical Center. Merry was seated in the Kaiser waiting room, having arrived before Christy, when the young woman, whose name Merry no longer remembers, approached her. She said that Christy was standing just outside the waiting room door but that Merry "was not allowed to speak to her."

Merry recalls exactly what she said to the counselor. "I don't want to speak with Christy. I don't want to speak with you. We're here to do what we have to do. Now bring her in."

Merry spoke privately with the Kaiser pediatrician before the examination. She explained the circumstances of Christy's allegation against her father, and her accounts of the gang rape and of being abducted and raped by a man in a green car. Merry told the doctor that she was sure Christy was a victim neither of rape nor of parental molestation, but that both she and Christy's father felt an examination was necessary. She explained that the young woman who had accompanied Christy to the medical center was an escort from Southwood, and she requested, rather adamantly, that this person not be present during the examination. The doctor listened carefully, then said, "But I think you should know,

Mrs. Scheck, that Christy doesn't want you to be in the examining room, either."

"Fine. Just let it be you and your nurse, then."

The examination showed no evidence of any sexual activity whatsoever. Christy's hymen was intact, and her vagina could allow only the passage of the doctor's index finger.

Merry is not sure whether Christy told the doctor that she had sexual relations with a twenty-one-year-old man she had said was her boyfriend or whether she talked about being raped. But she'll never forget what the doctor told her Christy said about her father. "She said that he had been penetrating her for two years."

The Schecks' next meeting with the CPS social workers brought in a new team of investigators. Merry insisted that the findings of Christy's physical examination be taken into consideration in relation to the molestation charges.

The next family session was scheduled for January 12. Up until that point, Bob, Merry, Christy, and Gary Juleen were accustomed to sitting around a kind of conference table as they talked. On the twelfth, Christy refused to take a chair at the table. When Merry asked her to move closer, Christy shook her head.

"I can't discuss any of this with men," she said.

Merry was unable to control a brief surge of anger. "Why not? You've made a very serious allegation against your father."

Christy went into a tirade. She restated, at top volume, her accusations of parental lack of concern and understanding. She accused Juleen of taking their part against her. Then she turned around and stormed out of the room, slamming the door behind her.

CHAPTER SEVENTEEN

APPROXIMATELY THREE WEEKS before Christy Scheck was first admitted to Southwood Psychiatric Center, an NME corporate release announced that a major realignment was under way: All principle health care operations would be centralized under a single management structure at NME's Santa Monica headquarters, with a number of functional and staff responsibilities (previously handled at the group level) consolidated into headquarters departments. Psychiatric Institutes of America (PIA) and Rehab Hospital Services Corporation (RHSC) would henceforth be known as the Psychiatric Hospital Division and the Rehabilitation Hospital Division, while NME's acute-care hospitals would operate as the General Hospital Division. Richard K. Eamer, NME's chairman and CEO, was quoted as saying, "This realignment will provide senior management with improved control as NME continues to grow, and will give us the opportunity to achieve significant reductions in overhead costs."

The release stated that the company would recognize, in its second quarter ending on November 30, 1991, the estimated reorganization and relocation costs due to the realignment, as well as unusual and associated costs relating to investigations and adverse publicity involving its psychiatric operations. The release went on to say that NME expected these costs to be substantially or completely offset by gains from sales of nursing homes to the Hillhaven Corporation.

These "unusual and associated costs" were perhaps more accurately described by Michael H. Focht, who replaced Norman Zober as senior executive vice president and director of operations for NME's Specialty Hospital Group (SHG) in October 1991 when Zober was placed on an indefinite administrative leave. Focht said that "the business was in a state of free fall." He credited this to "bad publicity and changes in the fundamentals of the business that had begun at that point in time."

There was the Harrell case (described in Chapter 6) at PIA's Colonial Hills Hospital in San Antonio, Texas. It was this case and subsequent others that would prompt the Texas attorney general to file suit against PIA in September 1991, alleging fraudulent conduct. On July 18, 1991, the ABC television show *Prime Time Live* aired a segment entitled "To the Last Dime," in which misconduct at other PIA facilities came to light. Among the people interviewed was Dr. Robert Stuckey, former medical director of the alcoholism unit of PIA's Fair Oaks Hospital in Summit, New Jersey, headquarters of the controversial 800-COCAINE hot line. Stuckey, who resigned his position at Fair Oaks in 1985, stated flatly that "everybody in the hospital understood the primary goal was to make money" and described how patients were moved from unit to unit in order to milk insurance payments.

Louis Parisi, director of the Fraud Division of the New Jersey Department of Insurance, told the TV interviewer that PIA had recently paid a $400,000 fine (the largest of its kind ever imposed in New Jersey) after a yearlong investigation for fraud. Parisi smiled thinly as he described PIA's response to the charge: "They blamed the overbilling on both human and computer error."

Former PIA employees, with a certain note of triumph, related illegal acts regarding CHAMPUS patients at PIA's Lake Hospital in Palm Beach County, Florida. One former staff worker spoke of required deductibles that went uncollected in order to keep beds filled. She also described billing alterations that occurred when patients' insurance companies refused to pay for certain procedures—for instance, biofeedback sessions would be rebilled as "psych testing."

A teenage girl and her father recounted a nightmare of overmedication and restraints that took place during an eight-month incarceration that began as a six-week weight-loss program at

PIA's Fair Oaks Hospital in Delray Beach, Florida, and ended at another PIA facility. The girl had been transferred to the second facility with a blanket diagnosis of "depression" after it was learned that her mother had unlimited insurance coverage. The total bill came to $240,000.

The Florida spokesperson for PIA, Caroline Guida, was asked if there was any truth to the stories that patients were kept in PIA facilities until their insurance was exhausted. She denied it vehemently. "We keep *many* patients after their insurance runs out."

Guida was then presented with a court document in which PIA attorneys admitted that patients were discharged when their insurance benefits expired. She glanced at the document and asked to be excused "for a few minutes, to leave the room and review something." The camera followed her as she got to her feet and walked away. Then the interviewer turned to face the camera and announced that this was the sixth time that Ms. Guida had asked to be excused during the interview. Guida reappeared to address the question: "We offered the option of self-payment or transfer to another facility."

It cannot be perceived as wholly coincidence that, shortly after the *Prime Time* segment aired, the signs in front of PIA facilities were changed to identify the hospitals as NME entities. This would become a part of the Scheck lawsuit against NME. Bob Scheck had seen the *Prime Time* segment but due to the recent name change was unaware that he was placing his daughter in a PIA facility.

In October 1991 the Newark *Star Ledger* published an article, written by respected syndicated journalist Herb Jaffe, that focused on PIA facilities and included comments made by Dr. Robert Stuckey concerning the PIA unit at Fair Oaks in New Jersey. Stuckey stated, in a letter to Jaffe dated September 25, 1991, that he had been "constantly pressured to keep patients longer, and to order more lab testing by the two doctors who ran the facility [and who, coincidentally, were the co-owners of the lab] and by Norman Zober, president of PIA." Stuckey, who had an independent contract with Fair Oaks, stated that he had been told by staff psychiatrists that "their bonuses were calculated according to the number of days they kept patients in the hospital, and by the quantity of the tests ordered." Stuckey further stated that these tests included sperm counts on male patients and "street drug testing" on elderly patients.

According to Stuckey, these staff physicians "admitted that the so-called 'Evaluation Unit' was often a rip-off. They said that even when the diagnosis of depression was clear, and the choice of medication was clearer yet, clients were told they needed the extended in-patient assessment. This, they were told, must be completed before the patient could be considered for transfer to a 'treatment unit.' "

Stuckey's letter went on to say:

When a patient called Fair Oaks, his insurance numbers were recorded. With that number, [the intake worker] researched the original policy until satisfied how the hospital could legally acquire every dollar that was still available that day, on that policy. The patient usually received the diagnosis that matched the category with the most available money in it.

Next, when a patient arrived before the phone research had been carried out, the choice of treatment was made by an admitting clerk without the patient ever seeing a physician. On the walls of the admitting office were cards for each bed in the hospital. When uncomplicated alcoholics were referred to me for alcoholic treatment, she [the admitting clerk] would interview them until they talked about their depression, then she could put them on the depression unit, where everybody made more money. If another unit had a free bed, she would question the patient until she found an answer that matched the vacant bed.

If the patient had Blue Cross or some other insurance that would not pay the full fair [sic], they were told there was no bed and put on a waiting list.

Stuckey was on the board of directors at Fair Oaks and, in that capacity, attended board meetings at NME headquarters in Washington, D.C. In the letter he described one such meeting chaired by Norman Zober: "I requested that the doctors at Fair Oaks be able to have an open staff meeting. Here we would be able to candidly debate the proper diagnosis and care of one patient each week—particularly those who were in the hospital for such a long time. I was told emphatically that the 'System' set up by Dr. Pottash [codirector, with a Dr. Gold, of Fair Oaks] would decide on the diagnosis and treatment."

Shortly after Stuckey resigned his position at Fair Oaks in 1985, he opened a successful outpatient program and within a short period was accommodating five hundred patients a week. "Norm Zober had a designate meet with me," he stated in his letter. "He insisted that we meet on the street and in no one's office. There, the designate told me that if I did not take my clinic out of Summit, they would smear me personally until I was ruined in the state."

Stuckey's outpatient clinic was ultimately shut down. Stuckey states, "It is the state's decision that [an] outpatient [facility] can only be owned by an inpatient unit."

Stuckey expressed concern "not only with the open and established greed of Fair Oaks Hospital. I am more concerned with the lack of regulatory agencies to monitor and prevent such insurance abuse." Stuckey made his point by describing a meeting he called with six physicians and several executives of Prudential Insurance. Stuckey had wanted to question Prudential about a $375,000 bill a friend of his had been handed after two years of unsuccessful treatment at Fair Oaks. The patient had continued to use cocaine after his release from the hospital and only conquered his drug dependence when he entered a Twelve Step program. According to Stuckey, the Prudential executives showed no interest in the Fair Oaks bill. "They made jokes about a recent bill of over one hundred thousand dollars submitted by Fair Oaks for a Prudential employee. I was dumbfounded. Then one of the Prudential physicians [one of Stuckey's former instructors] pulled me aside. He said, 'Bob, don't you know we like big bills here? Big bills mean big premiums and big bonuses.' "

Stuckey took his case to the New Jersey Health Commission. No results.

He wrote to New Jersey's governor, Thomas Keane. No reply.

He finally called the American Psychiatric Association. The man he spoke to was to retire the following year. "His response to my concern left me permanently disillusioned. He said, 'Well, Doctor, you know, we older fellows could learn a lot from these young kids.' "

For Stuckey, that was the final straw. He bought a sailboat and made plans to move abroad.

His letter ended with the following statement: "When greed is more acceptable in health care than sensitivity to suffering, I am out of step."

Greed was not only acceptable, it was spelled out in manuals and documents circulated throughout NME's psychiatric hospitals. A pamphlet entitled "The Administrator's Inquiry/Intake Focus Golden Rules" was sent out to hospital administrators in August 1991. The piece was written in the first person, so that it read like some kind of bizarre oath. Rule 3, according to this imagined top-notch administrator, states: "I've made it clear to everyone in the hospital that inquiry/intake is our most important system—nothing else matters if we don't do that well—and I foster an intake culture."

Rule 5 talks about goals: "My goal is to bring every inquiry caller in for an evaluation without regard to insurance/financial resources. If callers raise the question of cost, I want staff to explain that this will be addressed when they receive their evaluation, because it will depend on the services needed, and that it would help if the caller brought his insurance card or policy—but I don't want the staff to initiate these issues."

Other rules urge administrators to know the conversion rate (any inquiry that is converted to an in-person evaluation) of everybody in the hospital, to take the intake staff to dinner often, and to provide "a constant stream of little perks [inexpensive watches, radios, small-screen TVs] and recognitions to the staff who take calls and do evaluations." Rule 11 instructs the administrators to use a marketing tracking system to monitor inquiry/intake activity and individual performance weekly and to review such activity and performances on a monthly basis with the intake director. The intake staff must "enjoy their work, or do something else."

Included in the pamphlet is "PIA's Inquiry/Intake Performance Expectations." Twenty-nine points are delineated, such as all intake telephones being answered by the third ring, an expectation that 70 to 80 percent of all inquiries were to be scheduled for evaluations, and that 50 *percent or more of these assessments were to be converted into admissions.* (This figure was aimed at those PIA facilities that employed media advertising. *A 70 percent conversion rate was expected from nonadvertising hospitals.*) The final expectation was that all intake staff initiate calls (when time permitted) to generate admissions by contacting former patients as well as hospital emergency rooms.

Also provided was a "troubleshooting guide," which instructed administrators to "sit in on some evaluations of poor convertors" and to "ask staff why evaluations don't convert." A series of potential problem replies was supplied: "Do staff feel: 'They should try out-therapy first'?; 'They just want someone to talk to'?; 'I just don't see that many that are clinically appropriate', etc."

It seems clear that those intake workers who questioned the advisability of hospitalizing every person who called in, would fall into the category of employees who should "do something else."

CHAPTER EIGHTEEN

"AT SOUTHWOOD PSYCHIATRIC, marketing was God."

Alan Sidell, former Southwood marketing executive, is speaking. We are having tea in the lobby of a small hotel in San Diego. Sidell is a tall, rangy man who is probably in his mid-forties, although it is difficult to pin him with any degree of accuracy. He has a narrow face that appears boyish despite the deeply etched lines that travel a course along either side of his mouth, patient, intelligent eyes, and large, ivory-colored teeth that crowd unevenly against his lips. His voice is low-pitched, and he delivers each word as if it were encased in a silky membrane. It is the voice of someone who is able to make a living from the way he talks.

"I knew what the score was when I went to work at Southwood. I knew there was too much emphasis on marketing and not enough on patient care. I knew that Southwood was a proprietary organization that was basically just concerned with the bottom line."

Sidell began his career at Southwood in 1979 as a senior counselor on the adolescent unit of the residential treatment center. In 1982 he left the facility for a job in communications. He returned in 1984 as a program coordinator for teen substance abuse but left again ten months later. Sidell came back to Southwood in August 1991 as a coordinator for the dual-diagnosis program for child and adolescent services. If an adolescent could be tracked into a dual-diagnosis program (any primary psychiatric diagnosis that carried with it an attendant chemical-dependency issue, such as "behavior disorder with alcoholism"), there was the potential for more services and larger bills. After three months Sidell was made assistant director of child and adolescent services. He recalls that he was responsible for "anything and everything. And that included keeping the beds filled and revenues generated as well as clinical issues, clinical staff, training, program design and implementation. I was responsible for coordinating all the efforts of the psychiatrists, social services, and nonverbal therapies like art therapy and occupational therapy."

Six months later Sidell moved up to the front office in the hospital section as head of one of the marketing teams for child and adolescent services. His job was to guide the efforts of those staff members who were expected to make sales calls and any intake workers who fielded inquiries.

"Every morning we'd start the day off with an intake meeting in which we'd review marketing contacts, incoming calls, evaluations, and admissions from the previous day. And we'd look at the discharge calendar, to see who was getting out, and we'd look to see what patients would be left, and what their coverage was. The reimbursement rate was different for each company (the payor), and the payor mix was determined by which patients were covered by what policy. CHAMPUS, which paid approximately one thousand dollars per day for every CHAMPUS patient, was at the top of the list. MediCal, at about three-fifty per day, was at the bottom. All other coverage—Medicare, Aetna, and so on—was in between.

"An intake worker would probably have in his head the understanding of what the average daily census was on any given day, what discharges were coming down the pike, and what the payor mix was. And it was the payor mix that guided most of the decision making as related to admissions. The intake worker would look at the boards, which were up on the wall of the office, and the first board he or she would look at would be the one with the twenty-four-bed unit on it. Now, if you've got only six or seven beds filled, you'll bring in anybody. So, okay, MediCal only pays three hundred fifty a day, and that's not as good as a thousand or five hundred, but you've got eighteen empty beds: Let's get 'em filled with somebody."

Sidell looks sharply at me; he wants to make sure I'm getting all this. "Now, if you had twenty-one or twenty-two out of those twenty-four beds filled, you might not want to take the chance of filling one of the remaining spaces with a MediCal kid. Especially when initial grades were coming back from the schools. If you're in the middle of a school semester, there's going to be a lot of act-ing out, and we're expecting some admissions as a result. So let's not fill up those beds with MediCal kids. But if you've got some room, maybe only eighteen beds filled out of the twenty-four, you can fill up a bed or two. *But* if you've already got six MediCal kids out of those eighteen, then, uh-uh. That's too many. So that's the payor mix. What the mix of payors was out of what you already had in the beds."

I ask Sidell to give a couple of examples of intake calls involv-ing the mothers of troubled kids, asking about what help was available. Sidell nods, clears his throat, and, as if he were audi-tioning for a role, begins to act.

" 'Yes. Yes, this is Southwood and we provide services. Tell me what's goin' on.' " He pretends to listen to the person at the other end. When he resumes speaking, his voice is soothing, and he speaks rapidly. " 'Yeah . . . yeah. I understand. It's a tough time. We can help you out, that's why we're here. . . . No, no . . . don't worry, we'll find out what's goin' on and get you in an appropriate direc-tion. . . . No, no, no . . . he may not need hospitalization. We'll have to see what's goin' on. Let's take it one step at a time. Now, give me some basic information. Who am I speaking with? . . . Uh-huh. And your phone number? . . . And where do you live? . . . Uh-huh. Do you have any insurance? . . . Okay, what kind do you have? . . . Okay, CHAMPUS . . . Dad's out to sea? Well, that's part of the problem right there . . . Navy. No, no, we get a lot of Navy fami-lies in here, unfortunately. That military life, especially that Navy lifestyle, doesn't help with some of the family issues goin' on, doesn't help kids get their needs met. You, too, probably . . . ' " He chuckles softly, like someone who's in on a joke. His voice has as-sumed a folksy, chatty tone. " 'You know what might be better?

Let's do this: How about I set up an appointment? Let me see what's available. Do you think you can get your son in here? . . . Well, just tell him he's comin' in to talk to a counselor. Just tell him he's comin' in to rap. And we'll take it from there. You get him in the lobby, and believe me, we know how to deal with these kids. . . .

" 'How would we keep him from walking right out again? Well, we do it by listening. We're good at that, we know how to listen. And, from what you tell me, it sounds like this kid's just lookin' for someone he can talk to. He's throwin' out some signs and signals that he needs some attention. We'll give him some. . . . Well, yes, he may run away. But you tell me he's ditching school, and, well—that's running away, isn't it? It sounds like we're gonna have to take some chances here. He's already doing some things that aren't in his best interests.' "

Out of curiosity, to see how Sidell will handle it, I interrupt with a question, as if I were the mother at the other end. "How are you going to get him back if he runs to the nearest McDonald's?"

Sidell doesn't miss a beat. " 'Well, we'll just walk over there and buy him a Quarter-Pounder.' " He pauses, the way a comedian does, to give the audience time to laugh. Then he gets serious again. " 'We have our ways, trust us. Get your child in the lobby, and we'll come out and speak with him, and if you can't get him to the lobby, come on in yourself. We often find that when the kids know the parents are comin' in to talk about 'em, they want to come in, too. . . . But listen, that's why we're here. We're the professionals. Let's go ahead and schedule a time for tomorrow morning at . . . ten o'clock okay?

" 'Listen, he knows that somethin's goin' on, he's askin' for help. Just tell him you want to bring him in to talk to a counselor who'll be able to refer him somewhere for some support. Maybe talk to some other kids or something. I promise it'll be nonthreatening to him. You don't have a thing to worry about.' "

With the abruptness of a flicked switch, Sidell's demeanor changes. Now he's back to business, off the imaginary phone.

"Okay, that's the CHAMPUS kid. The guy on the phone, his obligation is to get an evaluation, get him scheduled, *get the bodies in there.* If it was a different payor mix, that conversation on the phone would take a different direction. The main objective would be to get off the phone, dependent on what type of insurance plan was presented in the initial information gathering. If the unit was too full, or if there were too many MediCal kids, then the caller would be channeled into the free community service, and you'd get off the phone so you could get a *real* phone call coming in. A money call."

And what if the next caller was without health insurance?

"There are dozens of resources in a community that are cost-free. You can refer someone to a church, if they have one. All they're looking for, when they call, is a direction. Their trust is in you, as a professional, to provide a direction. So, instead of directing them to 'come in for an evaluation and talk to some counselors, maybe some other kids, and we'll get started,' the direction goes toward an adolescent Narcotics Anonymous meeting, or some other support group, such as Al-Anon. And, as far as the person on the other end of the line knows, that sounds like exactly the right answer: 'Thank God I called you! You say there's a meeting right up the street from my house?'

" 'Yep.'

" 'And why is this a good meeting?'

" 'Well, because it's teenagers only, so it will be nonthreatening for your daughter. Yeah, they don't even let the grown-ups in. So the kids can really express their feelings.'

" 'Oh, God, you guys are wonderful. I didn't even know there were meetings like—what did you say your name was? May I call you again?'

" 'Sure. Feel free. But, look, check out that meeting. If I let you off the phone now, you can probably make the one that's starting in an hour. Thanks.' "

What if a patient calls with an emergency-room scenario?

"Well, you'd still look at the board, at the payor mix. Now, this is an acute-care situation, it's serious—'My child has just had his stomach pumped, and/or his wrists stitched, and they told me in the ER that I should seek psychiatric treatment, only the doctor didn't want to refer us to anybody.' *Or* it might have been a hospital ER that we had marketed. Which we do. Some hospitals wouldn't let us in the door, but others were appreciative of being able to provide their people with a range of options. So if we got in that ER door, our flyer went up on the bulletin board. And we'd get calls."

And your response?

" 'Well, Mrs. X, you certainly made the right decision to call us. It sounds like you could use some help. Let me get some information from you. What insurance do you have?'

" 'None. I don't have any—'

" 'Don't worry about it. That's not a problem. Our job is to provide you with a proper direction. Let me give you the number of County Mental Health.' " Sidell's words have slipped out like ball bearings, uniform and smooth from constant use.

"Because it's an acute-care situation," he explains, "you can't palm it off on an AA meeting, or tell them to see their pastor. But there are these cost-free, government-sponsored avenues for dealing with it. You know, let the county taxpayers foot the bill on this one.

"So, whatever was presented to us in terms of a telephone inquiry, there was an avenue to channel it into. And that channeling process was *entirely dependent* upon the insurance coverage. The payor and the payor mix. Be it no money, big pay, acute-care situation, or just some kid doing a teenage thing. It didn't matter. Let's say we get a call from a woman whose fifteen-year-old son just got suspended from school for riding around the school parking lot on the hood of another kid's car. Just normal kid stuff: dumb but not pathological. Okay, let's say we find out that this is a CHAMPUS-pay kid. You probe a little bit, find out the kid's been acting a little bit snotty lately. So you tell Mom it sounds like there's something goin' on, and why doesn't she bring him on in for a little meeting. 'After all, he *did* get suspended from school. Maybe he's starting to get the picture he could use some help.' Because, as an intake worker, your next job is to convert that call into an evaluation. A face-to-face evaluation, and as soon as possible. And the next obligation, after that, would be to turn that evaluation into an admission."

Sidell allows a flick of smile to move across his lips. "There was an intake worker, a guy named Harry,* and we worked well together. Okay, let's say it was Harry who took this call, and we've checked the kid's benefits, and now we know that none of them have ever been utilized. This hood-of-the-car kid is a checkbook whose account hasn't been cashed yet.

"So now we've got the kid and his mother in for the evaluation. Now, in order to admit him to an acute-care psychiatric hospital, the fundamental criteria would be 'a danger to himself or to others.'" Another smile appears and quickly fades. "Well, you take any normal teenage behavior today, or any day, and you can interpret that as self-endangerment behavior. You got a kid riding around on the hood of a car? 'He's a danger to himself. He needs to be protected—he's not safe right now. Because that's a self-destructive gesture if I ever heard one. The *hood* of a *car?* And there were other cars in the parking lot? Uh-huh. And they were moving, some of 'em, yes? What's he gonna do next? Step out into the traffic on the freeway as another high school prank?'

"The kid's in the other room, while Harry is talking to Mom; he's not hearing any of this yet."

Now, as if running through a menu, Sidell—as Harry the intake worker—begins to recite a list of possible symptoms. "'Let's see what we're dealing with here: Okay—depression. Does he drink or use drugs? Well, if you found a beer can in the car, he's probably smoking marijuana, too. And you say he's been acting kind of withdrawn from you and your husband lately. And then, of course, there's that ride on the hood: suicidal ideation. Gosh, you know, Mrs. X, any one of these'"—Sidell shrugs—"'Look, maybe we should take a time-out, see what's goin' on with this kid. Let me tell you something about behavior: It's gonna escalate until he gets attention.' " He pauses for dramatic effect. " 'So . . . we can let it go. But he's riding around on the hood of a car, he's probably smoking dope, he's not talking to you anymore, not communicating. You want to let all that go? You don't have to.' " He repeats the phrase. " 'Tell you what: One of the values of a hospital and an inpatient program is that we can run a full battery of tests. 'Cause this could be organic. He may be biochemically imbalanced, for all we know. But we gotta find out. Listen, that's one of the values of a hospital—in three days we can run the tests, do psychological testing, get some blood, get some serum levels—find out what's goin' on.' " Sidell allows his voice to trail away, leaving behind it a cloud of concern. Then he's talking again. " 'No, no, no. Don't worry about it. The insurance covers the full battery of tests. You're active duty, right? . . . Uh-huh, okay, non–active duty . . . twenty percent.' "

Sidell points out that he, as Harry, had dropped that 20 percent as if it were a minor detail. "But what it means is that CHAMPUS will only pay eighty percent of the costs in a non–active duty case. Twenty percent deductible. If this were an active-duty case, CHAMPUS would pay one hundred percent of the costs." He pauses for effect. "Active-duty military—that's a prime, prime payor.

"So now you sell the three-day stay, and now you bring the kid back in the room."

Sidell goes back into Harry mode, with all its carefully constructed beats and pauses, the sudden "inspirations"—all the details that make up the architecture of a snow job: " 'Okay, let's do it right. We got something here, we got some smoke. There's probably fire. Do you want to wait till there's a full blaze?' " A singsong delivery now: " 'I don't think so.' " Then, seriously again, " 'Let's do it.' "

Sidell addresses me now: "So now Mom's having second thoughts. She doesn't know—'a psych hospital' . . . and the kid's saying, 'No way, I'm not crazy.' And Harry's ready for him: 'No, it's not that you're crazy. You're obviously not crazy. But you've got something goin' on.' " A thoughtful pause. " 'Tell you what, I know some kids upstairs right now who are going through the same things. It might be helpful for you to talk to them. You don't have to listen to the shrink, just tell the shrink what he wants to hear. Talk to these other kids up there on the unit, they'll probably help you out more than the shrink.' "

But clearly the deal isn't clinched yet, Sidell tells me, so Harry tells everybody to hang on a second, and he picks up the phone and punches in an extension: " 'Hey, Al? Could you come down here for a couple of minutes? Yeah, I got someone in the intake office. I just wanted you to meet him, tell him a little bit about the program up there.' "

Sidell nearly smiles. "So I come on down for the close. And I was pretty good at it. Because I present well. I meet Mom, meet the child. I speak his language; I'm not threatening. I talk about the program. 'Hey, it's not about right or wrong or crazy. It's about just understanding what's goin' on, and feeling like you've got some support, and some avenues of talking about it, that's all.' " After one of those meaningful pauses, he continues. " 'I tell you what . . .' " Then, surprisingly, brilliantly, the thrust of Sidell's pitch switches. " 'God, when I was growing up I wanted to do the same thing. Hell, I *did* the same thing. They didn't stick me in a place like this, but . . .' " Now he swerves back. " 'Tell you what, come on, why don't we walk on up . . . you'll see what it's about.' " Then, in the just-kidding tone of someone punching the kid in the upper arm: " 'Yeah, yeah, yeah, we'll let you back out, don't worry about it.'

"I mean, we wouldn't kidnap the kid," Sidell tells me. "They had to sign papers and stuff. But I'd take him on a tour of the unit, and I'd take one of my prime kids—you know, a kid who's really strong, got his act together, and is protreatment. I wouldn't take one of the other kids who was antitreatment, who's gonna say, 'I don't need to be in here. It's my parents who need to be in here. This place sucks, they're just in it for the money.' But with the protreatment kid, it's: 'Hey, Chris, I'd like you to meet Matthew. How long you been in here, Matthew?'

"Do a little bit of that until Matthew, or whoever, is doing it for you: 'I was way worse than you, man. Didn't you guys have to wrestle me down?' "

Sidell nods solemnly. " 'Yeah, we had to drag you up here.'

" 'Well, if I had to do it again, they wouldn't have to drag me, man.'

Sidell shrugs. "So. You just closed the sale.

"Your first obligation is to get the head in the bed. Now, you got the kid in, but now that kid is going to be calling his parents every two hours: 'Get me outta here. This is crazy—they tie people down in here. They do this. They do that. How can you do this to me?' They play on their parents' guilt. So the first twenty-four, forty-eight hours are critical for cementing the sale. But you still have to deal with, 'Yeah, I know I agreed, but I still have twenty-four hours to back out.' That was in the contract, like when you buy a car. And that's why it was important for us program directors to start, at the first point, in forming that therapeutic reliance on the program. Because the early hours are going to be critical for the kid to be pulled out AMA [against medical advice]. It was called 'guarding the door,' and what it meant was that once you've got people admitted, *don't* let them leave early. Don't let them leave until their benefits are used up."

Now Sidell backtracks. Before his promotion to the front office as head of a marketing team, he had to interview with Charles Trojan, the Southwood CEO. "We talked for about an hour, and not once did we discuss my clinical skills, or my background in psychology and human behavior, or patients' needs, or how to effect treatment. What Charlie Trojan and I talked about was referral bases, marketing, and the insurance companies' pay-reimbursement rates.

"Charlie wanted to know about my previous involvement in the mental-health industry, and when I told him I had previously worked for a DUI program, with court-appointed offenders, he wanted to know how many, and if they all had alcohol or drug problems, and if I'd noticed other, attendant problems. He wanted to know if we ever referred people from the DUI program to psychiatric hospitals—how many, how often. We just sat there adding up numbers of potential patients, and how many I might be able to bring to Southwood through my contacts in the professional community."

I ask if Sidell got the feeling he was being promoted for his skills as a rainmaker more than anything else. He answers instantly. "Yep. And I knew the buzzwords that would make Trojan want me." He performs one of his two-person dialogues:

" 'Who's your best payor now? Is CHAMPUS still high?'

" 'Oh, yeah. CHAMPUS is real high. Aetna's pretty high.'

" 'Uh-huh. What're you getting MediCal for nowadays?'

"See, I was just talking the talk with him. The administrative language of what reimbursement rates he was getting. And he was eating it up. He loved it. He was looking for someone who knew how to present, and who had enough organizational ability to do it."

Sidell has been speaking in a slow, steady stream. Now he hesitates, squinting slightly, and I can almost hear the roll and tumble of his thoughts. "Actually, Charlie was appropriate enough. The program director and I had already covered off on all the clinical issues, before I got to Charlie." He nods in a terse little gesture. "Yeah. Trojan was appropriate enough in the context of profitability."

Now Sidell grins. It is something of a surprise; he is not a man given to wide expressions. "But I could tell he was loving every minute of that conversation. I knew exactly what he was thinking: 'Here's a guy who can put heads in my beds.' "

With his promotion to marketing, Sidell was required to attend weekly marketing meetings. "Meetings took up from fifty to seventy-five percent of your time if you were at management level. Clinical meetings, program-review meetings, quality-of-care meetings. And then there were the marketing meetings. That was the only two-hour meeting at Southwood." As Sidell speaks, an image of the finely tuned organizational system that was Southwood's marketing program begins to emerge.

"One of the first assignments handed to me, as soon as I joined the marketing department, was to make twenty contacts a month. And there was a strict criteria for what constituted a marketing contact. Each one had to be with a licensed professional who had referral power within the community. They had categories." He leans forward, ticking off on his fingers. "A would be a doctor. B would be a program director at one of the DUI programs, for example. C would be counselors and therapists. Because those people would all have well-defined systems."

What about schools as referral points?

Sidell nods. "School systems were very big marketing arenas. And not just unified schools; we worked all the school systems."

(Indeed, a director from one NME-owned facility testified, during the 1992 congressional hearing, that he targeted kindergartens as part of his marketing strategy.)

"Everybody had to do marketing," Sidell says, "from the executive medical director on down. Even David Bergman, who was medical director of Southwood and a renowned psychiatrist in his own right, had to report his contacts, five every week. Charlie Trojan, too. Charlie would be talking to county heads, working on contracts with the county." According to Sidell, the only staff who were exempt from the marketing requirement were the mental-health counselors and the nurses. But only because the clinical staff refused to market.

"One of the sorest points, and one of the baddest reputations that Southwood got, was trying to mix clinical with marketing. Because they *don't* mix. The people who gravitate to the clinical side of the profession are polar opposites from those who move toward the sales profession. The clinical people bucked the whole idea of trawling for patients. They felt very strongly that they weren't there to do marketing.

"Those people who did market were charted on inquiries, evaluations, and conversions, all part of the marketing machinery. Records are spit out every week, every day on these marketing numbers." Sidell pauses; he appears older when he talks about statistics. "You never saw a clinical report. You never saw a report on this program or that program. You never saw a report on patients' ongoing adjustments. All you saw was average daily patient census and length of stay." Sidell refers to the latter as "L.O.S." A thin smile licks at the outer edges of his lips; it doesn't make it to his eyes. "Of course, L.O.S. was determined by the amount covered by the insurance policy. *Until* Southwood started to catch heat. Then they decided not to run a policy all the way to the end."

Sidell's voice takes on the pitch of another persona again—presumably Charles Trojan this time. " 'That'll look bad. Let's leave four days out of thirty, in case we have to readmit. We don't want to look like we're exhausting insurance plans.'

"There was no free service. We just discharged. And, of course, the discharge date was established upon admission, based on insurance coverage. Up until the last couple of years there, when these things started to come to the forefront of unacceptable issues, you'd sit in the morning intake meeting, and you'd go over last night's marketing activity, and what patients had been admitted. And, of course, who was being discharged."

Sidell leans forward in his chair. He looks, at this moment, like someone who is about to impart a long-held and despised secret. In fact, he has spoken out publicly once before (albeit under cover of anonymity) on the practices at Southwood. "And God help you if you had a patient go before their insurance was exhausted. You're in trouble; you'd better be able to explain why. And if you kept one person past their insurance coverage . . . well, then you're providing free treatment, and that patient may still think he's a space traveler from Neptune, but if you're giving away free days . . ." He shrugs eloquently.

"Every morning, Charlie Trojan and some of the staff physicians would hassle over these issues. And sometimes some of the docs would go to bat, and sometimes they wouldn't."

Sidell goes into dialogue mode again; it is like watching a stream of mercury as it slithers back and forth from one end of a tube to the other. " 'Why the hell are we discharging this kid? Doesn't he have more time covered on CHAMPUS?'

" 'Yeah, but listen, Charlie—'

" 'I don't want to hear it. Just come up with some issues.' "

Sidell gazes steadily at me. "The directive was, 'We need to keep the kid as a patient in this hospital. So find a way to do it.' But there's more to it than that. It gets more complicated. For instance, one time we've got a full unit, all twenty-four beds filled. Trojan calls me down to his office. 'Al, listen, Harry's got a good private pay in the intake office. And we've gotta get him a bed. I was looking at the discharge sheet, and you've got a MediCal kid up there, supposed to be discharged next week when her thirty days are up, right?'

" 'Yeah. Amber.* She's working a good program.'

" 'Well, I've gotta get her out of there. Can you do it? She's got seven or eight days left. Can we get her out?'

" 'Well, Charlie, let me go upstairs and see what's up on her chart, see what we can do.' "

It is somewhat reassuring that Sidell is making no attempt to whitewash his part in this recalled conversation.

"So I go up to my office, and I check out the girl's mother. Mom's in a rehab herself, and Mom's not getting out for a week. It's a four-week program, because MediCal covers thirty days, and all the steps in that program are built around those thirty days. Exiting on Day Thirty. So I call the social worker managing the case. I don't talk to the doctor yet. Well, the social worker says that this isn't right, that we shouldn't be doing this. And I say: 'I know. But you know how Charlie is. It's business, and he's got a private pay sitting in his office. A thousand-a-day waiting for a bed. Well, let me call Amber's mom . . .' And the social worker yells at me not to dare call Mom, that Mom will hit the roof. So the social worker's not buying it.

"I go back down to Charlie's office, and I tell him that I can't get this one to wash.

" 'I don't care if you can get it to wash or not! I want this kid out of here. I don't care if you have to call the cops and file abandonment charges against the mother and have the cops come and pick the kid up.' Then he looks at me and says he doesn't want to tell me how to do it. Just to get that kid out of the hospital."

Sidell is watching me carefully for any reaction.

"This is pretty much verbatim," he continues. "At any rate, I went back upstairs, got the social worker, got the doc involved— and the doctor was a staff physician and wise to what the game was here. And, of course, the docs didn't like MediCal kids anyway. The doc would rather have a private payor too. So he wasn't bucking too much.

"Well, we ended up calling the Chula Vista Police Department, and we had them come pick the kid up, and we filed abandonment charges against the mother. So, we got the MediCal kid out of the hospital, and we got the private-pay kid in. A week later, this girl, Amber, was in a general hospital, near coma from an overdose."

There is a long moment of silence before Sidell speaks again. "That is human damage perpetrated for a six-hundred-dollar-a-day difference in a bed rate. That's a real story, and that's only one of them. Over a payor mix."

CHAPTER NINETEEN

ON JANUARY 16, 1992, four days after Christy Scheck walked out of the family session with her parents and nine days after Christy's allegation of sexual molestation by her father, Bob and Merry Scheck went to Southwood for an assessment meeting with Dr. Quinn.

Merry had been studying as much medical literature as she could lay her hands on, and now she had a list of questions about the medications Christy was being given. She was particularly concerned about the amounts of imipramine that had been prescribed for Christy on a daily basis. Merry quoted her sources, all of which clearly stated that in adolescent cases, use of the antidepressant should never exceed 100 milligrams per day. Merry wanted to know why her thirteen-year-old daughter was being given 150 milligrams of imipramine daily.

As Merry relates the details of her interrogation of Quinn, Bob begins to make a series of small sounds: "Uh-uh-uh-uh . . ."

Merry glances at him and nods emphatically. "That's *exactly* what Quinn did. He just kept going, 'Uh-uh-uh.' This man who's supposed to be an articulate practitioner of psychiatry, and all he can do is stammer. He simply could not answer my questions."

Bob picks up the thread. "There were other people at that meeting, too, some of those young women, the psych techs, or mental-health counselors or workers, or whatever they called themselves. Quinn looked around the room at every one of them, like somebody was going to provide the answers to my wife's questions. Nobody had a clue. Then I asked for a diagnosis on our daughter, especially in view of these terrible things she was saying, which nobody seemed to question. I asked what treatment was being planned." Bob's eyelids begin to flutter rapidly. "That was the only time I got upset in that meeting. Quinn looked at me and said, 'What your daughter said has the ring of truth.' "

"That son of a bitch." She has spoken in a whisper, but nothing could be a clearer indication of Merry's rage. This kind of language is virtually never spoken in the Scheck home.

She goes on. "I pointed to Rebecca, who was Christy's co—primary counselor. She had given Christy a crystal on a chain, which Christy now wore constantly. At any rate, I pointed at her, and I said, 'This is the most intensive form of peer pressure I've ever heard of. If a person does not have an issue when they come here, one *will* be created for them. In order to fit in.'

" 'Now, Mrs. Scheck. We don't do that—'

" 'Baloney! That's exactly what you do.' "

Merry's lips compress into a narrow line. "We learned later that Quinn was not running Southwood. There were treatment teams, made up of the mental-health counselors, and they were the ones who determined what went on in the meetings and at the residential treatment center. With the exception of medication and any other treatment that required a doctor's signature. All of that stuff was done by the book, but I found out later that Quinn was completely *re*active, instead of being proactive in his dealings with Christy. And, I guess, any other patient. He simply reacted to whatever the counselors told him."

Gary Juleen has a memory of a treatment-team meeting that took place on February 20, 1992. It would seem to bear out Merry Scheck's contention. "Before the meeting ever began," he recalls, "Rebecca Boyle, one of Christy's co—primary counselors, stood up, pointed straight at me, and made a dramatic accusation: 'I want everyone in this room to know, before we begin this meeting, that this man is trying to split the staff. And he is coercing staff members.' "

Juleen shakes his head. "I'll tell you, that was a bolt from the blue. I was so shocked I didn't know what to say, and apparently neither did anybody else in the room."

What about Dr. Quinn? As the psychiatrist in charge, didn't Quinn step in?

Another head shake. "There wasn't a peep out of him. And frankly, at that point, I didn't feel as if I had to defend myself, or justify what I was doing, either. But Rebecca Boyle wasn't done yet. She had more she wanted to say, and what came next was even more outrageous as far as I was concerned. She turned away from me and looked around the room, then she said, 'We *all* know that the issue with Christy Scheck is that she was molested by her father.'

"Well, people were struck absolutely stone silent—Quinn, everyone. Nobody even looked at anyone else. And then the assistant director of the RTC, a young guy named Frank, made a comment. He said that several months prior to this there had been another situation where a child on the unit accused his parents of molestation. And those allegations were found to be untrue.

"Now, every eye on the room was on this young guy. And you could feel a kind of . . . rustle through the silence. As if, without being spoken, the connecting thought was, 'Oh, God—what if this is the same thing?' But he immediately cautioned the staff in general not to draw any conclusions from this. That he didn't see that molestation was *not* the primary issue in the focus of Christy Scheck's treatment.

"Everybody just stayed quiet after that. The meeting may have continued, but I honestly have no memory of either Christy or her treatment being discussed from that point on."

I ask Juleen why Boyle would have accused him of such things as coercion.

"In reality, where Rebecca drew her conclusion was that Christy's other co–primary counselor, Bria Altshult, had come to me and asked for my opinion about Christy's alleged molestation. And my statement to Bria was that I didn't feel the allegation was true. But I also said that whether it was true or not, I felt that the focus of Christy's treatment needed to be off the abuse issues and directed on to the reunification of the family.

"The following week another staff member came to me and asked about Christy's treatment and the allegations of molestation and abuse. I gave her the same answer I gave Bria: I wanted the focus of the treatment to be on family sessions, that we needed to reinstate the opportunity for the parents to be able to visit and to be involved in Christy's treatment. And for me to continue to conduct family sessions, which were stopped after the allegation was made."

I ask Juleen if it was the frontline staff, the mental-health counselors, who made these decisions, rather than Christy's treatment team.

"Yes. But what was taking place in late February was a reconsideration—by the staff—that we could reinstitute family sessions on Southwood grounds. It was because of my statements about Christy's allegations, made to Bria Altshult and to that other staff worker, and my desire to treat Christy from a family perspective, that caused Rebecca Boyle to make her accusations against me in the treatment-team meeting."

Juleen is not familiar with Arthur Quinn's course of treatment for Christy. He has known Quinn for approximately twenty years, and he considers the Southwood psychiatrist to be "competent." Juleen adds that he "doesn't know another person who cares more about the individuals he works with." It is faint praise, and it leaves one with the impression that Juleen does not wish to go on record against a former colleague.

Was there a poisoned relationship between Christy and some of the frontline workers at Southwood?

Juleen feels strongly that there were people on staff who needed to believe that Christy had been molested and abused. "I suspect they already had that in their minds. That if a child has a particular set of problems, it follows that they were molested. It may be that an undereducated and undertrained staff jumped to those general conclusions." He is careful to say that he is not privy to any specific information, but he believes that "since the treatment never deviated from focusing on Christy's increasingly bizarre stories, it makes sense to me that the Southwood staff in general adhered to the belief system that Christy was molested. And it could have been that they tried to force that issue out of her. A kid who is uncomfortable with herself provides a fertile field for a staff member to implant the idea that that child was abused. I don't know if any staff member directly mentioned the issue of molest to Christy Scheck, but certainly if there was any innuendo or inference of the possibility of her being molested . . . well, most kids will take that information and think about it. And even if they don't come up with a specific memory, the child still feels uncomfortable. And if that particular issue is pursued— because 'this is my counselor or my therapist who's saying this, and they must know something I don't'—it actually pushes a child into believing she was molested, even if she was not. And she begins to make statements: 'Yes, I was molested. Yes, my father is the one who molested me.' And so on. And it's all because of a collusion that takes place between a particular staff member and the patient."

Juleen has warmed to the subject; he is speaking with more emphasis than at any time during the interview. "That ushers a girl like Christy into territory that is untrue. And Christy was bright enough to know that it was untrue. But the reality is that even if she thinks it might have been a possibility—and now that she has stated emphatically that it happened—she's confronted with the actuality of having to betray the counselor, or the therapist, in order to tell the truth.

"So Christy stayed with the story. And, unfortunately, when she 'confessed' her molest, it is my belief that staff came to her and wanted to know more and more details about that molest. And that placed Christy Scheck in quicksand. Because now she has to come up with the details of something that never happened."

Juleen is silent for a moment before he continues. "She is given literature to read. And she sits in groups and hears about the molestation of other kids, or maybe she hears stories on the unit: kids interacting about molestation. And she begins to incorporate these ideas into her story. There is the possibility, of course, that Christy just came up with ideas about ongoing penetration for a prolonged period of time, and about anal penetration, and so on. Even though there was absolutely no evidence that anything like that had ever taken place."

Juleen has no idea why Christy's stories were not compared to the physical evidence. He strongly feels that without evidence of penetration or molestation, the staff should have been informed that molestation was no longer an issue. His reasoning as to why that didn't happen is simple: "They didn't want to change their minds."

We discuss the psychological evaluation that was ordered by Dr. Quinn and performed on Christy on November 13 and 22, 1991. The evaluation stated, among other observations, that Christy seemed to deliberately seek the negatives, that she took gratification in being "a bad actor," and that a firm, almost authoritative manner would work best with her. (It was stated, in later depositions by various staff workers, that the psychological evaluation done on Christy was not referred to in the course of her treatment.)

Juleen has potent feelings about the report. "That particular psychological evaluation described Christy to a tee. If it had been utilized by the staff, they would have known what they were dealing with in Christy Scheck. They would not have entertained her stories, and they would not have pushed her for more and more stories, and more details." Juleen says he can't be sure, but it is his opinion that reports like the psychological evaluation done on Christy Scheck were "just chucked into the chart, and a possibly overworked staff didn't take the time to read all the documentation. In general, reports like that simply become part of the chart, seen by staff as just something that's there. I think they're told they can access those reports, and I think there are some staff members who do read charts, but in general, I think people are there to perform their required responsibilities, which are to take the kids to recreation, and to make sure they get to dinner . . ." Juleen shrugs. It is both an apologetic and a telling gesture.

CHAPTER TWENTY

AFTER THE ASSESSMENT meeting with Dr. Quinn on January 16, the Schecks were ready to transfer Christy to another residential treatment center, a facility in El Cajon. Merry spoke to a caseworker at Child Protective Services and said that she and Bob were extremely unhappy with the treatment Christy was being given at Southwood. Merry has a strong recollection of that conversation.

"I told CPS that I knew Christy couldn't come home yet. Told them I knew we had to work this whole thing out. I asked the caseworker if CPS had a problem with Christy being moved to another residential treatment center, and she was completely reasonable about it. She told me that would be just fine.

"So we left that meeting at Southwood on January sixteenth, and we were ready to transfer Christy. We were ready, if necessary, to have the people from the new place go to Southwood and pick Christy up there."

Merry sits quietly for a moment. There is a sense of time suspended in the room. As if, by remaining untold, the rest of the story can be somehow altered. When she begins to speak again, her words seem almost measured. "When we came home from that meeting at Southwood, I went to the baby-sitter's house to pick up Molly. The woman's daughter met me at the door. The girl told me that her mother was at Molly's school. Then she said, 'They're taking Molly.'

"I knew exactly what was going on. I'd said to Molly, a few days earlier, 'Honey, because of the things that Christy is saying, the police may come and take you away from us. But I want you not to be afraid. I want you to know that we will come and get you just as soon as we can.'

"Now, remember, I'm saying this to a six-year-old. And it was only in preparation. Just in case."

Merry manages a small smile as she tells me how she drove, literally, at ninety miles an hour to get to her younger daughter's school. "I screeched up in front of the school, and I parked right in front of a police car." The smile vanishes. "The police would not allow me to see Molly. According to them, Molly stood up in front of the classroom and said, 'I'm having sex with my father.' "

I glance over at Bob Scheck. He is listening intently, his face expressionless.

Merry goes on. "Now, I must tell you that Molly has denied that statement to"—she begins to clap her hands for emphasis—"social workers. To us. Has denied it to foster parents and to her therapist. She said, to me, 'Mom, I never said that.' And I could see that the child didn't even know what it meant. The police also told me that this child was suicidal because she said she wanted to go and be with her sister." Merry makes a small sound of annoyance.

"Of course she wanted to be with her sister. She loved Christy. And maybe she thought that Christy was living in a 'neat' place." Her voice lifts. "Molly was six years old!

"At any rate, I asked the police officers if they would just tell Molly that Mommy and Daddy loved her.

" 'No, ma'am. That would be tainting the case.' " Merry shakes her head. Then her shoulders hitch up in a nearly imperceptible shrug. "All those police officers at the school were men. And I remember one of them saying that he had a six-year-old daughter." She starts to say something else but stops instead and looks at me, squinting a little, thinking about whatever it is that has come to mind.

"Look, I want to plug in something here that I didn't find out until afterward. But I think it's important to mention now. On the fifteenth of January, the day before that assessment meeting at Southwood, some police lieutenant and Rebecca Boyle, Christy's [co–]primary counselor, met with CPS caseworkers to discuss what they were going to do with Molly." She pauses, then she begins to tap the palm of her left hand with the index finger of the right. "The fifteenth of January. The fifteenth. And then, out of nowhere, supposedly on the sixteenth of January, Molly makes these statements at school?" Merry makes a small chuffing sound. "Sounds fishy to me."

Bob nods solemnly. Merry sits still for a moment, then she clears her throat.

"So, I'm sitting in my car, and the tears are streaming down my face as"—there is a rasp in her voice now; this is the first time since we met that the need to cry has overcome this woman's will—"as I watch that little girl walk away, hand in hand, with a police-man." She is very close to tears now. Bob reaches across the table for her hand and she turns it under his, so that their fingers can mesh in a long, tightly held grip.

"And as I sat there, the only thing I could think of was that now both my girls were gone."

CHAPTER TWENTY-ONE

IT BECAME A police matter the moment Christy Scheck accused her father of sexual molestation.

Michael Duffy was the detective assigned to the case. Duffy had been working juvenile investigations in the Southeastern Division of the San Diego Police Department for eight years. He had seen many cases of parental abuse. And, in his capacity as lead detective, he had worked with several local hospitals, including Southwood Psychiatric Center.

Although he is retired now, Duffy still has strong feelings about the Scheck case. He was, and continues to be, convinced that Christy Scheck was telling the truth.

"I handled the Scheck case from start to finish," he says, "and I consider Christy Scheck to be a classic. Here was someone who had the very foundation of her stability pulled out from under her. The basis of her world was gone."

Duffy is reluctant to discuss particulars, but he is very clear about his feelings toward Southwood. "Southwood Hospital was hamstrung by the rules of confidentiality. There was never any argument, from any member of their staff, about allowing us to have access to Christy. But"—his voice rises—"everyone there strictly maintained the rules of confidentiality. They were hamstrung." He resumes a tone of chilly objectivity. "Christy Scheck's parents wouldn't talk to me at all. The foster parents wouldn't talk to me, either. They refused all my calls, and they refused to allow me any access."

When I ask a question about Charles Trojan, the Southwood CEO, Duffy declines further comment.

Rachel Penny is more than willing to discuss her conversations with Michael Duffy. "I spoke with him on the telephone. What he wanted me to do was to convince Merry to come to his office without legal counsel. He'd say to me, 'I only want to talk to her for a few minutes. I only have a few questions I need to ask her.'" Rachel says that when she mentioned Merry's attorney to Detective Duffy, his reply was that Merry didn't need an attorney. "'If her husband is innocent, Merry Scheck doesn't need a lawyer.'"

Rachel says that she told Detective Duffy that she would speak to Merry, but she added an opinion of her own: "'Christy is lying, you know.'

"'Children don't lie about these things, Mrs. Penny.'

"'Oh, yes, Detective Duffy, they do. And Christy had access to Shana King, one of the foster children who was placed in my home. As you probably remember, Shana was taken from her house and savagely molested. Christy Scheck is using Shana King's exact words.'

"'I've seen Christy. I believe her.'

"'Look, I've known Christy since she was six months old. Don't you have questions for me? For the Schecks' neighbors? For the pastor of the church the Schecks attend? For Christy's teachers?'

"'I've been in this work for years, Mrs. Penny. Children never lie about this.'"

Rachel Penny still feels passionately that if Detective Duffy had gone out and interviewed people who knew Christy, he would have seen a different picture. "The gaping holes in Christy's story would have been evident. She was smart, and she was manipulative." She pauses. "But he didn't."

Rachel is clearly disturbed by her recollection of the conversation. "I really had no intention of renewing my foster-care license after we went through that horrendous molestation case with Shana. We were all just worn out by that one. But when Molly was picked up at school that day in January, Merry called me in tears. She was as upset as I'd ever known her to be. She told me that Molly had stood up in school during show-and-tell and said that she'd been having sex with her father." Rachel Penny levels her index finger as if it were a pistol. "Now, to this day, Molly denies everything. She was in first grade at the time, and her definition of 'sex' was holding someone's hand and kissing them on the lips. And Bob would hold her hand when they were out walking, and they would give each other a smack on the lips before she went to bed every night. So"—she shrugs—"she was having sex with her father.

"Also, you have to remember that Molly had overheard her parents talking on the phone about the allegations Christy had made. Because no matter how private you try to keep a conversation, kids'll always pick up on part—or all—of what's being said."

Red has been listening quietly; now he makes a small, chuckling sound. Rachel smiles briefly at her son before she goes on. "At any rate, Molly overheard things, and she hadn't been able to see Christy since the allegations were made. She thought that Christy had gone away to camp, because that's what Bob and Merry told her. So, in her mind, she wanted to go away to camp, too. To be with Christy. And since Christy was saying she was having sex with her father, then Molly was going to say that *she* was having sex with Bob, too. And then she'd get to go to camp with her sister. Six-year-old logic." Rachel's tone darkens again. "But Molly has consistently denied that she ever said anything like that at school. At any rate, she was picked up, based on that, and taken to Hillcrest Receiving Home. Well, when Merry called me, I said, 'Look, I know the system. They don't have enough foster homes, there's no place to put her. Hillcrest is overflowing; they've got kids sleeping in the halls.' I told Merry that I'd call up and have them put my license on hold, and that I'd offer my home as an emergency shelter." She takes a deep breath. "And that's what I did."

I ask Red how he felt when Molly Scheck came to live with his family. He shrugs, grinning. "Well, my folks didn't discuss it with me—Molly just showed up here. But it didn't bother any of us kids at all. We were used to it. It's always been the-more-the-merrier type of thing with this family."

Rachel continues. "As I remember, it was a holiday weekend. I called on Friday, to try to pick up Molly that evening, but by the time CPS got back to me, the social worker on the case told me they couldn't move Molly because she was 'medically fragile.' I looked at my watch when she said that, and I thought, 'Medically fragile nothing, lady.' That social worker wanted to leave early." She pulls another tissue from the box on the table next to her chair. She doesn't use it, though; she wads it up in her hand. And when she looks at me again, her brow is flexed angrily above her eyes. " 'Medically fragile' is the standard line. At any rate, I had to wait over the three-day weekend, and when I finally got through to someone on the following Tuesday, I asked what 'medically fragile' meant. I was told that Molly Scheck was too emotionally upset to be placed in a foster home. I asked, 'When can I get her?' And the social worker said, 'We're not sure.' "

Rachel waited one more day. Then she placed a direct call to Hillcrest Receiving Home. She explained that she was a close friend of the Schecks', and that she was licensed both as a foster parent and for emergency care. She said she wanted to come and get Molly. "Do you want to know what the Hillcrest people said?" Rachel's tone is an odd blend of anger and triumph, like someone who has expected to do battle for a prize, only to find that she has won by default. "They said, 'Thank goodness! When do you want to come pick her up?' They wanted to know why I hadn't called earlier."

Rachel Penny picked up Molly Scheck on January 21. The little girl had been taken from her school on the sixteenth, five days earlier. In the interval, while she was in residence at Hillcrest, she was taken on two separate occasions to the Center for Child Protection for evidentiary hearings. The center is a San Diego County facility, on the same grounds as Children's Hospital. Christy, accompanied by a Southwood mental-health counselor, was at the first hearing. Both girls underwent physical examinations, and each girl was interviewed by a caseworker. The interviews were videotaped, and Merry Scheck was allowed to see the tapes before they were sealed.

"Christy sat there with her head down and her shoulders hunched," Merry recalls. "She kept her hands in her lap and her eyes averted from the woman who was asking the questions. Once in a great while Christy would sneak a look at the woman, just a quick little peek from under her bangs. One of those sidelong glances. She answered the woman's questions mostly in monosyllables, and she only responded to direct questions. She volunteered nothing, and when the woman asked her to describe something, Christy did not give her any specific details." Merry draws in a deep breath; even that small sound is forlorn. "She used words like 'privates,' and I recognized phrases I'd seen in that book about parental abuse that Christy brought home from the school library. She also mentioned some of the things she'd heard from Shana King when Shana was in foster care with the Pennys and the two girls had gotten so close. But Christy's story at that first evidentiary hearing was completely inconsistent with some of the things she had been talking about at Southwood. For example, at Southwood she had talked about being taken away from the house and molested in a green car, but she didn't mention anything about this at the interview. Her stories were so inconsistent, in fact, that Barbara Korda,* the CPS social worker who supervised my visits with Molly while she was in foster care at the Pennys', put that in her report after she went to see Christy at Southwood in February. Ms. Korda met with Bob and me and our attorneys, and after that meeting she went to see Christy. Her report, dated February 26, 1992, said exactly that: 'Christy's story is inconsistent.' "

Although Merry has been able to provide at least the name of a credible witness in order to cast some element of doubt on her daughter's accusations, the victory, if it can be described as one, is clearly Pyrrhic. As for Molly's interviews at the evidentiary hearings, Merry saw only the videotape dated January 17.

"Molly seemed to be playing a game with the social worker," Merry recalls. "She built a fort out of pillows and hid behind it.

And when she spoke you heard a six-year-old responding in a completely uninterested voice. You could see the caseworker becoming increasingly frustrated. It's not that Molly was belligerent or hostile. She wasn't. She was just not interested. The woman asked, 'Does your sister have a problem with touching?'

"Molly said, 'No.' So the woman waited a minute, and then she rephrased the question. This time she changed the word 'touching' to 'being bothered.' The answer was still 'No.'

"Then she gave Molly some anatomically correct dolls to play with. And, again, Molly wasn't particularly interested, but she looked at them, and she undressed them. The caseworker pointed to the female doll's genitals and asked Molly what that was. Molly said, 'That's where I go pee-pee.'

"Then the woman pointed to the male doll's genitals and asked what that was. 'That's where Daddy goes pee-pee.' "

Bob is, as usual, listening intently to Merry's recollections.

"By the time the interview was over," Merry continues, "the woman had asked one particular question a number of times. The question was, had anyone been 'bothering' Molly? Molly answered this question consistently in the negative, and the caseworker would go on to another subject. But she always came back to that one question: Had *any* person—any person at all—ever bothered Molly?"

Surprisingly, Bob Scheck has begun to smile.

"Well, the last time the woman asked this question, Molly said, 'Uh-huh.' And the woman leaned in real close to her, like this was it, and she asked, 'Who is that person, Molly? Who is it that's been bothering you?'

"And Molly looked her straight in the eye and said, 'You. You've been bothering me.' "

"She's a great little kid." The pitch of Bob's voice is soft enough to be considered a whisper, but his smile has broadened into a grin.

The results of Molly's physical exam showed that she was still intact, her hymen unruptured. The report on Christy's physical exam stated that she, too, was intact. But the report also stated that she had genital warts.

Christy's examination at Kaiser Medical Center, the one Merry Scheck had insisted upon at the beginning of January, had shown no evidence of genital warts. The Schecks remain convinced that if indeed Christy developed genital warts during the three weeks between examinations, she acquired them at Southwood.

On January 22, 1992, Bob and Merry Scheck went to court for their preliminary appearance. Neither of them had ever been inside a courtroom before; neither of them knew what to expect. Before the proceedings began, they were each provided with court-appointed attorneys, as were Christy and Molly, who were not present.

"Bob and I each had about two minutes with our respective lawyers before we went into the courtroom, and I have to tell you, my attorney, Marty Cruz,* was worth his weight in gold. He was an incredible man." She glances at her husband with a sorrowful little smile. "Bob's lawyer, on the other hand, was"—Merry's shoulders lift in a small, telling gesture—"well, maybe she was new to the job. Maybe she . . . I don't know what it was. What I did know, right there, was that if we were going to keep Bob out of jail, we were going to have to get ourselves a private attorney."

As terrifying as the proceedings might have been for the Schecks, this was a fairly typical hearing on a petition for termination of parental rights as a result of sexual molestation, with the Department of Social Services (of which CPS is a subdivision) filing an allegation under Section 300(d) of the Welfare and Institutions code. If the accused parent is exonerated in a 300 case, he or she can still be tried criminally.

The proceedings moved quickly that day. The judge was given, among other reports, the results of the evidentiary examination performed at Children's Hospital. Bob Scheck was not exonerated, and the case was continued for one month. Christy would remain at Southwood. Molly would stay in foster care with Rachel and Hal Penny.

Rachel Penny is still able to tap into the anger she felt after the preliminary appearance. "I asked the investigative social worker who was given Bob and Merry's case why the judge hadn't been given both the Children's Hospital and the Kaiser report." Rachel's lips are puckered, and her eyes have narrowed. "Do you want to know what the caseworker said to me? She told me it had not been necessary to hand over both reports. That they said the same thing."

Red Penny is listening hard. He has probably not heard these details before.

"I accused the woman of lying to me. Told her I'd seen both reports." Rachel's lips have relaxed, but her eyes remain slitted. "Well, her way of dealing with me was to say, 'Mrs. Penny, you must be objective about this. You cannot get personally involved.'

"And I said, 'Well, lady, I *am* going to get personally involved. Because I have to. These people are my friends; these children are like my nieces. How can I not be personally involved?' " Rachel shifts position in her chair, picks up her glass of water, and drinks. "I'll tell you, I was very glad that I took Molly in to see the pediatrician at Kaiser for a gynecological examination after she came here for foster care. Just to make sure the evidentiary done on her was legitimate. And I stayed in the room while she was being examined. The doctor said there was no way either of those girls had been penetrated.

"Then Hal and I went one step further: We wrote a letter to the judge, telling him everything we knew about the case. About Christy and her parents, and about those two evidentiary reports. Writing that letter was within our purview, as foster parents, and my husband took a day off work and went down to that courtroom and hand-delivered it."

She sets down the empty water glass with a thud. "Well, the judge wanted to know why he hadn't been shown that second evidentiary report, and he must have asked a question or two about it, because he called a continuance and set a hearing date for March ninth, and the next thing I hear from the social worker is how I'm not able to be objective, and they're going to have to find another placement for Molly. We had quite a little conversation. 'Are you threatening me?' I asked.

" 'No, no, no, Mrs. Penny. Of course I'm not threatening you.'

" 'Well, excuse me, but it sounds like a threat to me. You tell me I'm an excellent foster home. You know that, psychologically, this is the best place for Molly to be because we are her family. And yet you're going to remove her from this house because I'm not playing along with you? Sure sounds like a threat to me.' "

Rachel smiles gently.

"Molly stayed with us." The smile fades. "Well, listen, the truth is, most social workers are undertrained and overworked and underpaid. They have too many cases to deal with and, in my opinion, the wrong signal gets sent down from the administration at the very top to the grunts who do the actual work."

What does Rachel Penny believe that signal to be?

"The one that says, 'We have to maintain a certain number of kids in our program.' "

MARTIN CRUZ, MERRY Scheck's court-appointed attorney, does not agree with Rachel Penny's theory of a systemic conspiracy. "Both reports not being handed in is not unusual," he explains, "considering the time restraints in a case like this. And, you have to remember, the system always puts forward the stuff that favors their position."

Cruz considers Merry Scheck to have been "a terrific client." He recalls, "The first thing I told Merry was that this case was going to be her worst nightmare. I explained what she could and could not expect, and I told her that one of the things an attorney could do for her was to take the element of surprise out of that nightmare."

According to Merry, Cruz did more than erase the element of surprise. "Marty Cruz spent hours on the phone that he didn't even charge me for. To explain the system, and what was going on, and how it all worked."

Cruz himself does not recall if it was he who explained that when a child is picked up by CPS, the parents become responsible for all costs incurred: the attorneys, the courts, psychiatric evaluations, medical treatments, and foster care. This does not apply to those people who are jobless, or to those who do not own property, but Bob and Merry Scheck were both working, and they owned their home.

Merry remembers, "We weren't allowed to see, for example, the attorneys' billing sheets. We were simply advised that their bills had been paid, and we owed whatever amount had been spent by the county. Same thing with therapists' bills. We had to pay the fee without knowing the therapist's hourly rates or how many hours had been spent with our child. I made an agreement to pay off all the money—thousands and thousands of dollars—so much a month. But a lien was placed on our house, so there was the constant fear that our home could be sold out from under us unless that debt was paid. And, if the house did get sold, and if the money from the sale didn't cover the county's expenses, both my pay and Bob's pay would be docked, so much every month, until the debt was cleared. I received no accounting; it was just whatever interest was calculated, and another bill mailed to me. I never got an accounting of what I was paying for. I just had to pay it, or the lien would not be lifted off my house."

Then there was the matter of finding a private attorney for Bob. Merry equates that search with the family's pursuit of a therapist for Christy. "I made call after call after call. Finally, we found an attorney. Lee Selvig agreed to give us an hour, and he was literally our last hope. My attorney, Martin Cruz, had been appointed to me only, so Bob had to have his own lawyer. All I knew was that if this man didn't take us on, we'd be stuck with Bob's court-appointed attorney.

"Lee agreed to take on the case, but his retaining fee was fifteen thousand dollars, and we didn't have fifteen thousand, even though we only had to pay half that amount up front and then the rest as we could. My niece ended up funding the payment to Lee."

Merry smiles. "He has become a dear friend, and we couldn't have asked for more." The smile turns rueful. "Poor man. I'd write him letters, I'd hammer him with questions."

"And Marty, too," Bob cuts in. Merry nods emphatically.

"And Marty, too. Those poor guys, they must have thought, 'Get this woman off the line!' But they talked to me about strategy, and they explained to me that this was *not* about right or wrong."

Bob breaks in again. "Lee kept delivering one message to me from the minute he came on the case. He said, 'I don't care how innocent you are; don't think you can't go to jail. There are a lot of innocent people in jail.' " Bob is silent for a moment. "It took him a long time to get that through to me."

The fond expression on Merry's face changes now. Everything shifts and hardens. "The detective assigned to the case called Rachel Penny, telling her what a strong case he had against Bob, urging her to talk me into coming in to see him so that he could show me the strength of his case. Of course, what he didn't know was that I was the one who was building the case for my husband. He'd call me, too. Often. And the only thing I ever had to say to him was, 'Excuse me, Detective Duffy. On advice of counsel I will not speak with you.' And I had to keep saying that to him."

The Schecks' family room is darkening now; it is late afternoon. Merry continues, "Once Lee Selvig came on the case as Bob's attorney, I'd be talking to him, or to Marty Cruz, every day. Bob had no contact at all with either Christy or Molly. I was allowed one 'therapeutic' supervised hour per week with Christy. I'd call and set up an appointment, and then, on the day of the visit, I'd call to verify." A grimace pulls at the muscles around her mouth. "Well, sometimes, when I'd make that verification call, I'd be told, 'No. Christy doesn't want to see you. Call back next week.' *Not* 'Call back later in the week.' *Not* 'Call me tomorrow, we'll work something out.' Just 'Call back next week.' Now, mind you, I was getting all this through Christy's co-counselors, Bria Altshult and

Rebecca Boyle. I had no idea what Christy herself was saying. Bria, in particular, was sweet as pie to my face: 'Oh, yes, Mrs. Scheck,' and 'I understand, Mrs. Scheck,' but she either ignored everything I said, or it was used against me."

I ask for an example.

"During those weeks in February and March, when I wasn't seeing or speaking with Christy, it became clear that Bria and Rebecca were telling Christy everything I was saying. For example, at one point Bria told me, 'Christy knows you're angry at her.' How *could* she have known? I hadn't seen or spoken to her in two months." She turns up both hands in a gesture of helplessness. "And Bria reported that 'the mother refused to discuss the allegations.' No. No. No." Merry has clapped her hands together on each "no," for emphasis. "What 'the mother' refused to do was allow this girl, Bria, to pump me for anything she could reconstruct as an admission that my husband had molested my daughter. I just kept saying, 'It. Did. Not. Happen.' Not 'couldn't have happened.' Not 'possibility that it didn't happen.' It did *not* happen."

Merry is not crying, but she yanks a couple of tissues out of the box next to her and swipes angrily at her eyes, which have begun to tear. "I'd say, to Bria or to Rebecca, 'You're believing everything that Christy tells you as gospel. You're not checking anything out, you're not talking to her friends or to her school counselor.' And I'd always get the same reply: 'Now, Mrs. Scheck, we treat the child as if we believe everything they say, and that way they can build trust in us.'

"At any rate, we could have no contact with Christy, so I was wracking my brains, trying to find ways to communicate with her. The only thing I could think of was cards. You know, greeting cards. Because any handwritten note could have been turned against us. I scoured the shops for cards that said what Bob and I wanted to say, and we signed them just, 'Love, Mom and Dad.' You see, that way, we felt we could communicate to Christy how much we loved her, without the Southwood people saying, 'Uh-oh—look.' Because, you see, the message itself was written by Hallmark." She draws another tissue from the box.

"At one point Bria told me that Christy had received one of the cards and that she'd broken down, just crying and sobbing. And I remember thinking, 'Hope! Hope! Christy does realize that we love her.'"

CHAPTER TWENTY-TWO

BRIA ALTSHULT'S HISTORY at the Southwood Residential Treatment Center might easily, without danger of exaggeration, be described as dramatic.

Altshult, the bearer of a freshly minted degree in communications, was hired as an on-call mental-health counselor in the spring of 1990, a period described by senior counselor Brenda Willis-Hughes as "chaotic." Shortly after Altshult began her duties on the early-adolescent unit, she got in the middle of a fight between two boys and her leg was broken in three places. It is unclear whether one or both boys were among the children that Southwood had marketed from the juvenile-justice system, but it seems likely that they were. During this same time, another counselor had a chunk of flesh bitten out of his arm by a twelve-year-old boy he was trying to place in restraints.

Brenda Willis-Hughes began working as a per-diem mental-health counselor at Southwood in 1985 after completing a human-services education program at San Diego State University. She was also state-certified in chemical-dependency counseling. She left Southwood in 1986 and returned in 1988. She was promoted to senior counselor approximately a year and a half later, working primarily with adolescents, preadolescents, and children. She chose a position on the child unit upon her return from a maternity leave in 1990. Willis-Hughes and other counselors were often called to assist in stabilizing the early-adolescent unit of the RTC. When asked about the qualifications of the staff employed during that time, she said that it appeared that many of the people hired post-1990 had college degrees but were lacking in hands-on experience.

When asked to cite an instance (without criticizing any person individually) of what Willis-Hughes thought of as a consequence of inexperience on the early-adolescent unit during late 1991 or early 1992, the former senior counselor provided the following episode:

"Christy [Scheck] was threatening to run away and do drugs—overdose on drugs and throw herself in front of a car. The other counselors I was working with said something like, 'Oh, she's just attention-seeking. Ignore her.' And I said, 'No. We can't do that.' And when she attempted to run away, I initiated a restraint. I called for backup assistance, and she was restrained and brought to the time-out room, and I instructed someone to stay on a one-on-one with her, meaning at arm's length at all times, to make sure she was being safe."

In response to a query about her own style of management as a senior counselor, Willis-Hughes said her "style of maintaining control in the milieu was one of high structure, consistency, and with an emphasis on groups, and pushing residents to talk in groups." She went on to say that it appeared to her, in the time leading up to March 1992, that there was "less structure, fewer groups, less consistency, and a more lax approach." When asked if she had instigated any discussion between herself and any Southwood program director concerning her observations during this time, Willis-Hughes said that because of her per-diem status, she did not want to appear overbearing. When asked if this "lax approach" might have created potential safety problems with the patients, she admitted that was a concern she "had at the back of my mind."

She was not alone in her concern. It should be remembered that Health Management Strategies, the reviewing arm of CHAMPUS, conducted a survey at Southwood in February 1991. Of the myriad of deficiencies found, the ones that would relate most directly, a year later, to Christy Scheck were the low staffing ratios, the therapy sessions conducted by unlicensed mental-health counselors and other unlicensed personnel such as interns who led group meetings (particularly those groups involving sexual abuse), as well as staff members who were both unlicensed and untrained in CPR. Other deficiencies found by HMS were the presence of only one registered nurse for all three units in the residential treatment center and the use of involuntary isolation (quiet room; extended room time) as a behavior-management tool by child-care workers without the approval or analysis of the professional staff. HMS also made the observation that there was "a far greater percentage of severely disturbed children" than would have been expected in a residential treatment environment. It was suggested that the level of care and supervision at the Southwood RTC be correspondingly increased to meet the heightened needs of the patient population.

If CEO Charles Trojan and the powers at NME were aware of one thing only, it was this: If HMS barked, it was CHAMPUS that delivered the bite. Southwood was facing the very real possibility of losing its certification as a CHAMPUS-approved provider, which meant the loss of all federal funding for CHAMPUS-insured patients. And Southwood could not afford to lose CHAMPUS kids like Christy Scheck; they made up a large percentage of the patient population.

Trojan mounted up and rode into action. With input from the RTC administrator, Nadine Peck, he filed and submitted a corrective-action plan to HMS, promising in effect to correct all of the deficiencies HMS had noted and to meet all of the required standards. With this pledge in pocket, HMS allowed Southwood Psychiatric Center to continue operations.

Nothing improved. In fact, conditions at the RTC worsened. When HMS came back for another look in February 1992, there was even less staff, and the acuity level, which relates to the degree of illness and patient acting-out, had risen. There were more dangerously disturbed kids on the units (especially those culled from the juvenile-justice system in order to fill beds) and fewer qualified people to care for them.

Trojan, perpetually NME's creature, was ready. In response to

HMS's attempt to decertify the RTC for CHAMPUS benefits, a document was prepared that answered each point in both the first and second surveys. In response to the criticism that certain specialized therapies (such as for chemical dependency and sexual abuse) were being conducted by psychology students, Trojan's reply stated that "Ph.D. and master's-level psychology interns act as co-therapists in family sessions and group therapy." The document went on to state, "Licensed clinical social workers and licensed marriage, family and child counselors are now providing a specialized family and group therapy, such as chemical dependency groups and sexual abuse groups at the RTC."

This was untrue. Interns were actually running child-molestation group-therapy sessions at the RTC in spite of the specific promise, made after the initial HMS survey, that group therapy would not be led by interns because they had neither the qualifications nor the experience to perform such duties. Christy Scheck was a member of one of those intern-run groups and, in fact, made frequent complaints about being placed in molestation groups with boys who were known to be molesters.

The document acknowledged that only 75 percent of group therapy was being provided by licensed health care professionals but that the "remainder of the groups were run by qualified master's-level, Ph.D.-level, non–California licensed personnel under the supervision of a qualified licensed practitioner."

The latter statement would prove to be not entirely accurate, either. Both of Christy Scheck's primary counselors ran groups, as did most of the other mental-health counselors. Virtually none of them had Ph.D.'s, and neither Boyle nor Altshult had attained even senior-counselor status.

If the person in charge of any particular therapy group was not a member of the Southwood staff, he or she would be paid at an hourly rate of anywhere from $50 to $75. Each group session ran for approximately one hour, with anywhere from ten to fourteen patients. The insurance carrier for each patient would be billed at about the same rate the therapist was being paid, so if an M.F.C.C.

(marriage, family, and child counselor) or a psychologist, for example, got $60 for a group session with twelve kids, Southwood's profit was $720, minus, of course, the outside therapist's $60 fee. If the person in charge of a group was a Southwood mental-health counselor or an unpaid student intern, the patients' insurance benefits would still be charged at an individual rate. There were between six and eight group sessions held daily in both the early-adolescent and the adolescent units at Southwood Psychiatric Hospital and RTC.

Bob and Merry Scheck were unaware of the roiling controversy at Southwood. They had been given only crumbs of information about Christy from the time she entered the facility. Merry Scheck had, in fact, complained about "being stonewalled." The Schecks were kept particularly uninformed after the allegations of abuse and molestation were made. The subsequent lack of contact left them with only the weekly telephone call Merry was allowed to make to co-counselors Boyle or Altshult and whatever information either of them saw fit to dole out to her. The Schecks' contact with Dr. Quinn was minimal to a point just short of nonexistent.

Rebecca Boyle claimed she told Merry Scheck about certain "significant events . . . if [Christy] had to be restrained, if she was acting out severely on the unit. What her grades and levels were—her progress on the unit, her behavior." In truth, the information given to the Schecks was extraordinarily selective. Merry was told about Christy's "sullen and grumpy" attitude, her difficulties in relating to her peers, her "defensiveness."

Merry Scheck was not aware of Christy's tendency to "junior staff," a term used to describe a patient who, according to Altshult, "was telling other peers what to do, and coming to staff and kind of tattletaling all the time on other residents." Merry was told about some of Christy's AWOL attempts, but not all of them. And she was not told that Christy would often turn over her shoes to Boyle, as a precaution against further attempts.

Neither Bob nor Merry Scheck was aware of how many hours Christy sat alone in her room, sent there by staff members for infractions such as grumbling to herself or refusing to participate during group meetings. They were not aware of the long hours spent at "table time," a punishment in which the patient sat at a table writing essays on her conduct. The Schecks knew that such methods of discipline were brought into play at Southwood, but they had no idea that during one twenty-four-hour span at the RTC, Christy was given three separate stretches of table time.

Christy Scheck's parents were told about some of their daughter's "suicidal ideations," but they did not know how constant the threat was. Merry was told about the safety contract Rebecca Boyle had devised for Christy, but she was not informed that it was written up by Christy herself (dictated, it would appear, by Boyle) and then copied on a printer, each copy to be signed, when needed, by Christy and whichever counselor happened to be on shift at the time. Merry Scheck was not told that Rebecca Boyle initiated the safety contract without consulting any senior or medical staff member. It must be assumed that the safety contract was a well-meant, if naïve, maneuver to insure against AWOL and/or suicide attempts.

Between January 10 and March 5 of 1992, thirty-nine safety contracts were signed by Christy Scheck and various mental-health counselors at the Southwood Residential Treatment Center.

One of the events about which the Schecks were not told took place two days after Christmas, the day of the "transparency" family session, when Christy was able, for the first time since her hospitalization, to make real contact with her father, only to later describe that session as "horrendous" to a staff worker.

A "significant event" was written up by Brenda Willis-Hughes on December 27, 1991, at 4:25 P.M., a few hours after the family session. Willis-Hughes noted that Christy was talking about running away and killing herself. The counselor further noted that " 'sharps' will be removed from resident's room, and she will be placed on a Close Watch and 10' limits with instigating peers will be implemented. Resident has been instructed to approach staff when suicidal ideation occurs or when peers encourage AWOL ('Let's go AWOL together')."

The next charting was a nurse's note written at 8:10 P.M.: "Called counselor to report resident left unit without asking permission from staff. Intent to AWOL."

And, at 9:20 P.M.: "Counselor notified nursing staff that patient hurt arms with razor. Three abrasions cleaned with peroxide and triple-antibiotic ointment. No bleeding noted." At 9:15 P.M., however, Brenda Willis-Hughes had noted that Christy had "eraser burns on both arms."

There were other lapses in the information relayed to the Schecks while their daughter was a patient at Southwood. They were not told that after Christy accused them both of abuse and her father of sexual molestation, Rebecca Boyle suggested that Christy begin to document her memories of the incidents (referred to as "flashbacks") in a journal. Neither parent was aware, until after Christy's death, that their daughter had been supplied with books and articles that dealt with the abuse of children "in order to assist Christy in coping with her feelings." One of the articles Christy was given to read was entitled "Being a Battered Child Means . . ."

When asked in her deposition about the remedies that were used in terms of Southwood residents who raised molestation and/or abuse issues, Boyle claimed to be "really blank on what specific things we used." She did say, at that time, that she herself did not provide Christy with any reading materials regarding molestation issues. She was able to recall that Christy's other co–primary counselor, Bria Altshult, had given Christy "one article, or something, on surviving." Altshult, in her deposition, said she didn't remember assigning Christy any topics to write or read about. In fact, she stated that she had no memory at all of what she herself could have been thinking at the time.

When asked why Christy Scheck had been assigned two primary counselors, Altshult stated that "Christy was particularly needy, and she got two because Rebecca could deal with her on

A.M. and I could deal with her on P.M." Altshult went on to say that she and Boyle worked closely together, scheduling regular "staff meetings" in the adolescent unit. She failed to remember, however, if those meetings occurred daily, weekly, or monthly. Boyle, in her deposition, stated that these meetings took place once a month.

When Altshult was asked for a definition of Christy's particular neediness, the former counselor's reply was that "she just wanted to talk, and she always needed to have contact with somebody." Boyle was unable to recall any impressions she might have had about Christy's neediness, or lack of it.

When asked how she viewed her role as co–primary counselor regarding Christy's allegations of abuse and molestation, Altshult said that it was her understanding that she was not to "go into, like, any deep-seated feelings. That wasn't my job."

When Boyle was asked if she had any understanding as to whether or not it was proper for her, as a mental-health worker, to have formed a belief as to the veracity of Christy's allegations, she stated that it would have been "improper" for her to have formed a belief. And yet it was Boyle who, during a treatment-team meeting, accused Gary Juleen of "splitting the staff" when he did not agree with her blanket diagnosis that Christy's real "issue" was her molestation by her father. And it was Boyle who argued with CPS social worker Barbara Korda when Korda advised Boyle about "serious inconsistencies and exaggerations" in Christy's allegations, specifically those made against Bob and Merry Scheck. Boyle stated at that time that what Christy was saying was "entirely consistent and believable." This in spite of a counseling assessment written by her, and dated early January 1992, in which Boyle made the following notation: "Confront resident on her exaggerations."

When asked, during her deposition, what she meant by that notation, Boyle said she didn't remember. When asked if in fact she ever formed the belief that some of Christy Scheck's allegations were exaggerated, Boyle said no.

Christy Scheck was never confronted about her stories of abuse and molestation while she was a patient at Southwood Psychiatric Center. After Christy's death, Rebecca Boyle stated that it had been her job "to work with Christy, not to try and dissect whether it [the molestation] was true or not." When the former counselor was asked about Christy's reports of multiple rapes by multiple people, drug use, abandonment by her mother, being beaten at home with pots and pans, and being struck during a family-therapy session, Boyle's response was that "nobody ever told me to confront her. Nobody told me that was my place, my job, to do that."

Upon being asked the same question in her deposition, Bria Altshult said, "It wasn't my decision to make, whether or not [Christy's stories] were true."

Gary Juleen feels that Christy Scheck sought attention during her hospitalization in much the same way she did at school: "She liked to sit and talk, on a one-to-one basis, about herself. And as she talked, her stories became increasingly grandiose. It built a bonding relationship between Christy and the Southwood staff."

Again, it begs the question: Why was Christy never confronted on her stories, each one so clearly constructed to top the one that came before? Was Christy Scheck, in effect, handed a loaded gun by her primary counselors' willingness to buy into anything she told them?

Juleen thinks about this for a moment. Then he nods. "I believe so. Yes, I believe so. I don't think it was intentional, but certainly it was evil. The way Rebecca Boyle conducted herself during staff meetings made me believe she *wanted* Christy Scheck to have been molested by her father." Before I can say anything, Juleen holds up one hand to signal that he intends to go on. "Rebecca was heading toward her master's degree. She wanted to be a social worker. And the Scheck case was a stepping-stone. And, of course, there was the aspect of 'Look at me. I'm the one who uncovered all of this, where the rest of you couldn't. Or didn't.' "

CHAPTER TWENTY-THREE

WHILE MERRY SCHECK was waiting for the random conversation with Rebecca Boyle or Bria Altshult, a call came in from Dr. Arthur Quinn.

"Christy's having hallucinations," he said.

"You mean she's having bad dreams?"

"Oh, no. She's awake."

Merry's voice is thick with anger as she recalls the conversation. "Now, I'd been reading literature about the medication Christy was on, the imipramine in particular, and according to what I'd read, an indication of toxic dosage is hallucinations. I told that to Quinn, and I asked him what they were doing about these episodes." She pauses. "He skipped right over that."

Now she assumes a slightly condescending tone. "Then he said, 'Well, Mrs. Scheck, when Christy has one of these episodes, when she thinks she sees something, I have her go to a staff member. And then they go into her room and look around—really look. And then they explain to her that there are no monsters in the closet.' "

During this time, Bria Altshult wrote up a "significant event" in Christy's chart: "Resident reported that while walking back to the unit from school, resident 'saw' her parents and her sister's foster parents, then she shook her head and the people were gone. Resident reported that there were no other people behind her that she could have mistaken for her parents. The vision simply appeared and then disappeared. Resident said that this had happened once before, but it was just her father's face appearing over another resident's face."

Despite the hallucinations and the medical literature available, Christy Scheck's daily dosage of imipramine was never modified.

"So now," Merry continues, "Christy was supposed to be writing this 'flashback' journal of the horrendous things that had happened to her, and it had gone from just accusing Bob to accusing me, as well. One of the entries said that when she was five, and Bob was out to sea, I left her alone. For two weeks. She said that a babysitter was supposed to come and take care of her, but that the sitter never showed up, so she just took care of herself.

"Well, Quinn's response to that was, 'Well, Christy is a very intelligent child. It could very well have been that she did.' "

Merry pours mugs of freshly brewed coffee that Bob has made and brought in from the kitchen. "I wracked my brains to try and come up with *where* that story could have come from. And I finally figured it out." She takes a sip of her coffee. "When Christy was four years old and in preschool, Bob was out at sea and my father became very ill. I flew out to Florida, to see him. And while I was gone—about a week, it was—Christy stayed with Rachel and Hal Penny. The day after I got back home, my father died, and I had to fly right back to Florida. And I was gone for another two weeks. And Christy stayed with the Pennys again.

"Well, in thinking about that, I remembered that after I got back home, for about a month at least, every painting that Christy did at preschool was either black or brown. So clearly the child did feel abandoned. Even though she was staying with people who loved and cared for her." Merry shakes her head in a slow, solemn motion. "That's the only place I could put that piece of the puzzle that was listed in her journal that she wrote on March second. I tried to put the whole puzzle together like that, looking for the basis of each of the twenty-six items of abuse that Christy listed.

"Christy said I beat her daily with pots and pans and sticks and vases." Merry shuts her eyes and her head moves in a jerky little side-to-side movement that seems almost involuntary. Then her eyes flick open again. "Now, this child constantly wore shorts and T-shirts. Where were all the marks of all those beatings? Did I do it so it wouldn't show?" She stops speaking, color flaring across her cheeks. The line of her vision moves away from mine, and she brushes one hand through her hair in an impatient motion.

"When Christy first arrived at the hospital, they noted that her skin was remarkable for the bruises below her knees. Well, she told them she got those bruises from walking through a gang fight, and when the Southwood people told me that, I said, 'Let me get this straight: Were these midget gang members who beat her lower legs with teensy little martial-arts weapons?' "

ON FEBRUARY 24, the court-appointed lawyer for Christy Scheck and her sister, Molly, recused herself from the case, citing a conflict of interest. On February 26, the social worker investigating the case wrote in her report that there were certain inconsistencies in Christy's stories.

"Things were beginning to come out of the woodwork," Merry explains. "Big holes were showing up: Being raped at the age of nine. Being raped by gang members. Being kidnapped and raped by an eighteen-year-old who might—or might not—have been a boyfriend. Another story about a twenty-one-year-old boyfriend." It was with the kidnapping and rape story that Christy provided the detail about the green car. Shana [King's] story was all over the news at one point, and it was clear that Christy simply borrowed her story with all the details."

Merry starts to say something else, stops, looks at her husband. "Bob, I just thought of something. The street Christy said was the one where she was kidnapped was the same street where Shana King lived. I just now remembered."

Bob has been lying back in the lounger, eyes closed. Shadows of expressions have drifted across his face just often enough to make it clear that he is listening to everything being said. He now registers faint surprise. Merry turns back to face me. "At some point, our pediatrician, who had known the girls since they were babies, took it upon himself—without telling us—to write a letter to CPS, saying, in essence, that he had been treating the children in our family for most of their lives and that there had never been any evidence of any kind of abuse or molestation." Merry smiles. "Well, that didn't count for much, either. Because now the Southwood people were saying"—Merry simulates a purposefully overly theatrical gasp—" 'Look! We've got the father, and we've got a mother who's in denial . . . because . . . Look. What. She. Did.' It was just like one of those corny signs people in offices put on their desk: 'Don't confuse me with the facts, my mind's made up.'

"Then, and I must assume it was because the social worker was beginning to have problems with what the thirteen-year-old was saying, CPS decided to allow Bob to have a supervised meeting with the six-year-old."

Bob sits straight up in the lounger now. He is gazing intently at his wife.

"The instant Molly saw her daddy, she literally threw herself into his arms. He had brought a little stuffed dog for her, and she kept hugging Bob and the stuffed dog in turn.

"See, in every one of my weekly supervised visits with Molly over at Rachel Penny's house, Molly would always say, 'How come I don't get to see my daddy? How come I can't go home?' She was always saying how much she wanted to see her dad. Well, the first thing Molly did, after she hugged Bob, was to hold out the little toy dog to the social worker and say, 'I love this doggy, and I'm gonna call him Daddy.' " The expression on Bob's face is, if not exactly a smile, about as close as it gets for him. Merry goes on.

"That visit took place on a Tuesday, the second of March, and we knew that the following Monday, March eighth, we had this hearing coming up. Of course, our attorneys were working constantly on all of this, and we had absolutely no idea of what the outcome was going to be. Our lives were in complete disarray. But every day, Bob went to work. And every day, I went to work. We didn't know what else to do. The only thing we did know was that our house was empty. There were no children there."

CHAPTER TWENTY-FOUR

"THE MENTAL-HEALTH community in San Diego is very small. In a strange way, it can be compared to an old-time vaudeville circuit: If you're in it long enough, you meet all the acts. And sooner or later, everybody plays the Palace. For a while, the Palace was Southwood."

Flynn Davis* was a frontline worker at Southwood Psychiatric Center for eighteen years. He worked as a mental-health counselor, a position he defines as the equivalent of an orderly in a medical hospital. Davis began working at Southwood in December 1976, and his recollection now is that it was "a very informal atmosphere, with a frontline staff that was friendly and open and completely involved in the therapeutic community. They conducted group therapies and therapeutic encounters, and they were involved in family therapy with the psychiatrists and the patients. This was all a new concept for me—in the facilities I'd worked at before I came to Southwood, patients were just more or less warehoused. So it was easy to see why Southwood had the reputation, at that time, of being one of the best facilities in the country.

"About six months after I came on staff, the people in charge decided to drop the adult population and treat only adolescents and, eventually, younger children. That decision enhanced the Southwood reputation, because it became one of the first facilities in California to have an all-adolescent population." Davis pauses. "Even though they didn't do any formal follow-ups with their patients, the way some of the other facilities I'd seen did."

He pauses again, looking past me toward a bank of rain-swept windows across the lobby of the small San Diego hotel where we have met. It is a weekday, and we are the only people in the room, but everything seems crowded by Davis's bulk. He is a tall man, not exactly fat—more like an athlete whose musculature has begun to soften. Even his head appears to be larger than scale: heavy features surrounded by a thatch of light brown hair and a carefully trimmed beard. His voice is mild, almost soothing, and when he smiles there is a picket-fence lineup of teeth.

When did things begin to change at Southwood?

Davis thinks about it for a moment. "I'd say the decline started when NME came into the picture in about 1982. Staffing was always a problem, in that we were a business and, like any business, you wanted to cut costs. But when NME and PIA overlapped, even though PIA signed the paychecks as the corporate entity we worked for, NME started to call the shots. And cost cutting became more obvious. I won't say that safety was compromised initially, but any time you have less staff, you run that risk. And it became more blatant, and to my perception, more dangerous, during the period when PIA and NME were together, from the early eighties to the beginning of the nineties."

When I ask for a description of those dangers, Davis is ready with a reply.

"They were twofold: Undertraining and understaffing. When I came on board in '76, there was intensive, formal training done by other employees. Everything from drug education through how to conduct a 'forced seclusion' by utilizing a show of force by staff members to a kid who was acting out. But slowly the length of training diminished and, in order to cut corners, the staffing became more and more minimal with less and less training. For example: As staffing became tighter over the years, we were reacting much less often in a speedy, effective manner. It took longer to summon staff from other units when it was necessary to do so. People became less quick to recognize dangerous situations as those situations evolved." Davis shrugs. "Undertraining or inexperience—take your pick. There were people on staff at Southwood who had years of university training but absolutely no practical experience at all."

What about the dangers Davis mentioned in connection with understaffing?

"Well, for example, quite often, a kid who was acutely self-destructive or suicidal would be placed on a one-on-one, which was supposed to be 'at arm's length' at all times. Now, the policy of the hospital stated, very specifically, that if a patient was placed on a one-on-one status, the hospital would bring in another staff to deal exclusively with that patient. Without dealing with any other patient . . . with the single exception of a *dire* emergency. Well, as things progressed, and as more cost cutting went into effect, they stopped bringing in on-call people for one-on-one duty. Someone on staff would be assigned to the one-on-one patient, but that staff person would also have other patients they were responsible for moderating. One-on-ones became, to a large degree, a situation where, instead of the staff member staying with the kid, the responsibility shifted to the kid himself; it became up to the kid to stay with the staff member. So, if the staff had to go deal with some other patient, the one-on-one kid just had to trot along."

During the time Christy Scheck was a patient at the Southwood Residential Treatment Center, Flynn Davis worked the late-night shift, from 11:00 P.M. to 7:00 A.M. And he remembers very well the arguments he had with lower-level management personnel about one-on-ones assigned to Christy at night.

"Oh, I had a lot of conflicts about overnight one-on-ones, because the management people would not bring in another staff person to cover them. The mentality was, essentially, 'Nothing much happens at night. You can set up your charts and your paperwork next to Christy's room, and you can monitor her and do your paperwork at the same time.' " Davis shakes his head in a slow, negative motion. "I wasn't at all comfortable with that, and I went around and around with management on it. I said, 'Look, there's a strict policy on this, and if something happens, we're going to be in one helluva mess. Because I will not chart this as a one-on-one. I'll chart whatever I observe—if Christy slept all night, or if she got up to use the bathroom, or whatever—but I won't chart a one-on-one. You have to bring in a staff for that. There's a specific policy about one-on-ones, and I'm sure there's a legal policy as well, and you're messing with both of them.' " Davis's voice has assumed an intensity I have not yet heard. "Well, I got a lot of runaround from the management people. They said things like, 'Don't worry about it. We can cover it.' "

I ask Davis if Charles Trojan was the person he confronted at Southwood.

"Charlie? Well, ultimately Trojan would be responsible, of course." Davis grins sourly. "Charlie's a piece of work. He came on board as CEO in about 1990, and he was there for at least a month before I even knew who he was. He reminded me of the guy in *thirtysomething,* Miles Drentell. They even looked alike; they both had that same cold, cutthroat 'whatever works for the company' manner. But I had very little contact with Charlie. I just used to hear things from the day-shift people, like how much Trojan was hated and feared, and how Charlie's boss, Richard Eamer, was the highest-paid corporate CEO in California at a time when South-wood wages were being frozen and we were being told they had to cut staff. That was an ongoing process: They were constantly cutting back on staff, and there was a constant pressure to have less staff deal with more patients.

"At any rate, I was way too small potatoes to be able to take my complaints to Charles Trojan. It had to go much further down the line before anyone in management was available to me for any kind of confrontation, and the management structure changed so often at Southwood, it could have been a charge nurse, or a unit manager, or a program director I talked to. The titles—and the responsibilities—changed over periods of time. But the decisions came straight from the top. Above Charlie, at corporate headquarters. They were made out of financial considerations alone, and they took precedence over either therapeutic or safety concerns.

"You could see the kind of situation that ultimately happened with Christy Scheck coming for years before it actually happened.

It became so apparent that Southwood had gone from the business of patient care as a way to make profits to making money by doing patient care. I know that sounds pretty subtle, but there's a real difference between the two, and ultimately, at Southwood, patients stopped being the important element in the equation. They just became a way to make the big bucks. That was the topic of conversation on a whole lot of Friday nights when some of us frontline workers got together for a drink after work."

Does Davis think that the idea of parental molestation was implanted in Christy Scheck's mind by members of the Southwood staff? He thinks for a moment, then nods. "I think it's a distinct possibility. The repressed-memory syndrome has become a very big thing in therapy circles. And the accepted mind-set with the Southwood staff was, 'Kids never lie about these things.' "

Davis stretches out both arms along the back of the sofa. "Well, let me tell you something: It's been my experience that kids do tell stories that are not true. Sometimes the kid is angry. Sometimes they tell malicious lies. Sometimes the stories are just fantasies."

He mentions a couple of examples. One is the case of Shana King. "That little girl's abduction and rape were true, of course, but she was talked into blaming her father."

I ask if there was an emphasis on sexual-molestation survivor groups when Christy was at Southwood.

"It was beginning to be more and more emphasized. One of the things that would happen was that quite often it was assumed, by both doctors and staff, that if a female patient came in with an eating disorder, she had been sexually molested. It wouldn't be a formal diagnosis, but the way the system was set up, with the kids having to earn points so they could move up to better levels, one of the areas that weighed most heavily in the point system was what the staff called 'dealing with your issues.' " Adolescent patients earned points for cleaning their rooms, for not swearing, for going to school, for "keeping a good attitude," et cetera. When a patient earned enough points, he or she moved up a level, which meant they were given more privileges, such as home passes, time alone, going outside to the recreation field, and outings with other patients. Quite often, if a girl came in with an eating disorder, say, it was assumed that she was hiding, or had repressed, a sexual-abuse experience. She and other girls with similar problems would be encouraged to 'deal with their issues,' so if the staff asked if the kid recalled ever being sexually abused, and the kid said no, then quite often the staff would 'correct' the kid by telling her, 'Oh, I think you probably *were* abused and you just don't remember it.' Because that was the prevalent mentality.

"So, with the point system being set up in such a way as to earn privileges, the kid might figure maybe she *should* talk about being abused, if that was what the staff thought—whether or not it had actually occurred *not* being one of the 'issues.' It was a way to earn points, you see? And the more the kid was willing to talk about abuse, the more points could be earned. Or, conversely, if she didn't talk about it, it was assumed that the kid was either in de-nial or didn't *want* to talk about it. Didn't want to 'deal with her issues.'

"And it wasn't only eating disorders that got jumped on. It could be cutting on yourself, could be aggression, could be smok-ing dope." He shrugs. "Could be anything."

Whose responsibility was it to decide whether or not a patient was "dealing with the issues"?

"The primary counselor," Davis replies. "Each kid was assigned one." He delivers a piercing look. "And nearly every primary counselor at Southwood, and everywhere else I worked in San Diego, was completely unlicensed. In the days before cost con-tainment, when staffing was better, a primary counselor would es-sentially follow a patient throughout their course of treatment from beginning to end. Usually the primary counselor would work the day shift, because that's when treatment-team meetings would be held, and meetings with the school personnel, and that kind of hospital business. But as things began to slide downhill, a primary counselor became whoever was available on any given shift. I've been tagged as primary counselor to several kids."

Davis wants to revisit the subject of inexperienced and under-trained staff. Leaning forward, he explains that there is an area of "overzealousness" that we have not yet explored. "If you're one of the younger staff, in your early twenties, usually, and new to the field, you become a kind of star, in your own mind as well as to the other staff members, if you can have the kind of 'breakthrough' with a kid where the kid will tell you something they haven't told anyone else. You've got a real connection with that kid, because *you've* gotten him to open up. And, if nothing else, that's a real emotional payoff. From the kid's perspective, 'opening up' may or may *not* be dealing with the truth. But from the staff's perspective, especially the younger people, you'd get all kinds of recognition and feedback. Even from the psychiatrists."

Davis gets to his feet, walks to the bank of windows, and peers out at the weather. It is still raining. "It happened to me. A kid told me something concerning a molest issue, and I got all kinds of pats on the back from people who'd been on staff a lot longer than I had. And, like I said, when you're young, and new to the business, that makes you feel like a star."

But didn't anyone ever question the veracity of such statements?

"Not too often. You have to understand the overall mentality, going from the idea that if a kid came up with a molestation story, he or she must have been coming out of a nightmare about something that hadn't really happened, to the conviction that all children tell the truth about this kind of thing. It became a given: If there was a molestation story—no matter how far-fetched—it had to follow that it was the truth."

CHAPTER TWENTY-FIVE

MERRY SCHECK SAYS that on Friday evening, March 6, 1992, she had a sense that something momentous was about to happen. "I'd had the feeling all day," she recalls, "since the instant I woke up. I even made a note of it in my journal that morning. But as the day progressed and turned into evening, and as the evening wore on, I attributed it to the sense I'd had during this whole period, of things turning, changing." She has cupped her hands and is turning them, one around the other.

"At ten o'clock I was on the phone with my friend Helen, and I was telling her that the hospital staff had decided to set up a meeting for me to see Christy. With Gary Juleen there, as well." Merry looks at me for a long moment, but mine is not the face she sees.

"We have call-waiting on our phone, and I heard the signal, so I told Helen to hang on. It was Dr. Quinn, and he tells me there's been an accident at Southwood and they've taken Christy to Scripps Clinic. But that a team from Children's Hospital is on the way over to Scripps, to move her to Children's. Well, I didn't think anything of that, because my first thought was that, yes, Children's Hospital is considered to be the best facility for children, so that's where I'd want Christy to be."

I ask Merry what she thought might have happened to Christy.

She spread her hands. "I didn't know. She could have fallen and knocked herself out—Quinn told me she was unconscious. She could have broken her leg." Merry shakes her head. "To show you where my frame of mind was, before I even told Bob about the call, I got back on the line with Helen and said, 'That was the hospital calling. There's been an accident. Do me a favor and call the pastor and ask him to say a prayer.' Then I told her I'd call her later."

It is clear that as she speaks, Merry is reliving the event. And, at this instant, her voice is vital and unclouded. As if she is still only thinking of a broken bone or a bruised head. Unpleasant but manageable things.

"The first call I made, as soon as I hung up from Helen, was to my attorney." She notices my look of surprise. "Because, by *court order*, Bob had not been allowed to see Christy. And I had not been able to see her unsupervised. I said to the lawyer, 'We need to go and see Christy right now.' And he told me to go ahead, to do what we needed to do. 'We'll deal with it in court on Monday.' Which was the day set for the hearing.

"You see, I needed to hear him say that, because at that point I didn't want to do anything to jeopardize the probability that Molly would be coming home soon. And I didn't want to jeopardize the eventuality that Christy would come home. So we were trying to follow the rules, to jump through the hoops, to do everything correctly so that there wouldn't be anything that could be used against us."

Merry takes a moment to place each event in order so that she can relay them to me accurately. "Then I called Southwood and spoke to a nurse on staff there. Quinn had told me the name of the doctor on duty at Scripps, and I'm positive that I called there and spoke to him as well." Another small silence. "Yes, I'm sure I spoke to him, because I remember that I got almost no information from either him or the nurse at Southwood. Of course, the doctor didn't know me, didn't know even if I *was* Christy's mother. But he did tell me that Christy was being transferred to Intensive Care at Children's Hospital.

"Then I go into the other room, and I tell Bob that there's been an accident. And we get in the car and race down to Children's Hospital, and all I can think now is that Christy's in Intensive Care, so it must be serious."

Bob breaks in. "One more thing: It turned out that we were not called for one hour after they found Christy."

The words hang between us during a long, uncomfortable silence. Then Merry begins to speak again. "They found Christy at eight fifty-nine P.M. They called us at ten o'clock. The last person to see her saw her at eight-thirty. But I don't want to sidetrack into that right now. I really don't. I just need to talk about this in its proper sequence.

"Our pastor, Gene, and his wife and the children's minister met us at the hospital, in the waiting room of the Intensive Care Unit. It was awhile before they got Christy set up, so all of us just sat. I called my niece, in Michigan, and told her what I knew, and I asked her to call my attorney and tell him to get hold of Bob's attorney. We waited for a long, terrible time, and when we finally got in to see Christy, it was just"—Merry's voice falters for the first time in the telling—"such a shock.

"She was hooked up to a life-support system. Bob was so upset he was only able to stay in the room for a minute or two, and then he had to leave. And then I see this mark on Christy's neck.

"I asked the doctor what the mark was, and he—" Merry clears her throat softly. "The doctor was the first person to tell me that Christy had been found hanged."

Merry remembers that her anger broke then. All of the impotent rage that she had kept silent during the past months erupted. She shouted at the doctor, telling him that no matter who called from Southwood, he was not to give them any information. She told him that Christy was her child. That he was not to talk to *them.*

Bob and Merry, their pastor and his wife, and the children's minister sat in the waiting room through the night. At intervals Merry and Bob would spell each other in their daughter's room.

"I held Christy's hand, and I talked to her, and I told her that I forgave her. And I heard, as clearly as if she were speaking, Christy's voice. She said, 'Mom, I don't want to die.' And I couldn't tell her that she wouldn't die, because I knew that she would. There was no doubt in my mind."

It is only an extraordinary force of will that has kept this woman from weeping. Bob's eyes are reddened by the tears he seems equally determined not to shed.

"There was no movement," Merry continues, "and there was only minimal brain-scan activity. Christy was already as still as death." Merry's voice lifts slightly. "In the meantime, I'm speaking to neurosurgeons, and neurologists, and PICU (Pediatric Intensive Care Unit) physicians, and I'm taking notes. Because I knew if I didn't write it all down, I wouldn't remember any of it. The ICU staff talked to us about donating Christy's organs, and we thought, yes, that would, in a sense, give life to Christy. But when Bob's attorney called us at the hospital, and I told him what was going on, he said we couldn't do it. Had we signed the papers allowing the hospital to take Christy's organs for donation, it would have been used against Bob by CPS. Because, as the case was still open, he would have gotten rid of the witness against him." Merry sees my look of disbelief. "It wasn't only Bob's attorney who told me that. My lawyer, Marty Cruz, said the same thing. And it's something that I will always regret. That we couldn't donate Christy's organs."

The Schecks exchange a look. Their eyes connect only for an instant, but the energy in the room undergoes a subtle change. They both know what is coming next in Merry's narrative.

"Friends began to show up in the waiting room. From church, from work; neighbors came by. Most of them were people who did not involve themselves in difficult situations. But all of them showed up, and they simply . . . enfolded us. Somebody even brought in sandwiches." Merry is beginning to cry now. She apologizes softly.

"At eleven o'clock, on Saturday morning, I felt Christy's spirit leave her. And I knew, even though her heart continued to pump, I knew that she was gone."

Bob clears his throat. "I felt it, too," he says. "At the same time."

"And we were in different rooms when it happened." Merry swipes at her eyes with a tissue. "I have to say this for Children's

Hospital: The nurse who cared for Christy in the ICU was wonderful. We both knew that Christy was gone, but this woman was so . . . gentle with her. She treated Christy with such loving care. She even stayed on for another shift, just to stay with Christy. I can't say enough about the care she received . . ."

Merry is unable to continue; she can only weep now. For this moment, she has no more words. Bob goes on for her.

"We didn't stay at the hospital that night. We went back to our house. But, even at home, it seemed like I could still hear that terrible sound of the life-support system my daughter was hooked up to." He shuts his eyes. "It was awful. Like the sound Darth Vader makes."

There is a short silence. Then Merry begins to speak again. "We contacted family members, and one of our friends called other people and made all the arrangements for funeral services. We weren't at the hospital, because we knew that Christy was gone already.

"The next morning they ran the brain scan, and it was flat-line. So we didn't have to go through a court order to remove Christy from the life-support system. The doctor pronounced her dead. What was allowed for us to do was to say when she should be taken off the system. Not if—*when.* That would be our decision. And I was very grateful that the other decision, the *if,* had been made for us.

"We went back to the hospital. Hal and Rachel Penny and our pastor and his wife went with us. And we finally gathered the courage to tell them, 'Okay. Take her off the machines.'

"Bob just wasn't able to be in the room. It was more than he could handle. So I"—Merry can barely form the words she needs to say—"I stood and held her hand until her heart stopped. And then we said good-bye to Christy." Merry rests for a moment, folding and refolding the ever-present tissue in her hand. When she has collected herself, she goes on. "When I called Marty Cruz, to tell him that Christy was gone, he said, 'You don't show up for the hearing in court tomorrow. I'll take care of that.'

"We scheduled a viewing for Christy on the following Friday

evening, and then a memorial service, without a casket. The reason we had a viewing was so that the kids, who came by the busload from Horace Mann Junior High, would see that this was for real. This was final. We wanted the kids to be aware that this was not something you playact.

"The place was packed. And the next day, there were more than seven hundred people at Christy's memorial service. Her preschool teachers were there. And all her coaches. Her teachers from Horace Mann. Her friends." The tears are flowing again. Bob is silent; pain has cloaked his face like a visor.

"People got up and spoke about what Christy meant to them. Our friends were at our side, supporting us." Merry hesitates. "Rebecca Boyle, Christy's primary counselor, called Christy's school counselor, Ed Dueñez, and asked if we would allow her to come to the memorial service, but I don't remember seeing her. We never heard anything from Southwood. Not a phone call. Not a card. Nothing." Another pause. "CPS called up Rachel Penny and told her that she could send Molly home."

Bob's voice cuts across the room. He has apparently gained strength from his recalled anger. "It was like Christy Scheck and her family no longer existed. Southwood brought in a suicide counselor for their staff, they contacted all the counselors for the patients, and we heard they had a memorial service there for Christy. None of which they bothered to tell us." He pauses. "Well, somebody, one person, came out from Southwood to our home. We don't know who it was; he was turned away."

Merry shakes her head. "I don't believe he came as a representative of Southwood. I think he came on his own. But, because what had happened was so monstrous, my niece met him at the door and she and my brother just kind of shuffled him out. I didn't even find out about it until months later."

There is another break, then Bob leans forward in his chair. "The big reason I wasn't in there when they decided to turn off the life-support system was because I was talking with a large group of men from our church in the waiting room, trying to figure out among us how, and why, this terrible thing had happened. I didn't understand why, at that moment, but at two forty-seven I felt the need to ask what time it was . . ." He is unable to continue; he drops his head and covers his face with both hands.

Merry finishes for him. "That was the exact minute Christy's heart stopped beating." Bob looks up again, and when he speaks it is without anger or pain or even grief. All of these emotions will surely return to him, will come at him like birds flying in a true line toward their nesting place, but at this moment the only thing I can detect in his voice is a note of bemused acceptance.

"You know, there were so many people affected by this. So many lives that Christy touched. It wasn't just a little girl dying."

And he retreats once more into silence.

CHAPTER TWENTY-SIX

TARA DAITCH* WAS the last person to see Christy Scheck alive.

Daitch traveled west from Kansas in May 1991 (after earning a bachelor's degree in psychology) because she wanted to work with the dolphins at Sea World. By the end of May she had two part-time jobs, one at Sea World (although not with the dolphins) and the other at Southwood Psychiatric, where she was an on-call mental-health counselor in the residential treatment center. Daitch worked most often in the early-adolescent unit, where, according to her deposition, taken in May 1994, there were "usually about three regular staff per shift, with an on-call counselor." Daitch also stated, however, that "sometimes [there were] two regular staff with two on-call counselors." Daitch worked "mostly at night," often more than five eight-and-a-half-hour shifts a week. She also worked "some days."

During her deposition in the case of *Scheck* v. *Southwood,* Daitch recollected, under questioning, that she had been given "some form of orientation" before beginning work in the RTC, and that the orientation lasted for "a day or two." She was unable to remember, however, what form of orientation was provided other than several hours spent practicing the use of restraints. Daitch stated further that she never had a regular supervisor during the time she worked at Southwood. "There was a head counselor every shift, and whoever that was, you could always talk to them, if you had an issue with anything." Daitch recalled, when she heard his name, a senior counselor named Andy Michaels. She said that Michaels provided her with some supervision when they worked shifts together.

Daitch described her duties and responsibilities as supervising patients in activities "such as going out, playing, group activities, volleyball, basketball, supervise them at dinner or any meal . . . and have shift meetings, as we called them, [of] which . . . each child needed to have three a week signed off on their book."

Daitch described shift meetings as "basically just little sessions they'd have with the counselors that were working that day, to talk about a specific issue that they [the patients] had, or whatever they felt like talking about. The reason for these was because a lot of children didn't talk, so we needed to have—they needed to have at least three a week."

Although Daitch stated that she had been given "two files'" worth of written procedure manuals upon being hired by South-wood, she did not recall reading anything titled "Suicide Precautions" or "Special Procedures" at any time before the death of Christy Scheck. She did not, in fact, recall any of the names of any of the policies and procedures she had looked at before beginning work. She said that she never referred to any of the manuals before the death of Christy Scheck.

Daitch said she had never had any interaction with Dr. Walter Miller,* the clinical director of the Southwood Residential Treatment Center. When asked if she had had any interaction as a counselor with Dr. Russell Lebow,* the RTC medical director, she said that she had not, although they had exchanged "formal greetings." Daitch did remember Dr. Arthur Quinn, Christy Scheck's psychiatrist. "He actually asked my opinion once in a while, about Christy. How she was doing this day or that day." Daitch added that "he was very nice. If that matters."

Did she recall anything else about Dr. Quinn?

"The kids loved him."

Daitch remembered Christy Scheck's two primary counselors, Rebecca Boyle and Bria Altshult. She had talked with both women about what was going on with Christy; her general overview of those exchanges was "that [Christy] was a really great kid whose parents seemed to be the root of her depression," and that she "was very needy for affection and attention, but out of most of the children there, I thought that she had a lot of potential to grow up and have a 'normal' life."

When reminded that she had "shared opinions" with the other counselors, Daitch said that was in reference to "the new things that were coming up in [Christy's] treatment of abuse" and "her father molesting her." Daitch's opinion, "for what it was," was that Robert Scheck had not molested his daughter.

Had she shared that opinion with the other counselors?

Yes, she had.

With anyone else at Southwood?

She could not recall.

When asked why she had formed the opinion that the molestation charges were not true, Daitch stated, "It seemed to me, as an on-call counselor, there was things just building and building, like on top of each other, that were just so horrific that it seemed like the first things when [Christy] came in, the first allegations she had, weren't enough, and she didn't think that they were as bad as maybe some of the other kids' there. You know, what had happened to them." In her opinion, Christy was so needy for attention that "maybe she made things worse than they really were, to get that attention she needed, because she didn't think that maybe the emotional abuse, or the lack of love from her family, was as bad as being sexually abused."

When asked if she had read the psychological assessment done on Christy upon her admission to Southwood, Daitch said that she did not recall. "But if it was in her record, I did."

The former counselor stated that she believed the allegations made by Christy upon her arrival at the RTC—that she had been raped by different people on different occasions. "I believed it at the time because it was right when she got there. As time went on, it may or may not have been true . . . because more stories were coming out from Christy. Not that Christy necessarily told me, but that I read in her chart, or [heard] from other counselors. It put a little doubt in my head that a lot of this stuff that she had told me when she first got there had happened."

Daitch could not recall whether she had discussed the issue of credibility with Rebecca Boyle, but she said she may have expressed some doubt to Bria Altshult and a couple of other counselors on the night shift.

Daitch was one of either three or four mental-health counselors on duty in the early-adolescent unit of the residential treatment center on the night of March 6, 1992.

She noted a "significant event" on Christy's chart at some point that afternoon: "Resident has been asking for a shift meeting from this writer since approximately 3:00 P.M. [the beginning of Daitch's shift]. Her mood for most of the shift appeared to be pretty happy as she was laughing and smiling with the other residents. She did not seem to be isolative or looking sad, although she was needy of the staff's attention."

The notation went on to relate that, at approximately 7:00 P.M., Christy Scheck got her shift meeting with Tara Daitch. It took place in the quiet room, "because that's the only place we could find that was quiet to have a shift meeting." Daitch noted, "We talked about her family issues. Resident expressed that she was worried about her sister going back home to be with her parents. Our shift meeting lasted about one-half hour. When we were finished, she gave this writer a hug. Resident did not express to this writer that she was feeling unsafe. This writer then went to have a shift meeting with another resident, and during that time, a note was slipped inside of the door."

According to her statement at the deposition, Daitch did not know who placed the note under the door, and she did not open it until the other patient's shift meeting was finished, about fifteen minutes later. The note, in Christy Scheck's round, schoolgirl's handwriting, read:

Dear Tara,

After you're done with Don and Rick will you please do my safety contract with me because I'm feeling very unsafe. I don't want to run I want to hurt myself. You don't have to believe this is what I really want to do right now but I had a really bad flash-back and some other things and I want to do my safety contract.

Christy

Tara Daitch had first learned about Christy Scheck's safety con-tracts on the previous night, March 5, when Daitch went into Christy's room to say good night. Earlier that evening, Christy had requested a shift meeting with Daitch "for the whole shift," but Daitch was not able to accommodate this rather unusual request. There were other patients and other shift meetings, other respon-sibilities to be met. Daitch promised that she and Christy would have their shift meeting the following evening.

But when Daitch went in to say good night, Christy said she felt like hurting herself, that she wanted to sign a safety contract "because she would feel safer that way."

Daitch had no idea where such a document might be kept; she had never heard of one being used with any other Southwood pa-tient. She would learn, later, that the safety contract was created based on a specific understanding between Christy and her co–pri-mary counselor Rebecca Boyle. Christy's need seemed urgent enough for her to reach into the folder she kept next to her bed and bring out a previously signed safety contract. She and Daitch read through the contract together, and then she re-signed it and Daitch added her signature.

After Daitch read Christy's note the next night, March 6, she decided to look for a fresh copy of the safety contract. She went into the counselors' office and searched through the file cabinet, thinking that it might be in among the general contracts and other forms, like the Feelings chart, which showed, through a se-ries of cartoon happy/unhappy faces, the patients' emotional lev-els. No luck.

When Daitch left the counselors' office she saw Christy in the hallway, with the other kids, all of them coming back from receiving their medications. It was, according to Daitch's statement, between 8:32 and 8:35 P.M. Daitch observed that "the resident . . . looked sad in that her shoulders were hunched over and she was talking very softly."

According to her deposition, Daitch then went to stand behind the windowed counter of the workstation. It was time to hand out the evening snacks. At some point Daitch told Christy that she had not been able to find the safety contracts, and she asked if Christy knew where they might be kept. Christy told her, "Look in Rebecca's box."

But another ten minutes elapsed before Daitch left her post at the work counter. She finished handing out the snacks, and she had a conversation with another patient on the unit. Then she went back into the counselors' office and looked in Boyle's box. There were no safety contracts there.

During her statement, Tara Daitch read her notations aloud. At this point in the narration, she found a discrepancy in her notes: " 'This writer then decided to go and check on the resident, which was at approximately . . .' " Daitch hesitated. "I wrote eight-fifty, and it says eight fifty-nine here."

Nine minutes.

One of the Scheck family attorneys, Christopher Cody, asked, "You wrote eight-fifty and it says something different?"

"I don't know. Well, it looks like it . . . I don't know."

"Do you know who wrote—made it an eight fifty-nine?"

"Nope."

Cody told Daitch to continue. Reading from her notes, Daitch stated that she tried the door to Christy's bathroom. It felt like something was holding it back, she said, so she pushed. It didn't move. Another push, harder this time, and then the sound of something falling. Daitch was alarmed now, so she leaned against the door, shoving and pushing until it gave.

Christy was lying on the bathroom floor. The sash of her terry-cloth robe was wound tightly around her neck. She was unconscious, and she did not appear to be breathing. Daitch turned and ran for the counselors' office, yelling at senior counselor Jeff Harding* and another male counselor that Christy was in trouble.

Then she dialed 911.

While Daitch waited for the arrival of the medics, Jeff Harding knelt over Christy's motionless body. As he opened her mouth to begin CPR, he saw that some object was lodged in the girl's throat: It was a sucker, a Tootsie Pop, and it was all the way at the back of the throat, as if a sudden, urgent need for air had propelled it there. Harding reached in and pulled. The sucker came loose, followed by a gush of vomit. The vomit was cleared away, and CPR was begun.

At some point, two nurses were summoned from other units. There was no nurse on duty in the early-adolescent unit of the Southwood RTC on the night of March 6, 1992.

After Tara Daitch read her notation, Cody asked if she had been asked to prepare it. Daitch stated that she could not recall.

When did she write the note?

At 7:00 P.M. on Sunday, March 8, 1992.

Did somebody review the note immediately after she wrote it? Daitch could not recall.

Did Daitch discuss the note with anyone before she wrote it?

Again, Daitch's memory failed her. She was able to recall, however, something she had said to Christy during that final shift meeting: "Sometimes we say things, maybe, because we don't think our own problems are big enough." Daitch went on to state that she told Christy that however Christy's problems made her feel, Christy "was the world to us." She further told Christy that she could "come to us with anything, for attention, any time you need to." Daitch also stated, in her deposition, that her intentions on the evening of March 6, 1992, had been "for [Christy] not to exaggerate."

CHAPTER TWENTY-SEVEN

"WE LEARNED A few very disturbing things from the court documents," Merry Scheck says. "The paramedics got to Southwood at approximately nine-oh-two on the night of March 6, and they attempted CPR on Christy. They took her to Scripps at nine thirty-four; we were not contacted until ten o'clock. We learned, when we read the documents, that the Southwood staff called every insurance provider of every one of the other patients, and all other administrative staff was on site within that first half hour. From the time the paramedics left with Christy, it was an additional half hour before we were called.

"Bob and I were shut off completely from the process of getting information about what had happened that night. So I requested, through Gary Juleen, because he was our family therapist, that I be allowed to come down to Southwood, to the unit, and walk through the hospital. I didn't want to talk to the staff. I didn't care if I even saw any of them. I just wanted to go down there and walk through, because that was the last place I ever saw Christy alive."

Merry is not crying now. There is a quickened light in her eyes, but it is not a reflection of tears. "I couldn't figure out why they didn't find Christy for so long. The times don't jibe, and that was a big consideration." She pauses. "Also, Christy's room was located just off the right of the community room, where everybody watched TV, and played cards, and so forth. I just couldn't figure out why people—who would have to be going back and forth in front of that room all night—wouldn't have noticed."

Bob Scheck has been listening intently. Now his voice, rusty with disuse, breaks in. "Also, during the whole previous week, before"—he clears his throat—"this tragedy, Christy was on a suicide watch."

Merry looks at me for a long moment. *"A suicide watch,"* she says. "And thirty-nine safety contracts that were supposed to keep Christy from committing suicide. And a sash from her bathrobe left with her." There is a brief, nearly palpable silence. "I just could *not* figure out why it took so long for them to find her." Merry shifts her body, moving forward until she is perched on the edge of the sofa.

"I found out later that this child, this child who was on a suicide watch, was moved to a room farther away. Down the hall and away from the staff room. *That day.* The day she killed herself."

What could have been the reasoning behind such a move?

"We were never able to get a straight answer. Supposedly, according to what information we were able to get, they made changes in procedure, quote, 'which had nothing to do with Christy Scheck's suicide,' quote."

Then there was the matter of Christy's effects. The clothes she was wearing when she hanged herself were taken by the Chula Vista Police Department as evidence. Included was the sash from Christy's bathrobe, which had been found tied around her neck. The Schecks were informed of the whereabouts of Christy's things. But their grief was too fresh; they would collect everything in time.

A year passed, and Bob and Merry Scheck felt the time had arrived when they could bear to look at the clothing Christy was wearing that night, including the pink sash that had made that deadly mark around her neck. Merry called the Chula Vista Police Department and was told by a sergeant that he would check it out and get back to her.

A few hours later, the Schecks received a call telling them that the evidence had been destroyed.

The Schecks went down to the police station for a meeting with the head of forensics. They were told that evidence in misdemeanors and felonies is warehoused for three and seven years, respectively, and all evidence involving murders is kept indefinitely; however, there was no explanation of why Christy's effects—which were evidence in a suicide—had been destroyed. A year later, in September 1993, police lieutenant Dan Wolf was quoted in the Chula Vista *Star News* as saying that "the girl's clothes, sash and other items were supposed to be kept by the police for six months but were destroyed two weeks prior to the end of that period." The article continued, "[Wolf] also said that the police department has a policy requiring them to send a letter informing family that property is to be disposed." Merry Scheck had never received such a letter. That day at the police station, she asked to see the order for the destruction of the evidence. It was unsigned, and nobody had any answers to give her.

The Schecks filed a complaint. According to Chula Vista police chief Rick Emerson, an internal-affairs investigation got under way, and all department policies were updated "to prevent this kind of thing from happening again."

The Schecks would not learn until September of 1993 that Chief Emerson had been a member of the Southwood board of governors for several months.

The Chula Vista Police Department did not respond to my requests for interviews.

CHAPTER TWENTY-EIGHT

AS MARKETING EXECUTIVE for Southwood's adolescent unit, Alan Sidell was required to take a turn leading group sessions at the hospital, a duty he shared with the social workers and other Southwood program managers. Saturday, March 7, was his day. We are still seated over tea in the hotel lobby as he recalls that morning.

"As soon as I got in, the nurse on my unit told me what had happened the night before. I called my supervisor immediately.

" 'She's in a coma, Al,' he told me. 'She's probably not going to make it.'

" 'How do you want me to handle it?'

" 'Well, what would you advise?'

"I told him I thought we should gather the community together and tell them something had happened at the RTC. Nothing specific, of course. Just, 'There's been some self-destructive type of behavior.' "

Sidell bites into a piece of pastry, chews appreciatively, and brushes crumbs from his fingertips. "My style has always been to deal with issues head-on. Because pretenses and counseling don't mix. So our posture was always, 'Let's deal with it on our terms.' I called a community meeting and told the kids—very briefly, and in a businesslike fashion—what had happened. I simply said that one of the patients in the RTC had apparently been suicidal last night, that we weren't going to mention any names, but that the girl was in the hospital. Well, right away, everyone started asking questions."

Sidell begins to replicate the moment by addressing a phantom group of kids. " 'No, she's not dead. But it doesn't look good.

We're doing everything we can to take care of the community over there, and as you guys know, that's why you're here. Tiffany, you had a suicide attempt and you slashed your wrists, so you guys know what's goin' on. What we need to do, when you guys see the other kids down in the lunchroom, is to be aware that everybody needs plenty of support right now.' " Sidell drains his teacup and sets it back in the saucer with a hard little click. Then he looks at me again. "My objective was to introduce the issue, and introduce it in the context of, 'Hey, this is a psychiatric facility. That's why *you're* here, isn't it?' "

I ask about the responses among the staff to Christy's suicide attempt.

"For the frontline staff, it was a tragedy. These were the people who were there, not for profit, but to help the kids." He pauses. "I didn't even go down to the RTC, because I knew the police were down there, and the hospital administrator and the associate administrator were down there. Charlie Trojan wasn't there. My immediate superior didn't have to come in." Another pause. "All the third-party people were there.

"Up in my part of the hospital, nobody was blaming themselves. But there was plenty of that going on in the RTC. A group meeting was convened, and a social worker was called in. Most of that was about damage control, of course. Especially from the corporate angle."

Was any staff member dismissed?

"I think some of the staff were put on administrative leave. But there were no immediate suspensions or dismissals." There was only the slightest shading of emphasis on the word "immediate."

When I mention that I had heard about an in-house editorial written by Charles Trojan after Christy's death, Sidell thinks for a moment. "He could have. Saying that these kinds of incidents happen. We counseled our staff who had been traumatized by the event. Paid some lip service to it. And tried to project a sensitivity, a compassion around it. And"—he hesitates rather awkwardly—"a lot of it was genuine."

I ask about the response, at the upper echelons, to Christy Scheck's death. Was it any more than a blip on the corporate screen?

Sidell doesn't need time to think about this one. "The blip was not for the Scheck family, or for the Southwood staff workers, I can tell you that. The blip was the same one that I realized. And that was, that at the same time I was dealing with the issues of community and staff, and the issue of the child herself, there was also the sense of, 'Oh, my God . . .' Because I was aware of what was going on in terms of cost containment and the risk involved."

Sidell pours out another cup of tea, takes a sip. "So, one part of me went to damage control and making sure it was processed in a way that was still beneficial to the community that I was in charge of, and part of me said, 'This is going to be some serious, *serious* shit happening.' When I said that to myself, I didn't know just how serious things were going to get."

Within two days of Christy Scheck's suicide, Southwood Psychiatric Center lost its CHAMPUS certification. (It would reapply a year later and be recertified). That decertification eliminated 60 percent of the patient population, and, in the residential treatment center alone, over half the revenue ceased as reimbursement checks were halted. Southwood had one week to present its case against the decertification, and when the case was presented, the decision went against the facility. According to Alan Sidell, the hearing judge deemed Southwood to be "an unsafe place."

"The whole thing made for front-page news. Newspapers quoted Southwood officials saying, 'We will follow through with our quality treatment in spite of the other political and financial issues involved. No one will be discharged as a result of this issue.'" Sidell chuckles softly. "That was the public posture. But the attitude around the hospital was, 'As therapeutically as we can, let's get these kids out of here and into other CHAMPUS-certified NME facilities.'"

We have been sitting in the hotel lobby for hours, but Sidell shows no sign of fatigue. On the contrary, the conversation seems to have energized him. "You have to keep in mind that Southwood Psychiatric Center was the flagship out of fifteen or sixteen NME facilities in the western region. Charlie Trojan and Southwood Psychiatric were held up as models to the rest of the corporation." Sidell stops, thinking. "Hell, did I say we were the flagship of the western region? Wrong. Southwood was the model for all the NME hospitals around the nation. Because it was the best producer. But Christy Scheck's suicide was the beginning of the end. And it was a slow, painful death.

"The cutbacks and the layoffs began almost immediately. The tone became, 'Rally round the flag, and those of you that are still going to have a job left need to sacrifice. Those of you we're laying off, sorry.'

"Charlie would call a meeting with the heads of the different departments, and he'd look at each of us in turn: 'Ben, we need four from you. Sidell, we need five from you. Head of social service, we need three of your social workers because they cost us too much money. We're also going to start laying off these licensed people—they cost us too much money. And we're going to provide in-house cleaning from now on instead of using a contractor. Same with housekeeping.'

"Once the suicide happened, and the decertification and loss of revenue, a very bad morale began to generate until there was just constant fear among the employees. People saw empty beds—a twenty-four-bed unit with three or four kids on it—and it scared them. They saw people being laid off and hours cut back. They saw services being restricted and limited. Cost containment at every angle."

As Sidell speaks, I am reminded of something said to me by Flynn Davis, who remained at Southwood, working the late-night shift, after the death of Christy Scheck. Davis recalled how the place began to acquire a seedy, run-down look: frayed upholstery left unmended, stains allowed to collect on carpeting, dust balls under beds. He told me how he sat in the dimly lit hallway after the patients were asleep and watched mice scurry in and out of the unit bathroom.

Sidell goes on. "The managers and administrators were also under an even clearer understanding that the corporation wasn't going to take it. Corporation doesn't like even a single quarter of loss. You get two quarters of loss and that's always been a reason, in the past, to take a look and see if that facility is viable. And if it's not, start cleaning house. Now Southwood was faced with *four* quarters of loss, and the adverse publicity was ongoing." Sidell is silent for a moment. His eyes have slid away from mine, and he is quite clearly lost in his own thoughts. Then his focus snaps back and he looks at me again.

"You have to remember that my first introduction to Charles Trojan was as someone kicking ass, taking names, and cleaning house. He was the hired gun shipped in to straighten up shop. But where NME fucked up was by allowing him to remain in that role for so long. Because that's a limited value. You bring in someone to clean up, but then you have to lock in somebody else to maintain. The cleanup person, the gunslinger, well, he's not too good at maintenance after a year or two. That cold-blooded talent for firing people is good on the front end, when you need it. But it was pretty bad at the end, when Charlie was even laying off marketing people and cutting the budget for marketing." After a brief silence, Sidell says, "It was amazing to me that the place was able to last as long as it did."

When I ask about NME's final implosion, Sidell laughs. Not falsely or bitterly; he simply unleashes a long, low ripple of sound.

"Let's see. Was it the wrongful-death suicide that should never have happened? Was it the drug-dealing program director? Or was it the FBI raids?"

CHAPTER TWENTY-NINE

THE NME OVERLORDS, the people in the windowed offices at corporate headquarters, had been uneasy for some time. When Texas state senator Frank Tejeda obtained that writ of habeus corpus in order to secure the release of fourteen-year-old Jeremy Harrell from PIA's Colonial Hills Hospital in San Antonio after the boy was ambushed by a hired goon squad, a virtual domino effect of investigations spread across the state.

In July 1991, state senator Judith Zaffirini, chairperson of the Health Services Subcommittee on Health and Human Services, flew in from the capital to conduct a two-day "exploratory hearing" in San Antonio at which the Harrell family and Frank Tejeda testified, and at which Senator Tejeda assured Senator Zaffirini that not only was Harrell's abduction and unwarranted hospitalization not an isolated case, but that the problem ran statewide and nationwide. Tejeda further stated that insurance coverage was the common denominator in every instance.

The hearing kicked off another investigation, which pried the lid from a multioffice hot line that was found to be primarily funded by NME: Recovery Line. This call-in service was known to "suggest" hospitalization for nearly every person who called in. (In a subsequent lawsuit, filed by eight major insurance companies, Recovery Line was charged with conducting "a massive fraudulent scheme" skewed, nearly without exception, toward the referral of patients to NME-owned psychiatric hospitals.)

After the San Antonio hearings, Lieutenant Governor Bob Bullock appointed state senators Zaffirini, Mike Moncrief (who had at one time served on the community advisory board of a CareUnit hospital in the Dallas–Fort Worth area), and Chris Harris to head up a traveling interim committee, the purpose of which was to elicit testimony from people throughout Texas about abuses suffered in psychiatric hospitals. By September, as a result of the San Antonio hearings, a new law was passed by the Texas state legislature outlawing bounty payments for referrals to hospitals.

The event that created the most fallout for NME was the July 18 broadcast of ABC's *Prime Time Live,* with a segment on misconduct at Colonial Hills Hospital as well as other PIA facilities around the country. Shortly after the program aired, the president of the American Psychiatric Association, Dr. Lawrence Hartman of Harvard Medical School, issued a statement denouncing "bullying outreach tactics."

In October 1991, *The Wall Street Journal* reported that a five-state investigation for fraud had been launched targeting NME's psychiatric hospitals. At approximately the same time, a criminal investigation of CHAMPUS billings was begun by the Justice Department. Claims in Texas came under particular scrutiny: In that state alone $132 million had been paid out by CHAMPUS for private mental-health services in 1990.

NME scrambled to offset the potential surge of lost revenue with full-page newspaper statements proclaiming corporate innocence. Additional press releases announced internal investigations. Richard Eamer spoke out to NME shareholders, pledging that there would be "no material impact on the company's earnings." Nevertheless, NME stock plummeted: 20 percent on a single day in October 1991.

Some of the more beleaguered PIA hospitals, including the notorious Colonial Hills, were shut down. This was perhaps more a gesture than an actual corporate sacrifice; admissions to PIA hospitals in Texas had fallen by at least 30 percent. As the adverse publicity snowballed, heads began to roll: Norman Zober, CEO of the Specialty Hospital Group and president of PIA—the man who had placed himself squarely behind the 800-COCAINE hot line in 1985—was placed on an indefinite leave of absence, with pay (more than $2 million in salary, bonuses, and stock options), for the remainder of the fiscal year. Four other NME executives were fired.

By the end of October, the statewide hearings had produced witness after witness, all of whom testified about incidents of abuse in psychiatric hospitals that included bounties for referrals, overprescribed medications, exhaustion of insurance benefits, and patient care delivered not by the physician on the case but by para-professionals.

In mid-November, NME cofounder and senior executive vice president John Bedrosian sent a rather conciliatory letter to Texas senator Mike Moncrief, admitting that corporate mistakes had been made even as he stressed NME's high standards and unyielding principles. Mention was made of the "shame" experienced over the ongoing situation in Texas; however, Bedrosian went on to urge Senator Moncrief to take into consideration that much of the testimony at the hearings had been presented by former psychiatric patients. For good measure, Bedrosian took a swipe at the press, complaining that local newspaper stories mainly favored those reports that were unfavorable to NME.

The truth was that NME's troubles in Texas were only the continued rumblings of an approaching storm that would spread out across the country. Within a year, the psychiatric industry in general would find itself at the eye of a roiling controversy.

CHAPTER THIRTY

ON THE MORNING of April 28, 1992, a congressional hearing was convened before the Select Committee on Children, Youth, and Families. Congresswoman Patricia Schroeder, the committee chairwoman, made the opening statement, in which she shared her hope "that the shedding of light today will help to stop what I think is one of the most disgraceful and scandalous episodes in health care in America."

Schroeder went on to deliver an alarming statistic: In 1991 the United States had spent an estimated $800 billion on health care, and 20 percent of that sum—$160 billion—had quite possibly been "ripped off by questionable practices within the mental health care industry."

When Texas state senator Mike Moncrief took the floor, he briefly described the public hearings in Texas, then said, "We have uncovered some of the most elaborate, aggressive, creative, immoral, and illegal schemes being used to fill empty hospital beds with insured and paying patients." Moncrief spoke about the Jeremy Harrell case, and quoted the boy's grandmother, who had compared Jeremy's abduction by security guards to "her childhood in Nazi Germany." Senator Moncrief further stated that the same security firm was being paid "between one hundred fifty and four hundred fifty dollars for each patient delivered to certain psychiatric hospitals in [the San Antonio] area."

Moncrief continued: "What was once thought to be a very serious local problem in San Antonio quickly exploded into a statewide problem and then became national, and even international in scope." He talked about Canadian patients "enticed by the prospect of complimentary airfare, limousine services and luxury accommodations in treatment programs in sunny California, Florida and Texas. . . . One man was referred to as a 'half-million-dollar man.' He reportedly received over twenty months of treatment in five different Houston hospitals and returned to Canada a cocaine addict." Moncrief described the plight of dozens of Canadian patients "dumped and stranded at the Houston airport with no return tickets" after the Canadian government placed limits on reimbursements to U.S. hospitals. He added that bounties paid for Canadian patients ranged from $1,500 to $4,000 per patient.

Moncrief gave other examples of abuse, providing the panel with copies of patients' bills from three separate facilities in Texas: Willowbrook Hospital in Waxahachie; Brookhaven Psychiatric Pavilion in Farmers Branch; and Baywood Hospital in Webster. On the Willowbrook bill, for September 6, 1991, there were *twenty separate entries* for twenty separate "Group Psych" sessions listed as half-hour segments at $40 per segment. Individual and multifamily sessions were billed in the same fashion, with eight sessions notated for August 17; those sessions were billed at $62.50 for each half hour. Psychodrama sessions cost $50 per half hour. The so-called "account episode" for this patient's bill ran from July 8 to August 23, 1991, and the total charges came to $32,538.25. At Brookhaven, a patient's pharmacy bill showed wildly fluctuating daily costs for the same medication: A single 2-milligram tablet of Immodium (an antidiarrhea medication costing approximately $3.99 for six 2-milligram tablets in a drugstore) was billed, on separate days, at $35.10, $44.95, $10.60, and $23.40. However, Thorazine, one of the megatranquilizers, was relatively inexpensive, although it too was subject to capricious pricing: $3.30 for a 25-milligram tablet one day; $1.65 for the same amount the next. (The Brookhaven billing sheet is the only one that lists the patient's insurance carrier; in this instance it was Aetna Life and Casualty.) At Baywood, an adolescent patient was charged $625 per day for a semiprivate room from August 24 through September 5, 1991. On September 1, the patient's bill showed seven separate group counseling sessions, one hour each, at $80 per session. With seven hours of group counseling in a single day, one must wonder when—and if—the mandatory educational classes were provided. This same patient was charged $53 for something called an "adolescent general patient text," and $41.90 for a single paperback copy of a book entitled *Broken Toys/Broken Dreams,* which retailed for $10.95. This book was sold *twice* to the same patient within a five-day period, as her bill reflects, for a total of $83.80. All told, the charges came to $14,356.87 for a hospital stay of less than two weeks.

It should also be noted that, according to Senator Moncrief's statement to the committee, one of these patients "was billed, on one day, for thirty-six prescription drugs. Her itemized statement shows 8,400 milligrams of Lithobid [lithium; most commonly used for the suppression of bipolar disorders]. The *Physicians' Desk Reference* lists the maximum dose at 1,800 milligrams. This amount of lithium alone, or in combination with other drugs, would have been lethal had it actually been given to the patient."

Senator Moncrief did not specify the corporate ownership of the aforementioned facilities to the committee, and the billing sheets did not reflect it. Calls made to the telephone numbers listed at the top of each separate billing sheet turned up the following results:

• The Willowbrook Hospital number was assigned, by August 1996, to a private citizen in Waxahachie. He had never heard of the facility. Information for Waxahachie had no listing at all for a Willowbrook Hospital.

• The Brookhaven Psychiatric Pavilion in Farmers Branch was an NME-owned facility in 1991, located on the grounds of the Robert H. Dedman Memorial Hospital, which is still in operation. According to the RHD Memorial business office, Brookhaven went out of business shortly after the Texas statewide senate hearings began; soon afterward, the building that housed the Pavilion was torn down. Dedman Memorial is now owned by Tenet Healthcare, formerly known as National Medical Enterprises—NME. In reply to whether a psychiatric wing is still in operation at Dedman Memorial Hospital, the person in the business office said, "We're out of *that* business."

• The telephone at Baywood Hospital in Webster is answered by a machine. Callers are informed that the Charter/Baywood Behavioral Health Services of Clearlake are no longer providing services. The message goes on to inform callers that the building that housed Baywood is for sale (with a realtor's number provided), and that the Baywood school (the Academy of Clearlake) has already been sold. Another referral number is given to anyone calling for medical records or "personal issues." The caller is thanked for having called Charter Hospitals. Calls to the Charter corporate offices in Macon, Georgia, failed to provide information pertaining to the year Baywood was purchased by Charter. Baywood was, however, an NME facility until well into 1993.

AFTER SENATOR MONCRIEF'S address to the Texas state senate committee, Congresswoman Schroeder introduced Louis Parisi, director of the Fraud Division of the New Jersey Department of Insurance. Parisi's opening statement described health care fraud as "a time bomb waiting to explode." He expressed grave concern about the low priority given fraud prevention and detection by insurance carriers, and he stated that "fraud can easily become an acceptable cost incurred and passed on to all consumers."

Next, he provided a shocking statistic: In eight years of operation, the New Jersey Department of Insurance Fraud Division had never received a single complaint from the insurance industry concerning any aspect of a particular hospital that was then under investigation. Parisi said that twenty-one health-insurance companies paid over $40 million to a two-hundred-bed facility in one year without reporting a single questionable claim.

As a possible remedy, Parisi cited the Fair Automobile Reform Act, signed into law in 1990, which requires every insurer writing private passenger insurance in New Jersey to file a comprehensive plan for the prevention and detection of fraud. In 1991,

Parisi reported 14,635 cases were referred to the Fraud Division for investigation, but during the first three months of 1992, more than 10,000 cases had been referred. This dramatic increase was due to a single factor: More people were on the lookout for auto-insurance fraud because it was mandated by law and was backed up by stiff penalties. Parisi informed the committee that the state of New Jersey was "in the process of attempting to get similar legislation passed that will require the health care companies to institute mandatory fraud prevention and detection plans. [This bill was signed into law in January 1994.]

"Depending on whose numbers you wish to use, health care fraud is a $16 [billion] to $80 billion industry. . . . State and federal authorities must have the political will to pass tough laws and provide the tools to remove those health care professionals that don't belong in the system."

Parisi closed by stressing the urgency of adding to the fourteen states already on the lookout for health care fraud. "A consumer must learn that it's not a victimless crime, and it is not just an insurance company that loses."

A series of testimonies followed Parisi's speech, including an address made by Curtis L. Decker, executive director for the Washington-based National Association of Protection and Advocacy Systems (NAPAS). Although Decker did not name specific hospitals, he cited some examples from a Congress-mandated nationwide investigation into charges of abuse and neglect in both private and public institutions providing psychiatric services. Included was the case of a sixteen-year-old boy in San Diego who was "plucked from class" without his mother's knowledge and taken to a psychiatric hospital where he was held for five days, until doctors at the facility discovered that the family's insurance would not cover the treatment.

Decker quoted a report from the Los Angeles Patients' Rights office about the "Teen Shuttle," in which teenagers were surprised at home by strangers who then proceeded to carry them off to psychiatric hospitals, often in handcuffs.

From Nevada, the state protection and advocacy investigation reported "some of the more disturbing examples of aggressive marketing on the part of private hospitals. Due to the highly lucrative tapping of insurance benefits for adolescents labeled as 'mentally ill,' and overt marketing techniques employed by two hospitals in the Health Corporation of America chain in Reno and Las Vegas [no longer listed in 1996], it is estimated that hundreds of children with 'conduct disorders,' 'adjustment disorders,' and 'attention deficit disorders' were admitted for inpatient treatment and often lengthy stays in these facilities as a result of poor report cards."

Decker provided an instance of unethical conduct whereby "an administrator of one of the HCA centers in Nevada was investigated by a multidisciplinary team who found several instances of abuse, including children who were subjected to a disciplinary practice that called for them to bend from the waist and hold their ankles for periods of up to one and a half hours, and children who were deprived of meals by the staff."

As a result of the state P&A investigation, the license of this hospital's administrator was severely restricted. He tried to set himself up in the recovery business in Maine, but the Maine P&A offices, alerted by the Nevada board, opposed his licensure with the Maine Medical Board.

Reports from Wisconsin included one in which a sixteen-year-old boy involved in the delinquency and mental-health system was admitted to a psychiatric hospital and placed in an adult forensic unit because "it was considered the best place to manage his aggressive behavior." The prescribed treatment for this boy, according to the report, consisted of being held in four-point restraints for twenty-two hours per day, with two hours "out" in the unit's dayroom.

In Kentucky, Decker stated, the state P&A office there was representing a ten-year-old boy "who was forced to eat by a nurse who held a hypodermic needle over his head and told him he would be given an injection if he did not clean his plate."

Also in Kentucky, the investigation turned up the case of a teenage boy "who was forced to drink a quart of water and was not allowed to use the bathroom until he 'confessed to the group' that he was planning to escape."

The Cabinet for Human Resources in Kentucky concluded that 40 percent of private-hospital admissions in that state were either questionable or inappropriate. At one facility alone (also unnamed to the congressional committee) 80 percent of the children admitted were diagnosed as having "conduct disorders." Decker then pointed out to the committee that the problems were not restricted to private hospitals alone. "The abuse within state hospitals is staggering."

Decker cited the case of a fifteen-year-old boy in Oregon who had been caught up in the web of that state's Child-Adolescent Treatment Program for the past seven years, passed from doctor to doctor, each of whom came up with a different diagnosis. By 1992 the boy was "completely institutionalized." He had attended school for only approximately 10 percent of the time he spent in the state's treatment program, and although he was finally diagnosed with attention-deficit hyperactivity disorder and severe oppositional defiant disorder, a then-current psychological profile emphasized that the boy "needed to transition out of the hospital immediately while there is still some of his youth left." Decker found, through investigation, that there was no place in the outside world for this boy. His mother was unwilling to take him, and neither the state nor the hospital would place him with his father. Without advocacy or mandatory reviews, the boy remained in a state mental hospital, and his condition worsened.

Another disturbing case was reported by the Alabama P&A agency: When a set of foster parents had trouble reinforcing bathroom habits in an eight-year-old boy in their charge, they took him in for counseling. After an initial session, the boy was taken out of foster care and placed in a seven-month inpatient program where, the foster parents alleged, he was placed in isolation and overmedicated. The boy was returned to the family only after they sought legal and political help.

Decker ended his statement to the committee with a series of recommendations stressing expansion of community services, liaison between educators and the mental-health system, and the utilization of review by insurance providers focusing on individual diagnoses and need. Decker also strongly recommended that the Health Care Financing Administration be given the authority to hold both private and public hospitals accountable for all inappropriate treatment, abuse, and oversights. "There are excellent programs out there, and there are youth with a range of emotional problems who are in need of them. The challenge is to assure that the population is not jeopardized by programs whose main concern is profit."

As if to highlight Decker's remarks, two former employees of NME/PIA hospitals delivered statements.

Russel D. Durrett was the comptroller of Twin Lakes Hospital in Denton, Texas, from November 1988 through July 1989. On April 28, 1992, Durrett spoke to the committee of his "personal knowledge" that coercive techniques were employed at Twin Lakes in order to keep patients who had already signed papers of intention to leave the facility within ninety-six hours hospitalized. Durrett stated that discharge planning would, as a rule, only be discussed for those patients for whom insurance coverage was running out.

Speaking as an accountant, Durrett asked for the committee's indulgence to permit him to focus on the violations of the Medicare, state, and Internal Revenue Service regulations, as well as the violations of "accepted business practices" about which he had firsthand knowledge. "The bottom line was the driving force behind almost every decision. Profit and cash flow created an environment where the incentive for money clearly exceeded considerations of proper patient care and/or their rights."

Durrett described an ongoing practice in which Twin Lakes Hospital recruited psychiatrists by picking up the bills for the establishment of their private practices and throwing in the title of "unit medical director" as a further fiscal embellishment. The monthly fees for these recruited psychiatrists, according to Durrett's statement, ranged from $8,000 to $15,000 as renumeration for approximately ten hours of work per week. As patients were admitted to the hospital they would be assigned to one of these psychiatrists, who could then bill a daily charge (usually $100 to $150) per patient.

"There were so many occasions when a physician would have more than twenty-five patients in the hospital. As you can see, if the physician spends only a couple of hours a day in the hospital, and that physician has twenty-five or more patients to see and document . . . the physician could not be spending much time, or any time, with the patient. In addition to the daily charge, the physician could bill for any additional individual-therapy sessions that were needed during the patient's stay. If you calculate the above numbers, you will find that a psychiatrist could easily make between six hundred thousand and nine hundred thousand dollars a year from the hospital."

Durrett described an incident in which the medical director of the Twin Lakes drug- and alcohol-abuse program was given a $35,000 loan with the understanding that as long as the number of patients on the program was kept above a certain level, a portion of the loan would be written off. "This was not included in the contract, as it is in direct violation of Medicare regulations. The loan was totally written off, and the physician was never given a 1099 [tax form]. The hospital took the loan as an expense, which means that the physician should have picked up the proceeds of the loan as income."

Durrett told the committee about cases of potential Twin Lakes patients who, although they had lost their jobs, still had insurance benefits available under COBRA (the Consolidated Omnibus Budget Reconciliation Act, which allows an ex-employee of a company with more than twenty people on the payroll to maintain eighteen months of continuous health insurance, provided the former employee pays all premium fees previously paid by the employer). At Twin Lakes, according to Durrett, if the potential patient did not have funds available to pay for the COBRA policy, the hospital wrote a check, which was then taken to the bank and cashed. A money order was then purchased, usually at a post office, and mailed in to cover the COBRA policy without reflecting that the payment had actually been made by the hospital itself. The person was then admitted to the hospital, which would subsequently collect on the policy. Durrett said this practice was "a regional call."

Durrett also described some of the billing practices where "demands were made on us to be creative." He cited therapy sessions billed according to a daily schedule sheet that stipulated which sessions patients were to attend. However, if a patient was away from his or her assigned unit (for any reason, including a necessary hospital procedure), the patient would still be billed for scheduled therapy sessions. According to an explanatory letter sent by Durrett in reply to a letter from Congresswoman Schroeder after his testimony, "There were probably between 15 to 20 therapy sessions a day that were billed when, in fact, the patient did not attend the session. On weekends the number would be even higher. In addition, any time the revenue was down, the schedule would be changed to include more therapy sessions. Therapy sessions would even be added in the evenings if the sessions were needed to bring up the revenue per patient day. It was not uncommon for the adolescent program to have 8 therapy sessions a day and also to have the patient attend high school classes (in house) for a half of the day."

In his statement to the committee, Durrett said that there was a use of uncertified employees who would come in to the hospital to provide group-therapy sessions as part of Twin Lakes' network and referral system. The hospital would pay a consulting fee, but because of the unlicensed status of many consulting personnel, it was necessary to have a *certified* hospital employee sign off on any group-therapy session conducted by an uncertified person. In this way, the bill for the session could be sent on to the patients' insurance providers, and if the medical records were checked, the signature would be that of a licensed hospital employee.

Other enlightening statements made by Durrett were related to a problem at Twin Lakes Hospital (as well as other NME/PIA facilities in the region) that he described as "too much profit." He explained: "At month-end, a preliminary close was used to determine the profit of each hospital and region. These numbers would be given to PIA in Washington, D.C., and the following day, or day after that, the regional vice president of finance would call each hospital in that region and inform the hospital where to create additional expenses if the profit was too high." In one ten-month period, according to Durrett, $670,000 was added to Twin Lakes' expenses. He added that the amount of expenses that were unsupported by proper expense documents "had to be in excess of several million for our region alone."

Although Durrett claimed that he had not been contacted by either the Internal Revenue Service or the Securities and Exchange Commission at the time of his testimony, it seems clear that the covering of profits was a corporate effort to decrease tax liability and show a constant growth rate to NME/PIA shareholders rather than risk what might appear to be aberrant profits.

Durrett continued his statement: "This fraudulent accounting technique was used to hide the true profit, but also to manage the continued rise in profits in order to keep the [NME/PIA] stock prices increasing. Twin Lakes was budgeted to make $2.7 million for the fiscal year June 1987 to May 1988. The actual profit was $4.2 million even with the additional expenses added. The rate of return was in excess of 32 percent."

Then Durrett put those figures into perspective: "A healthy rate of return in the health care industry is 8 to 10 percent."

PSYCHIATRIST DUARD BOK testified to the committee as a former executive at PIA's Psychiatric Institute in Fort Worth, Texas. In April 1991, Bok informed the hospital administration, through a series of letters from his attorney, of his concerns, "which involved dangerous practices and ethical abusive practices occurring with frequency at the hospital."

In his statement at the April 1992 congressional hearings, Bok described some of the practices, which included untrained and unlicensed therapists working with patients who often fell into hypnotic trances; possible false-memory implantation under trance, and "the most heinous of all: rage-reduction therapy which was later euphemized to 'trust-development therapy' after some of my complaints." Dr. Bok went on to state that "there is no professionally recognized validation of rage-reduction therapy, but it involves holding the young person down by one or more adults while another person usually verbally taunts them and beats him or her in the rib and chest areas, often causing severe bruising."

Bok's employment at the Psychiatric Institute was terminated after he made his complaints, and he filed suit against the hospital, claiming that he was fired because he had spoken out. The hospital denied all of Bok's allegations, but the administration took things a step further: A letter was written by Dr. Al K. Marshall, chairman of the executive committee of the institute's medical staff, and addressed to the Impaired Physicians Committee of the Texas Medical Association. In the letter, Dr. Marshall wrote that it was "the unfortunate and unpleasant responsibility of this facility to report our concern that a member of our Medical Staff [Duard Bok] is likely impaired." The letter went on to state that, in Marshall's opinion, Bok was not "capable of conducting himself in the manner appropriate to a member of the Medical Staff of a hospital or clinic." The Psychiatric Institute officials further requested that Bok, whom they accused of "having a bi-polar personality disorder which impairs his judgement," undergo a mental examination. To that end, the institute authorities attempted to enlist the help of a state judge in this plan. The judge declined.

. . .

THE CONGRESSIONAL HEARINGS went on for days, with statements from physicians, former patients, politicians, and federal
employees. The most succinct observation, made after listening to
hours of testimony, came from Brooklyn congressman Charles E.
Schumer: "This is the closest to ultimate evil I've seen."

CHAPTER THIRTY-ONE

IN JUNE 1992, less than two months after the congressional hearings, National Medical Enterprises reached a settlement with the state of Texas for $1.1 million in legal fees, $2.6 million to be used for charity care, and $500,000 to be set aside in trust to help those patients whose medical histories had been tainted by inappropriate psychiatric treatment. A further sum of $5 million was placed on waiver for claims billed to the Texas crime victims' compensation fund.

NME then made a move toward redeeming its sagging corporate reputation: The company hired Richard Kusserow, former inspector general of the Department of Health and Human Services and, in 1992, president of Strategic Management Systems, a Virginia-based company. Kusserow's task for NME would be to review contracts, joint-venture agreements, and compensation plans and to develop a general corrective-action plan. The result was NME's adoption of a revised code, the establishment of ethics-information offices with toll-free call-in numbers, and the formation of an ethics steering committee that reported directly to the NME board of directors.

But the move was too little too late. Insurers remained unconvinced about NME's billing practices, and continued rumblings about fraud and billing improprieties made it clear that the storm was far from over.

In a preemptive strike that proved to be disastrous, NME filed a suit against the Travelers Group insurance company for withheld payment in July 1992. Less than two weeks later, eight of the insurers fired back with a civil RICO (Racketeering Influenced Corrupt Organizations) suit against NME. The insurers' suit alleged

$490 million in fraudulent claims from 1988 to 1992. Following Travelers' lead, two other insurer groups, Aetna Life and Metropolitan Life, also filed suit, as did Connecticut General Life, all within a matter of months. The sum alleged by the combined insurers came to $750 million in fraudulent claims.

That was just the beginning: Aside from the civil and insurance companies' suits, others would file against NME before the end of the year.

In December 1992, National Medical Enterprises, its cofounders, Richard Eamer, Leonard Cohen, and John Bedrosian, and a lengthy list of NME/PIA board members, management directors, and physicians were hit by a shareholders' derivative action. The list of defendants also included Norman Zober, the CEO of NME's Specialty Hospital Group, who had been placed on indefinite leave the previous year. According to the action of the filing, NME "owned, operated or managed 86 psychiatric hospitals and substance abuse facilities and 29 physical rehabilitative hospitals, all of which NME classifies as its 'Specialty Hospital Group,' many of which NME has been forced to close as a result of the misconduct alleged herein. In addition, the Specialty Hospital Group manages 49 psychiatric, rehabilitation and substance abuse units in other acute hospitals."

The allegations made against the corporation and the defendants listed in the suit included insurance fraud and insider trading involving "sales of over 2.9 million shares of [the defendants'] personal holdings of NME stock at grossly inflated prices, reaping profits to themselves of tens of millions of dollars." The suit alleged that "these insider sales did not conform to past patterns of sales by insiders and indicate that the defendants knew that once the adverse information reached the public, the price of NME stock would plummet."

Other allegations listed as defendants' violations were: false and misleading public statements in press releases, newspaper and magazine articles, and interviews, as well as filings with the Securities and Exchange Commission (SEC) and reports disseminated to shareholders and the public that were materially false and misleading. The allegations went on for 127 pages and included, under the subheading of "Predatory Marketing Practices," the description of an internal PIA memo that recommended staff training in discharge-intervention techniques and that social activities such as picnics and barbecues be "stepped up during weeks of fluctuations to discourage premature discharges." Another memo recommended bringing in Santa Claus by helicopter as a census-related activity "that increased the length of stay for three children by five days each."

Under the heading "Defendants' Wrongful Course of Conduct," there was an especially revealing statement: "During fiscal 1990, NME's Specialty Hospitals accounted for 37% of NME's net operating revenues of $3.9 billion and 54% of the Company's overall profits." And there was more: The filing reported that NME's psychiatric hospitals in Texas alone accounted for 20 percent of NME's psychiatric-hospital capacity.

Under the section entitled "Insurance Scheme and Financial Reports," there were alleged reports that "when the number of patients [in an NME facility in Oklahoma] exceeded census expectations, the hospital illegally put more patients in a room than the room was designed for and would charge the additional patients for rooms that did not exist."

Also: "It was the PIA psychiatric policy that patients would not be discharged on Friday, Saturday or Sunday. This assured additional patient days at a much lower cost as weekends were staffed at a greatly reduced level. NME/PIA would pick up 3 additional days of revenue, plus NME/PIA would have higher profit margins due to lower staffing levels on the weekend. Patients were also allowed 23 hour passes on weekends. Some patients were even given back-to-back 23 hour passes. As long as the patient was at the hospital at midnight, the patient was charged for the day."

The suit alleged that Norman Zober, in his former capacity as CEO of the Specialty Hospital Group, reported to an audit committee of the NME board with figures on the daily census, admissions and discharges. Zober, it was alleged, had been instructed to extend hospital stays, delay patient discharges, and "go after the insurance companies." Zober, it was claimed, had also been instructed by senior board members including Richard Eamer and John Bedrosian to instill the "fear of God [or] lose your job" in PIA employees.

The shareholders' derivative action should not be confused with the shareholders' suit that was brought against NME a few months later. The difference between the two suits, both class actions, is that a derivative action is filed on behalf of the corporation (in this case, NME) against the perceived wrongdoers, for example, the directors and officers of the company who put plans into place whereby "the corporate coffers were emptied as a result of actions perpetrated by these officers and directors." A shareholders' suit is brought on behalf of the shareholders against not only the officers but the corporation as well. In the shareholders' suit, NME was one of the defendants. The main distinction between the two suits is where the settlement goes. In a shareholders' action, the recovered money goes to the shareholders to compensate for loss of value to their shares. In a shareholders' derivative suit, the money goes into a corporate account to compensate for corporate loss.

According to California law (both suits were filed in that state), the plaintiffs do not need to obtain the permission of the corporation to sue its officers.

The initial trial court dismissed the derivative complaint for failure to be specific about acts engaged in by each defendant. This suit was later won on appeal with a settlement in the amount of $11 million, paid by the defendants to the corporation.

The shareholders' suit, citing the same alleged actions and the same alleged conduct by the same defendants named in the derivative suit, was upheld and proceeded to depositions.

NME settled for an amount exceeding $50 million. The value of NME stock had dropped from $24 to approximately $12 per share in direct relation to the egregious conduct of the NME officers.

.   .   .

ON JANUARY 8, 1993, a front-page story entitled "Abiding Suspicion" appeared in *The Wall Street Journal.* In the piece, written
by Sonia L. Nazario, National Medical Enterprises was described
as "a 4 billion-a-year behemoth with 143 hospitals on four conti-
nents . . . whose future remains clouded by its past." Nazario detailed NME's past and current problems and provided an overview
of pending issues, including fourteen separate federal and state investigations, as well as preliminary inquiries by the Federal Trade
Commission and the Securities and Exchange Commission.

An interesting picture of chief executive Richard Eamer
emerged in the article. He is described as a self-made man who
dropped out of high school and became a truck driver until he
could jump-start his education again in order to acquire a law degree. According to former NME executives interviewed by
Nazario, Eamer's position within the corporation was structured
to provide him with enough freedom from the daily operational
grind to permit him to disappear, without explanation, for weeks,
showing up at company-owned condominiums in London and
Aspen. Eamer's response to these statements was that he was never
gone for more than one week at a time, and that all trips unrelated
to NME business were paid for out of his own pocket.

Those who were willing to be interviewed described Eamer as
the kind of employer who would "castrate you if you make any
errors," a man who didn't hesitate to refer to his subordinates as
"morons" during executive meetings when his ambitious profit
goals were reported to be unmet. Yet, according to the interviews, there was also what appeared to be a strangely whimsical
side to Eamer's personality: He often brought his dog to the office, and he was occasionally seen pedaling a scooter through the
corporate hallways. He lived high, buying an estate in the Pacific
Palisades, one of Southern California's wealthiest enclaves. He in-
vested in thoroughbred breeding farms, drove fancy cars, wore a
ponytail.

The article also mentioned an affliction of which Eamer had

spoken openly, referring to himself as a "hypomanic depressive" who controlled his symptoms with regular doses of lithium.

According to the article, Richard Eamer described himself as the "hardest-working executive in the health care industry," a man determined to return his company to an unsullied reputation by the selling-off of many of its psychiatric hospitals and by the return of corporate focus to NME's thirty-five remaining general hospitals.

Eamer was quoted as saying, at a 1992 shareholders' meeting at which the atmosphere was one of distrust and anger, "Our focus is on the patient. We know everything else will follow."

Despite such avowals, by spring of 1993 NME had set aside a reserve fund in the sum of $65 million to cover defense costs alone.

CHAPTER THIRTY-TWO

IN THE EARLY morning of March 16, 1993, Southwood marketing executive Alan Sidell was driving to work when he saw the pulsing flare of red and white lights in his rearview mirror. He pulled over to the shoulder of the highway and got his wallet out of the glove compartment, figuring maybe he hadn't quite come to a full stop at that last stop sign.

As Sidell pulled his driver's license out of his wallet he could hear the slam of a car door and the crunch of footsteps as the driver of the black-and-white walked toward his car. At the same moment, another, unmarked car slid up and parked just ahead of him.

"Would you mind getting out of the car, sir?"

Sidell was presented with a search warrant for his car and another for his apartment. (He would learn later that the police had awakened a judge the previous night in order to obtain both documents.) Sidell looked at the warrants and got into the backseat of the detectives' car. There had been no raised voices, no threats. The only attitude displayed on either side was one of unfailing courtesy.

Sidell made only one remark, and that was delivered the instant the door to his apartment swung open: "There's a pound and a half of pot in the living room closet."

Sidell says that he didn't want the police to tear his place apart looking for drugs. He told them they were welcome to get out the dogs, but all they had to do was open the closet door. The police did search further, however, and they came up with a gun that was in the nightstand next to Sidell's bed.

"It was a legally registered firearm," Sidell says. "I was living in the South Bay of San Diego, and I had a weapon for self-protection. I know how to use a gun, and it was fully loaded, as it should have been. I didn't have any kids in the house." He smiles ruefully. "But, technically . . . possession of a firearm . . ."

Sidell was placed under arrest and booked into the San Diego county jail. Bail was set at $5,000; Sidell called a friend, who came down and got him out. He was back in his office at Southwood by late morning.

The arraignment was scheduled for four o'clock on March 18, two days after Sidell's arrest. By noon of that day the following in-house memo appeared in every Southwood staff member's mailbox:

> Due to unexpected circumstances, Alan Sidell will not be continuing his employment here. Al has contributed greatly to our organization and we will miss him greatly on our Southwood team.

Sidell has always found it odd that the memo appeared four hours earlier than the slated arraignment. He had not mentioned the arrest to anyone at work, and the friend who had arranged for bail didn't know anyone at Southwood. Sidell himself first saw the memo when another staff member walked into his office and handed it across his desk. "But then, of course, the chief of police chaired the board of governors at Southwood Hospital . . ." He allows the words to trail off into silence.

"The next morning the front-page headline in the San Diego newspapers described how a 'Southwood exec' had been arrested on a drug charge during 'an early morning raid.' That 'early morning raid' stuff was stressed, along with 'possession of a firearm during a felony.' The impression given was that I was selling heroin to babies."

I ask Sidell how the police knew about his connection with drugs.

"The guy who sold me the pot got busted, and when he got squeezed, he gave my name to the cops. Instead of handing over up-line names, he went down-line. The cops were pissed off, but the guy knew I wasn't a criminal. He knew I wasn't going to kill him." Surprisingly, Sidell smiles. "The police came out of my pad cussin'. They were expecting hundred of pounds of pot."

Once again, Sidell acts out a dialogue.

" 'What'd you find?'

" 'Well, we found some marketing material from Southwood Hospital in his car.'

" 'He works at Southwood?' " Sidell pauses dramatically before he continues. " 'Whoa! He works with kids at Southwood Hospital . . . *whoa!* He even does drug counseling . . .' "

I ask why Sidell got into marijuana sales while he was employed at Southwood.

"Well, I'll tell you this: It wasn't about the money. It was about smoking pot. I handed over pot and took money back in return. Basically, it was a co-op."

Who was included in this co-op?

"Why, my . . . friends. . . . You could write a whole book on sex, drugs, rock and roll, and the psychology of the psychiatric industry. I could give you names of doctors I smoked pot with, snorted coke with, rocked and rolled with. Doctors at Southwood, mental-health workers, counselors, psychologists." His hand makes a rolling gesture to indicate a lengthy list of drug consumers.

What about the "felonious amount of marijuana" mentioned in the newspaper in connection with Sidell's arrest?

"I had a pound and a half of pot in my living room closet. For this reason: Instead of spending a hundred dollars an ounce, sixteen times a year, making sixteen criminal activities, I'd buy a pound of pot for six hundred bucks and get the ounce for forty bucks. It was economics. And I had six or seven close friends who were pot smokers." He anticipates my next question. "And, yes, a few of them were in the mental-health community."

Any from Southwood?

"Yeah. A couple of them."

Any kids?

"No. I just co-oped with professional friends for a couple of years. Not drug addicts, not bad people. These were just people with jobs and families who happened to like getting high."

All of this begs the question: Were people getting high at work?

Sidell doesn't even have to think about it. "Oh, yeah. We'd had problems before, between '79 and '82, before stricter controls were implemented at the RTC. With some kid's Dexedrine [a highly addictive medication often prescribed for children with 'attentional disturbances'] that was being used up faster than the kid could use it on his prescribed dosage. Not to excuse anything, but within the context of the eighties, no one even missed a beat. Psychiatrists, administrators, nobody blinked an eye. And my interpolation is that's just the tip of a very large iceberg beneath the surface. I've seen too many lines on mirrors, and too many joints at too many parties with these professionals."

I ask Sidell if he ever saw lines on mirrors at Southwood.

"No. But that's just a matter of protocol—not because it wasn't happening. I know for a fact that some counseling was being done under the influence." He glances down at the table between us and brushes a scattering of crumbs off the surface. "But maybe that's just my frame of reference as someone who was partying too much. Drugs might not have permeated the facility, but that was my impression."

Is there a common thread here?

"If you're asking whether this is a profession, and an industry, escalating to an out-of-control point . . ." He moves his shoulders in a slight shrug. "The drug involvement is there in the industry, but I can't really say how pervasive it is. It's there. But it is not a causal factor for all the other out-of-control things that have happened. Nor is the use of drugs—prevalent or not—completely unrelated.

"It's an intriguing industry."

CHAPTER THIRTY-THREE

BY JUNE 1993, with NME attorneys already in negotiation with federal prosecutors over pending civil and criminal charges, Richard Eamer and Leonard Cohen announced that they were giving up their major operating posts with the corporation. The board then named an outside director as the new chairman and CEO. This was Jeffrey C. Barbakow, a former investment banker and onetime president and CEO of Metro-Goldwyn-Mayer/United Artists. Eamer, however, retained a five-year consultancy contract, and Cohen a three-year one. For the year ending on May 31, 1993, Eamer's total compensation was valued at $9 million, while Cohen's came to $2.9 million. At the time NME was being sued by several insurance companies over an alleged $1 billion in fraudulent claims.

August 1993 would prove to be even more disastrous.

The Department of Defense had been aware of overbilling of CHAMPUS patients in some of NME's facilities around the country, but by August 1993 the sheer magnitude of what could only be perceived as billing fraud created the need for serious investigation. To that end, the Department of Defense called in the FBI.

On August 26 more than six hundred federal agents raided twelve of NME's psychiatric hospitals as well as regional offices in California, Arizona, Colorado, Texas, Missouri, Indiana, Florida, Virginia, Louisiana, Michigan, Minnesota, Wisconsin, and Washington, D.C. Telephone lines were disconnected and staff workers and executives alike were ordered to stay away from their computers as FBI agents swept through the facilities, hoisting file cabinets onto dollies and dumping thousands of corporate documents

into legal-sized cartons, which, in turn, were loaded into the backs
of waiting vans.

At Baywood Psychiatric Hospital in Webster, Texas, fifty federal agents arrived at 10:00 A.M. on August 26; they would not
leave the premises until one o'clock the following morning. The
CEO at Baywood on the day of the raid was Charles Trojan. He had
been transferred, at his request, to that facility from Southwood
Psychiatric Center and had been on the job at Baywood for four
days when the FBI raid took place.

THE PRICE OF NME stock fell to $6.50 a share after the FBI raids,
and the company quickly adjusted its credit line. If the allegations
of overbilling and fraud could be proven, chances were that NME
would be excluded from Medicare, Medicaid, and CHAMPUS.
NME attorneys released statements in which terms like "prompt
resolutions" figured prominently. Everyone concerned was aware
that the future of National Medical Enterprises rested in the hands
of the United States government.

The hard, fast decisions fell to Jeffrey Barbakow. By the end of
September 1993, John Bedrosian, the last of the three NME
founders still actively employed, was relieved of his duties. Under
terms of an agreement effective until 1995, Bedrosian collected at
least half of his $510,000 annual salary and retained the legal
right to remain employed by NME until he reached the age of
sixty-five.

Barbakow's next decision was to settle the federal lawsuits by
nineteen insurers for a sum approaching $215 million. Settlement
was really the only available option if the insurers and the prosecutors were to be persuaded that NME was undergoing profound
changes, both ethically and in the corporate sense. The question of
how to pay for the settlement was solved by selling off NME's psychiatric division.

By March 1994, NME had sold forty-seven psychiatric facilities
for the sum of $200 million to Charter Medical Corporation,
which had, ironically, only recently settled fraud allegations of its

own concerning Charter psychiatric hospitals in Texas. Earlier in the year, 80 percent of NME's physical-rehabilitation hospital business had gone to Health-South Rehabilitation Corporation, an Alabama based company, for $350 million. A number of prospective buyers, including groups of independent operators as well as corporate chains, looked at the Southwood facility, but there were no takers until September 1994, when it was bought by a physician who promptly turned it over to a medical management company. Southwood kept on doing business during the changeover but under a different name: Bayview Psychiatric Hospital. Some of the old Southwood staff stayed on, including Flynn Davis, though he would leave a few months later. In January 1997, less than three years after the sale, a psychotic male patient who was described in the March 27, 1997, *San Diego Union-Tribune* as "burly" was accused of raping a ninety-seven-pound, "severely developmentally delayed" female patient whose room at Bayview was across the hall from the male patient's room. According to the *Union-Tribune,* the male patient pulled the twenty-one-year-old female into his room and sexually assaulted her after a brief conversation in the hallway. "That night, [the alleged rapist] sneaked into her room and raped her again, according to testimony. The woman said she told [him] to stop and tried to push him off . . . but she did not tell anyone what had happened until police arrived."

It was another Bayview patient who called the police, the day following the attacks, after he got no response from the staff when he alerted them about "inappropriate behavior." As of March 27, 1997, the alleged rapist had been ordered to stand trial on sixteen felony counts of sexual assault. As of this writing, county, state, and federal authorities are investigating Bayview, which, despite a filing for bankruptcy by its parent company, California Medical Services, continues to remain open for business.

BY THE END of June 1994, Jeffrey Barbakow had formally announced that NME would plead guilty to seven counts of

Medicare fraud and conspiracy. Additionally, NME agreed to pay the federal government the largest fine ever levied in a medical-fraud case in U.S. history: $379 million to settle all criminal charges. CHAMPUS was awarded $54 million, from which the Justice Department took 3 percent. NME also agreed to make yearly contributions to the Public Health Service and to set up a model compliance program at all of the corporation's acute-care hospitals. NME further agreed to cooperate with all government investigations of anyone involved in illegal conduct in its psychiatric division. In return, it was stated in the settlement that NME, its affiliates, and its divisions could continue to participate in Medicare, Medicaid, and CHAMPUS programs.

Barbakow's announcement paid off: NME's stock rose, closing at $15.50 per share on the New York Stock Exchange.

Hundreds of civil suits against the corporation remained, however. And among them was the case of Christy Scheck.

CHAPTER THIRTY-FOUR

BY THE END of March 1992, three weeks after the death by hanging of Christy Scheck, Bob and Merry Scheck approached Bob's attorney, Lee Selvig, about instigating a lawsuit against Southwood Psychiatric Center and its corporate owner, National Medical Enterprises.

"We knew something was very wrong by the way we were only able to contact anyone at Southwood through letters after Christy's death," Merry recalls. "We weren't able to even pick up her things from her room. It was clear to us that we were being stonewalled. We felt so strongly that this should *never* happen to any other parent, and we knew the only way we could bring it to the attention of other parents was by a lawsuit."

Selvig accepted the case and handled all the staging aspects of the suit, but it soon became clear that it was too big and too broad for one man. Selvig recommended the San Diego–based firm of Coleman & Shelstad to the Schecks.

"Actually," Merry says, "it was Lee's paralegal who recommended Michael Coleman to us, when we were doing research for the lawsuit. Mike Pritchard was doing volunteer paralegal work for Coleman & Shelstad, and he told us that Michael Coleman had been in the trenches with cases against NME for a long time. And Pritchard had already done an incredible amount of legwork, digging up information based on other cases involving NME. That information helped us immeasurably, as I'm sure our case will help others. I can't tell you how much information got pulled together for our lawsuit against NME."

MIKE PRITCHARD IS tired, but whenever he speaks about the war with National Medical Enterprises, his voice lifts and resonates, making him sound like a preacher talking Scripture. He has taken the train to Los Angeles from San Diego after several hours spent in depositions for other cases, and we are now sitting in my living room. "When the Scheck case began, I'd already been involved in the NME mess for about a year and a half, two years, maybe. We didn't know anything about NME when we took our first two NME-related cases. We didn't know that Alvarado Parkway and Southwood were owned by parent corporations. All we knew was that we had two different hospitals, and both of them were locking people up against their will."

Pritchard tells me that he himself has done time in rehab. In 1987 he signed up for treatment when it became clear that he was addicted to both alcohol and amphetamines. He was working as a title searcher at that time, but upon his release from the hospital he became a volunteer worker with the San Diego County Department of Mental Health, and he offered himself as an unsalaried part-time paralegal, researching cases of mental-health patients who had been unjustly treated.

In 1991 the firm of Coleman & Shelstad took on two cases against NME. "In both cases the patients had asked to be released. One of the cases involved a minor whose mother demanded that her fifteen-year-old son be released after he was admitted to Alvarado Parkway before being seen by a health care professional. The hospital wouldn't let him go, and this woman was willing to take her son to any other facility. She just didn't trust the people at the NME hospital." Pritchard cocks his head to one side. "You have to ask yourself this: Why would they have kept the boy? There was something inherently wrong in the situation.

"At any rate, that's what got me interested in the cases. Well, as things progressed, the litigation began to take an ugly turn. We'd send out some standard interrogations with standard queries. Stuff like, 'Who were the officers of the corporation?' And we'd get back some very nasty responses, and suddenly the whole timbre of the defense changed, and suddenly a new law firm was being brought in. We were, like, 'What the heck is this?' These were simple false-imprisonment cases, and suddenly these big heavy hitters from L.A. were being brought in. And the strong-arm tactics began."

Pritchard grins. "Well, I have a tendency toward being slightly anal-retentive, so I went down and pulled some files from the Department of Licensure. And I see that both these hospitals are owned by the same group." The grin intensifies. "So we sent out some additional queries asking what their relationship was with National Medical Enterprises. And things got even uglier."

Pritchard straightens his back and moves his head from side to side in a slow, rolling motion. "Now, remember, we still don't know anything that's going on with National Medical Enterprises. But I guess *they* thought we knew stuff and that we were trying to get on some big thing.

"Then, next up, we're contacted by an attorney from some Washington, D.C., firm who tells us *they're* suing NME, representing an insurance company." Pritchard shrugs. "And we're like, 'Big deal.' But we agree to meet with them, and they tell us there's this nationwide conspiracy." Pritchard is speaking at a fast clip now, gathering momentum as he builds his background story.

"Then this D.C. attorney hooks us up with a guy in Texas who's working with a law firm that's got about thirty or forty suits going against NME. And now I *know* that something big is going on. I mean, I start hearing about all these different places, and all the stories are basically the same, and I'm saying to myself, 'These cannot all be coincidences. This isn't just about a few bad employees, or a few greedy employers. There's something—a big something—more going on. I knew these guys at NME were vulnerable. I knew they were dirty. And I just figured if we hung in there long enough, the pressure would . . .'" He doesn't finish the sentence. He simply makes a crunching, pressing motion with both hands.

Meanwhile, Pritchard continued working as an unpaid volunteer paralegal for the firm of Coleman & Shelstad.

AFTER A SERIES of amendments, a fourth and final complaint for damages was filed by Michael S. Coleman, of Coleman & Shelstad, in the names of Merry and Robert Scheck versus Southwood Psychiatric Centers; Southwood Residential Treatment Centers; Southwood Hospital; National Medical Enterprises; NME Psychiatric Properties, Inc.; NME Psychiatric Hospitals, Inc., formerly known as Psychiatric Institutes of America; and a series of defendants including Arthur Quinn, Norman Zober, Charles Trojan, Bria Altshult, Rebecca Boyle, and unnamed "Does," 1 through 100, inclusive. The date of the filing was March 7, 1994.

The factual allegations were that "each and every defendant, and their employers and agents (whether or not named as defendants herein), embarked upon a plan and scheme to enrich themselves by artificially increasing their revenue and profits through, among other things, an insurance fraud scheme comprised of creative marketing, admissions, retention, treatment, accounting and other practices of the NME Institutions, including defendants SOUTHWOOD, SOUTHWOOD RTC, SOUTHWOOD HOSPITAL, NME, PIA and NME PROPERTIES."

There followed a list of further, more explicit allegations, including artificial increase of revenue and profits, insurance fraud, "crafted diagnoses to meet patients' insurance coverage," parents prohibited from being involved in their children's treatment, fostering an environment wherein false allegations of abuse and molest could be raised "so that the children would be reported to Child Protective Services and be held for additional treatment," failure to properly train staff, the use of unlicensed, unqualified staff in capacities for which licensed staff was required by regulation, the decrease of patient-staff ratios to unsafe levels, and bounties awarded as incentives to get and keep patients longer than medically warranted.

Next came nineteen separately named causes of action. This list included: *Fraud and Deceit/Conspiracy* (related to the February 1991 survey performed at Southwood by Health Management

Strategies (HMS) of CHAMPUS and the "serious deficiencies" found, which Southwood management "falsely promised to correct"). These deficiencies, which included overcrowding and inadequate staffing, were not corrected at the time of Christy Scheck's hospitalization at Southwood. This action was further related to the unfitness of Southwood employees who caused Christy's emotional condition to worsen, caused the relationship with her parents to worsen, caused Christy to make false allegations of physical abuse against her parents and sexual abuse against her father, and caused Christy's wrongful death by ignoring her pleas for help, by being unable to "properly or timely respond to Christy's suicide attempt, including, but not limited to, 1) the removing or even loosening of the sash Christy used to hang herself, and 2) the initiation and administration of CPR and other emergency procedures."

There was *Breach of Contract,* which related to the failure of the defendants to comply with CHAMPUS standards after the HMS survey, by their failure to remedy the deficiencies noted, thus resulting in a failure to deliver the promised medical services. Mentioned in the list were the cost-cutting measures "that directly affected the quality of patient care and safety" and "practices to increase lengths of stay without regard to clinical need."

Another cause listed was "that in order to maximize its profit defendant SOUTHWOOD RTC inappropriately mixed children and adolescents who were victims of abuse and/or molest with children and adolescents who were not victims of abuse and molest, such as CHRISTY SCHECK, which was therapeutically harmful to the children and adolescents who were not victims of abuse and/or molest."

And "that, for the sole reason of maximizing its profits, and without regard to the harmful effects to its patients, defendant SOUTHWOOD RTC actively recruited juvenile offenders from outside of the state of California with histories of gang and drug involvement, violence and sexual offenses, and placed them with the general population, including CHRISTY, and that exposure to juvenile offenders could and did lead children, including CHRISTY, to copy, adopt and embellish the stories and histories of these juvenile offenders."

There was *Negligent Infliction of Emotional Distress* and *Intentional Infliction of Emotional Distress.*

There was *Premises Liability,* in which "the [defendants and their employees and agents] knew or in the exercise of reasonable care should have known that the lack of adequate supervision, in view of the physical structure of the premises, constituted a dangerous condition and unreasonable risk of harm of which plaintiffs . . . were at all times herein mentioned unaware . . . all of which created a situation in which CHRISTY SCHECK was able to successfully attempt suicide."

There was *Medical Malpractice,* in which "the defendants . . . so negligently failed to exercise the proper degree of knowledge and skill in examining, diagnosing, treating, and caring for CHRISTY SCHECK that they negligently caused her to suffer additional emotional problems, failed to prevent her from attempting suicide, failed to revive her after she made a suicide attempt, and caused the plaintiffs to suffer the injuries and damages previously alleged in this complaint."

And there was *Wrongful Death,* in which "the defendants . . . had knowledge or notice from decedent's prior attempts and/or threats to commit suicide that decedent was likely to harm herself unless preclusive measures were taken, [however,] defendants, and each of them, and their employees and agents, negligently and carelessly failed to attend and supervise decedent while she was under their care and control [and] as a proximate result of this negligence, on March 6, 1992, decedent hanged herself while inside of defendant SOUTHWOOD RTC, and eventually died."

Shortly after the suit was filed, Coleman & Shelstad would bring in Rick Seltzer and Christopher Cody, of the Oakland law firm Seltzer & Cody, as part of the legal team representing Bob and Merry Scheck. Seltzer handled all motions and negotiations pertaining to the suit, and Cody took charge of all discoveries and depositions as they prepared for trial. Southwood Psychiatric Centers, Southwood Residential Treatment Centers, and Southwood Hospital were represented by Craig Dummit of Dummit, Faber & Brown, a Los Angeles firm, and Scott D. Buchholz of the San Diego branch of Dummit, Faber & Brown. National Medical Enterprises and NME Psychiatric Hospitals, Inc., were represented by Robert H. Fairbank of Gibson, Dunn & Crutcher, an international law firm.

CHAPTER THIRTY-FIVE

ON MARCH 23, 1994, nearly two weeks after the filing of their suit against NME and Southwood Psychiatric Center, Bob and Merry Scheck appeared on a syndicated television show called *The Front Page.*

The segment opened with a home video of Christy, her parents, and Molly seated around a birthday cake ablaze with candles. The next shot was a sweeping view of verdant grounds, a new, three-story building, and a sign proclaiming that this was Southwood Hospital and Residential Treatment Center. The segment correspondent, Tony Harris, was heard, in voice-over, detailing some of the violations reported by CHAMPUS/HMS nine months before Christy Scheck's admittance into Southwood. Among the violations was the report of "unlicensed personnel conducting group-therapy sessions."

Next on camera was a man whose features were obscured by shadows and whose voice had been electronically altered. He was asked, by Tony Harris, how it was possible for the Southwood management to okay the use of unlicensed counselors. The faceless man, who had been introduced as a former Southwood employee, replied: "Licensed people cost more. Profits came first in terms of priorities."

Two other families (besides the Schecks) allowed themselves to be interviewed for the show. The first case was that of a young woman who, in 1992, had taken her four-year-old daughter to an NME facility in Shenandoah, Texas, to be checked for suspected sexual abuse. The woman's husband was at sea with the Navy at the time, so CHAMPUS covered all medical costs.

The young mother was persuaded by NME staff workers to voluntarily check herself into the hospital to "help her child adjust to treatment." However, once they were both admitted, the woman was kept from seeing her daughter. On the third day, when the woman tried to check herself out of treatment, she was told that "she wasn't ready." Her next move was to try to stop the insurance payments to the hospital; for this she was put into a straightjacket, wheeled into Isolation, and sedated. It was only after the young woman contacted the local police that she and her daughter were released. The bill for eight days came to $8,000. It was sent to CHAMPUS.

The next case involved a high school boy from San Diego who had written an antiwar poem at the time of the Gulf War. After reading the poem, the boy's school counselor sent a brochure from NME's Alvarado Parkway Hospital to the boy's mother. Subsequently, a barrage of telephone calls to the boy's home from the hospital repeated the same message: "Your son is suicidal." The boy was finally sent to the counselor's office, where he was interviewed by an Alvarado Parkway caseworker, deemed to be "a danger to himself" (although he had never mentioned any thoughts of suicide), and committed to Alvarado Parkway Hospital for seventy-two hours. The boy's mother begged for her son's release and promised to take him to the family physician, whom she trusted. She was told, by Alvarado Parkway staff workers, that the hospital had the legal right to hold her son. He was released only after the hospital discovered that an intake worker had incorrectly listed the boy as a CHAMPUS beneficiary.

One of the program's most shocking moments was the showing of a videotape of a staff meeting at an NME facility in Indianapolis that was being used as evidence in another civil suit. Approximately eight people are seated around a conference table. A bearded man says, "We've got five empty beds. What're you going to do?"

The camera pans to another man, seated opposite the bearded man, who says, "Well, we're gonna fill them."

The camera moves jerkily around the table. The bearded man

speaks again. "Make sure the docs aren't discharging prematurely. Tell 'em to guard the door.

"All right. Let's go through marketing facilities."

The segment's most disturbing image was a still photograph of Christy Scheck's lifeless body with the red mark of the sash with which she had hanged herself showing lividly against the whiteness of her throat.

The disguised former Southwood employee made another appearance, talking about the insufficient staffing and the lack of "safe units" at that facility. Then a post-FBI-raid press conference was shown in which Jeffrey Barbakow stressed "the company's emphasis on the past as the past" and made mention of NME's agreement to "a settlement of $265 million."

Finally, NME cofounder Richard Eamer appeared. He had been tracked down to the driveway of his home after he denied access for an interview, and he is shown at the wheel of his car, reluctantly answering Tony Harris's queries. Eamer is not a bad-looking man: He is in his early sixties, with silvery hair and a clipped mustache that would have been described, in an earlier era, as dapper. His slightly protuberant eyes were veiled behind the lenses of wire-rimmed aviator glasses. Clearly disconcerted at having been caught on camera, he stammered slightly as he spoke. He said that to his knowledge he was not under current investigation by the Justice Department but that there were "several people in Psychiatric who were determined to enhance profits, primarily in marketing rather than patient care." Eamer said he thought "the care was good."

Harris then asked Eamer if it was the people subordinate to him who were responsible for the kind of fraud that had been reported as rampant at NME.

"I was not aware of what was going on. My philosophy has always been 'patient care first and profits would follow.' " The stammer increased. "I'm sorry about what happened. It changed my life all around, changed a lot of people's lives around. We run a won-

derful company—I-I had no knowledge—it was not my philosophy . . ."

Harris's final question was whether Eamer felt that he had been
set up by the people under him.

"I don't know if I was set up. But the company was used."

The segment ended with a short disclaimer read by the show's
host, Ron Reagan: "'NME denies any wrongdoing toward the
Schecks and others, and intends to fight their losses in court. NME
has announced plans to sell all its psychiatric hospitals, and is also
negotiating with the federal government to head off possible
criminal charges involving patient care.'"

CHAPTER THIRTY-SIX

WITHIN THREE WEEKS of the Schecks' appearance on *The Front Page,* a letter arrived at their home. It had been written in a scrawling hand on a single sheet of white copy paper. It read:

To Bob: I saw you on TV and everyone is sorry about your daughter. If this case goes to court, details of her medical records will come out, and details of your relationship with her will come out. The lawyers only want money—settle now and save your family more heartache.

The letter was unsigned, and the envelope bore an out-of-state postmark: Little Rock, Arkansas. Merry Scheck placed the letter and the envelope in a plastic bag and took it to the law offices of Coleman & Shelstad. When Coleman's paralegal, Mike Pritchard, saw the postmark, he confirmed Merry's suspicion that interstate threat mail was a federal offense.

The next move was to call the FBI.

On the same day, Alan Sidell received a similar letter, bearing the same hurried handwriting and the same postmark and mailed the same day: April 11, 1994. But the message for Sidell was even more ominous:

Does sitting in the shadows on TV telling lies make you feel like a man? Lowlifes like you get only what you deserve. You would be wise to leave San Diego, otherwise, watch your back. Your lies cause people to do things that they ordinarily wouldn't do. The value of your life decreases every day. We have your address, so expect company one dark night when you least expect it. Your life is worthless now. You're a piece of shit that is waiting to get stomped.

REMEMBER—YOU WERE WARNED ASSHOLE!

Sidell, who was considering a suit (since dropped) against NME after his dismissal from Southwood, called Mike Pritchard, who gave him the same advice he had given to Bob and Merry Scheck: Call the FBI.

Alan Sidell had spoken with FBI agent Keith Moses on two previous occasions related to the ongoing federal investigation of NME, but the contents of the anonymous letter made him nervous. After handing over the letter and envelope to Moses, Sidell pulled up stakes and relocated to the East Coast.

CHAPTER THIRTY-SEVEN

THE PRETRIAL DEPOSITIONS in the Scheck suit continued. Christy Scheck's Southwood psychiatrist, Arthur Quinn, was deposed on February 10, 1994. He offered up a virtual litany of ignorance and memory loss in response to Christopher Cody's questions. Quinn recalled that Christy had been transferred to the Southwood Residential Treatment Center on December 13, 1991, at his suggestion. He had no explanation, however, as to why the records produced by his office showed no billing for sessions with Christy after January 6, 1992.

He was equally lacking in any knowledge of the qualifications, educational requirements, experience, or training of any staff member employed on the early-adolescent unit of the Southwood RTC. He claimed not to know whether the nurses or the mental-health counselors were responsible for contact with the RTC patients in matters regarding emotional issues, and he said that he was unaware of how many nurses or mental-health counselors were on staff on any typical day during the time Christy was a patient at Southwood. Quinn denied having any knowledge that student interns were employed as mental-health counselors in the early-adolescent unit of the RTC.

Dr. Quinn further stated that he did not maintain an office at Southwood, that his visits to the residential treatment center added up to approximately eight to ten hours a week, and that this time frame incorporated visits with patients on all three units of the RTC, conversations with nursing staff and mental-health counselors, and sitting in on group meetings. Quinn was unable to recall, however, if any of those group meetings dealt with sexual-molestation issues.

When questioned about his treatment of Christy Scheck, Quinn said that he believed his approach could be described as "supportive psychotherapy, dealing with here-and-now issues." He added that he "was not doing major unearthing of skeletons in the closet."

Regarding the sexual-molestation charges that Christy had leveled against her father, Quinn revealed that he had formed an impression that some of Christy's counselors assumed that the alleged conduct had occurred. But he quickly added that he did not know if anybody at Southwood "ever said they were completely convinced that a sexual molestation had taken place." He himself was not convinced that such an act had ever occurred.

The man in whose professional hands Christy Scheck's life had been placed spoke at some length about his long experience at Southwood Psychiatric Center as well as other residential treatment centers over the years. Yet he pleaded ignorance to such concerns as the policies and procedures relative to suicide precautions at Southwood, didn't know if there was any procedure for a licensed nurse to be brought in to observe patients who exhibited suicidal tendencies, and didn't know if Bob and Merry Scheck had ever been notified about their daughter's self-destructive threats. Quinn said that he had not been contacted by any staff member after an exhibition of such tendencies by Christy Scheck, and upon further questioning, he admitted that he had never made any requests that he be contacted in an instance of suicidal behavior.

When asked if Christy had been delusional, if she had been influenced by hallucinations, Quinn stated that there was no evidence of "any active hallucinations." When presented with a portion of Christy's hospital records that clearly stated that "behavior is considerably influenced by delusions or hallucinations," Quinn countered by saying that "someone in medical records must have added that [notation] as a part of the diagnosis."

If Arthur Quinn accompanied his depositional responses with a shrug, Charles Trojan served up his answers with a sneer. Trojan was deposed on May 18, 1994, only days after his resignation from NME's Baywood Hospital in Texas. According to paralegal Mike Pritchard, who attended as part of the plaintiff's team, Trojan played small word games. At one point, when Scheck family attorney Christopher Cody asked a question about the staff at Southwood, Trojan asked what Cody meant by "staff." When asked about directives, Trojan requested a definition of that word. Pritchard claims he even saw a look of annoyance pass over the face of Trojan's attorney. And, at some point in the deposition, Trojan jabbed his finger across the table at Pritchard, yelling about a perceived expression on Pritchard's face.

Pritchard now recalls, "That was the moment I knew Southwood was everything we had ever heard about it."

The tough stuff began when Cody took Trojan through the so-called corrective-action plan that Trojan had prepared in response to the CHAMPUS/HMS criticisms (and potential decertification) of Southwood Residential Treatment Center in February 1991. Cody then produced a declaration Trojan had prepared, under penalty of perjury, in April 1992, after the death of Christy Scheck and in response to the second CHAMPUS survey. When confronted with the untruths contained in his declaration, Trojan pleaded an all-consuming ignorance of the facts except to say that they had been provided to him by Nadine Peck, the associate administrator of the RTC, and other personnel, both clinical and administrative. Trojan's attorney, Craig Dummit, raised continual objections regarding the relevance of Cody's questions as they pertained to Christy Scheck. Cody's reply was that Christy Scheck had, in fact, attended molestation group-therapy sessions led by interns, and that specific promises had been made, by Southwood, that group therapy would *not* be led by interns, but that those promises had been broken. Cody continued: "Did you have any knowledge at any time before you left Southwood that psychiatrists were signing treatment-team meeting notes even though they weren't attending treatment-team meetings?"

Trojan admitted to having heard about this misbehavior, but he claimed that the responsibility to correct it belonged not with him but with the medical director. Trojan failed to remember from whom he had heard about psychiatrists dodging meetings for which they signed off later, nor could he recall if he had heard about it before the death of Christy Scheck. He claimed to have no knowledge of whether this situation was remedied, and he forgot that according to the HMS survey of February 1991, a recommendation had been made that Southwood Psychiatric Center follow a policy stipulating that unless psychiatrists attended treatment-team meetings, they would not be allowed or permitted to attend patients.

Cody then questioned Trojan about a former Southwood employee who had been the director of psychology at the RTC until 1991, when his position was eliminated. According to Trojan, this man's duties had been to "provide supervision to the psych interns [and] run groups." Cody asked why the position had been eliminated.

"Because of cost reduction."

Was that part of the cost-reduction program?

"That's what I just said."

When Cody pressed, trying to pin Trojan down as to whether this was the specific cost-reduction program that had been implemented by PIA, Trojan waffled, saying that he didn't remember "a specific cost-reduction program."

When asked who, if anyone, assumed the duties of director of psychology at the residential treatment center, Trojan wasn't sure. He named two members of the hospital staff and the director of psychology at the hospital.

Were there any complaints from this person, whose duties were at the hospital, about being overextended by assuming similar duties and responsibilities at the RTC?

Again Trojan suffered memory loss.

There were endless wrangles between opposing counsel: about one-on-ones, and whether or not Charles Trojan recalled expressing a view that they needed to be closely monitored due to the associated costs; about whether or not the RTC director had tried to dissuade Trojan from admitting certain patients with acuity levels so high as to create a risk for both other patients and staff; about previous testimony that Christy Scheck had been treated along with known molesters; about a 1991 corporate memo from Bill Vickers, regional administrator and Trojan's immediate supervisor, that included an order to reduce all Southwood full-time and part-time employees to 75 percent of staffing and to increase the per-diem staff to 25 percent. The memo also stated that "the corporate goal was to have 60 percent of our staff being part-time/-full-time, and 40 percent of them being per-diem."

Charles Trojan, former CEO, the man about whom there was a legend concerning Christmas Eve firings, simply could not remember whether or not this recommendation had been implemented during 1991. It was a puzzling lack of recall, considering that Bill Vickers positioned himself in front of a huge blowup of a photograph of Charles Trojan at the Spring Administrators Conference on April 30, 1991, and praised Trojan for decreasing staffing ratios (among other things) and for bringing Southwood from a corporate loss of $350,000 a month to a monthly corporate contribution of $400,000.

Christopher Cody's final series of questions concerned an order given by Trojan in March 1992 that all medical charts related to patients at the RTC be "audited" to comply with HMS recommendations. Trojan couldn't seem to remember whether that order was given before or after the death of Christy Scheck. According to Trojan's testimony at his deposition on May 18, 1994, in Houston, he never reviewed Christy Scheck's chart, had no knowledge of the identity of her primary counselors, and didn't know who her therapists had been.

The single most emphatic response delivered by Charles Trojan during the deposition was in reply to whether or not he had any plans to return to California in the summer of 1994: "Never again in my life."

He was mistaken.

CHAPTER THIRTY-EIGHT

MIKE PRITCHARD LIKES to talk law, particularly as it applied in the suits against NME.

"There was a gentleman by the name of James Keppler," he recalls, "who was the comptroller at Southwood. Well, Keppler had testified under oath in one of our other suits against NME, and the whole time he was being deposed, I kept getting the strongest feeling that this guy was very uncomfortable with what was going on. I had the sense that he wanted to tell the truth, but that we just weren't asking the right questions in the right way." The intensity of Pritchard's tone moves up a notch. "I could almost hear his thoughts: *Ask better questions.*

"But we didn't know very much at this point, and every time we asked a question, the NME attorneys would object, and you could see that this guy, Keppler, wanted to answer more. You could see it physically, by his body English." Pritchard shakes his head. "But he could only respond to the questions that we asked. Nothing more.

"Well, when we got to the Scheck case, I spoke to Rick Seltzer about Jim Keppler, and Rick thought about it for a second, then told me to give Keppler a call. We made an appointment for him to fly up to Oakland and meet with Rick. Then, about an hour or so before he was to arrive, a call comes into the office. Mr. Keppler's sorry, but he has to cancel.

"Well, I called him immediately. And he told me that he had been told not to talk to us, and when I asked him who it was that told him, there was a long silence at the other end of the line. Then, in a whisper, Keppler told me that the NME attorneys said that if he spoke with us, they would not represent him in any further proceedings."

At this point, Pritchard backtracks. He is a precise man, and he wants to underline the timing. "Now, remember, at this time the FBI raids had already taken place. And, as Southwood's comptroller, Jim Keppler was very likely facing some legal problems. That was quite an effective hammer over his head.

"Well, we finally got him to come in and make his deposition anyway, and when we asked him about the cancellation of our first meeting, and his remark that the NME attorney told him not to talk to us, he shook his head. 'No. I never said that.' "

Pritchard smiles. "All of us knew he was lying. Because I'd put him on the speakerphone when I called him. Rick Seltzer heard the entire conversation. So now Rick begins to press: 'Who was it told you it wasn't in your best interests to meet with us, Mr. Keppler?'

"And finally, Keppler identified Michael Hunn, the former assistant administrator at Southwood Psychiatric at the time of the 1991 HMS/CHAMPUS survey. In fact, Hunn was one of the people who signed off on the infamous corrective-action plan. He was also slated to be a material witness in the Scheck case, even though he was gone from Southwood by the time Christy Scheck was admitted. Hunn had been promoted to NME's Los Altos Hospital in Long Beach. As administrator.

"We set up a deposition with Hunn, and Dummit, Faber & Brown objected. We asked if they were representing Mr. Hunn, and they said no, they had just found him and were going to speak with him themselves.

"Then, all of a sudden, they *are* representing him. Well, we went back and forth with that one for a while. Until the judge issued an order that either Mr. Hunn or his deposition be produced."

Finally a call was made to Rick Seltzer's office. It came in on a Sunday, and the message left on the answering machine was that

Dummit, Faber & Brown had been dismissed by Michael Hunn, making it impossible for the law firm to guarantee that Mr. Hunn would show up for his deposition the following morning.

"Michael Hunn," Pritchard continues, "who was also part of NME's federal plea agreement because he had been paying out over three hundred thousand dollars a year to physicians for referrals to Los Altos, was never deposed, never even located for the Scheck case. Even though he was under a court order to appear at the trial. He remained simply unfindable."

The firm of Seltzer & Cody made a strategic move to drop Southwood Hospital and Dr. Arthur Quinn from the Scheck lawsuit. Their reasoning was that both the hospital and Quinn would be covered under the Medical Insurance Compensation Reform Act (MICRA), enacted in 1975. MICRA caps medical damages to $250,000 and limits the amount of money that the consumer can recover for injuries.

But the Southwood Residential Treatment Center was not a medical facility. It was classified not as a health care provider, but as a group home. According to Pritchard, the Southwood RTC could have been licensed as a health care provider "if they had been willing to part with the hundred-and-twenty-five-dollar licensing fee."

Pritchard's gut instinct was to lean in on a premises-liability strategy. "See, I had gotten the idea that if you, as an RTC, have been written up for an unsafe condition at your facility, and if you've filed a corrective-action plan, and if, a year later, the inspectors come again and you still haven't fixed anything—in fact, conditions have gotten worse—and now, a couple of weeks later, some injury occurs, to me, this is premises liability. Well, everybody at the firm kept telling me no, that wouldn't fly. But Rick Seltzer kind of liked it, and after a lot of back-and-forth, we kept it.

"But first we had to get rid of all the medical actions. So, little by little, we dropped them until, by May of '92, we had gotten rid of the hospital and Quinn, and we were suing the RTC."

Pritchard grins all over his face. "It turned out to be a winning strategy. Rick said, 'This is the way we're going to get into their backyard.'

"But, at first, we lost the motion. So Rick got up in court and argued, and he got the judge to give him a week to file a supplemental brief as to why the premises liability is not covered under MICRA. A week later, the judge read the brief, looked up at Rick, and said, 'Mr. Seltzer, you are absolutely right.'

"That was the turning point. The defense kept whittling away, which is what the best defense counsel does, and we just kept letting them think they had us befuddled, kept letting them think they were winning, that this was going to wind up as a two-hundred-fifty-thousand-dollar medical-malpractice case. We simply held back and held back, and then we drove home the premises liability." Pritchard doesn't even try to keep the note of triumph from his tone. "And we got 'em."

His expression sobers. "I don't think there's another attorney around who would have listened to some low-grade paralegal's passionate argument for premises liability. But it made common sense to me. And on some level I have always believed that common sense must prevail over special-interest law."

CHAPTER THIRTY-NINE

THE CASE OF *Scheck* v. *Southwood* never made it to a courtroom.

The week before the trial was to begin, in July 1994, Bob and Merry Scheck were flown to Washington to testify before a House Judiciary subcommittee on crime as it relates to health care fraud.

Merry recalls, "We flew back on Thursday to find that the judge assigned to our case would not be able to preside over the trial because she had been appointed to the appellate court. A new judge was assigned, which meant delays while records and transcripts were forwarded. The other side knew we wouldn't be going to trial that coming Friday, because of the change in judges, and they had already made a settlement offer, which we refused. Then somebody suggested mediation."

The Schecks, with attorneys from both sides, met with an arbitrator who was a retired judge. Within days, Southwood came up with an acceptable offer.

"And, more importantly," Merry says, "they accepted responsibility for Christy's death."

Bob Scheck breaks in. "They offered that. We didn't press it. The arbitrator listened to both sides of the case, and he let the lawyers know the ballpark figure the case should be in. So they went back and hammered everything out, including the restrictions imposed on us, as the plaintiffs. Things we can't discuss, like the dollar figure of the settlement, and not going off on a crusade against other psychiatric hospitals. What we considered minor things, easily agreed to."

NME's admission of corporate responsibility was described as "extraordinary" by David R. Olmos, who covered the case for the *Los Angeles Times:* "It was the first admission of responsibility in any of the nearly 150 lawsuits alleging physical mistreatment and abuse of patients that NME has faced since the late 1980's."

In June 1996, Rick Seltzer was willing to discuss the case he would have brought to trial. "Parents like the Schecks are in such a vulnerable position when they need to turn over their child for someone else to take care of, and this corporation was set up to make as much profit as it could from that scenario. There was a huge push from the upper levels of this company to reduce expenses, including the hiring of qualified medical care. While they had employees [at Southwood] who were well intentioned, the patients were shortchanged on the kind of experienced staff that Christy Scheck needed."

Paralegal Mike Pritchard agrees with Seltzer's assessment and has adamantly maintained that there was a great disparity in attitude between the corporate officers at NME and the frontline staff at the facilities.

Seltzer continues, "What I believe happened is that Christy became involved in a game of one-upmanship with her peer group and created this completely false fantasy about an abusive life she had undergone at home. The well-meaning but inexperienced staff not only seemed to believe her, they encouraged her to continue her creation in ever more elaborate and ghastly acts. They were convinced that Christy's problems could only have stemmed from abuse suffered at her parents' hands. They, and her support group, convinced Christy this had to be the case. And they created a kind of saving-face for Christy by which all her problems had to have stemmed from abuse that would have screwed anyone up.

"There were so many inconsistencies in Christy's stories, so many obvious exaggerations and falsities, that experienced professionals would have cut through everything and tried to redirect her to the truth.

"The truth was there had been no abuse by either of Christy Scheck's parents. When Christy's fantasies started having real-life consequences, and there was going to be a hearing, and whether or not her sister could continue to live at home, Christy knew, within herself, that what she had done was wrong. That it was a lie. But that lie was the entire basis for the 'love' and support she was getting at Southwood. And, knowing that the whole thing was going to come to issue in the real world, in that hearing, it became something Christy couldn't face.

"This was the case I was going to take to court. I guess NME didn't like it."

CHAPTER FORTY

DECEMBER 13, 1994. Houston, Texas. Charles Trojan was just sitting down to breakfast with his wife and six-year-old son when the doorbell sounded. Trojan said he'd get it.

Three people were waiting to step into the entryway of the house: two FBI agents and an agent from Defense Criminal Investigation Services (DCIS). Charles Trojan was about to be arrested as the alleged author of the two anonymous letters sent, eight months earlier, from Arkansas, to Bob and Merry Scheck and to Alan Sidell.

Trojan's rights were read to him, and then he was handcuffed and taken into custody. He appeared before U.S. magistrate John Froeschner of the South District of Texas for arraignment, and he was charged with mailing threatening material, aiding and abetting, and witness tampering. His bail was set at $250,000. It was, coincidentally, his forty-first birthday.

CHARLES TROJAN LOOKS pretty much the way I expected him to when I see him at his trial in San Diego a month after his arrest. He is narrowly built, with rather rabbity features framed by ginger-colored, thinning hair and a carefully trimmed beard. He wears a blue suit, a power tie. His shoes could use a shine. He has arrived at the courthouse with his attorney, a sleekly dressed man with silvery hair and the look of someone who watches his weight.

The trial is being conducted in a handsomely paneled courtroom in the Federal Building. There are seven men and five women on the jury; they seem too casually dressed for the severe elegance of the room.

Prosecuting attorney Tom MacNamara begins his opening

statement: "This is a case about threats of violence and attempted extortion." MacNamara tells the jury about the letters sent to the Schecks and to Alan Sidell, and he talks about the ongoing investigation of Southwood by the federal government as well as the lawsuit brought by the Schecks. He informs the jurors of the seventeen separate search warrants executed on Southwood and other PIA hospitals. Then he describes the *Front Page* episode featuring the Schecks. "The show was a watershed for the defendant. It is what made him write those letters."

Huge blowups of the two letters are placed on easels facing the jurors, and MacNamara gives them a moment to finish reading. Then he continues: "The defendant now admits he wrote and mailed those letters. He mailed them away from his home in Texas while he was still an employee of PIA and NME so that suspicion would not fall on him. He knew there was a federal investigation of those companies. That investigation is still ongoing."

MacNamara takes his seat at the prosecuting counsel's table, and defense attorney Peter C. Hughes gets to his feet. He greets the judge and jury, then launches into his opening statement: "I would like you to focus on the contents of these letters. I would like you to focus on what else is involved in this case. And keep in mind what *your* initial interpretation of these two letters is, without the interpretation given to you by the government. What was Charles Trojan's intent? What was his state of mind? Please keep an open mind."

Now the parade of government witnesses takes the stand; Carol Lam, from the U.S. Attorney's office, asks the questions.

The first witness is Keith Moses, the FBI case agent in the investigation of NME and the search-warrants executive in the August raids on Southwood. Moses states that he was aware of the overbilling and maximizing in order to exhaust patients' insurance at Southwood, and he tells the jury that he interviewed Alan Sidell on two previous occasions concerning the Southwood facility.

Now the courtroom lights are dimmed and a large-screen television set is positioned in front of the jury box. The March 23, 1994, episode of *The Front Page,* videotaped by the FBI, is about to be shown. Before it begins the judge leans over to speak to the jurors: "What you will see is hearsay. No one was under oath."

I watch Charles Trojan as the tape unreels. He is alone at the defense counsel's table; his lawyer has taken a seat next to the jury box, on the other side of the courtroom. Trojan stares straight ahead, tapping out a jittery rhythm on the tabletop with the pads of his fingers. He cannot see the TV screen; he can only hear what the Schecks and Alan Sidell are saying. He hears the voices at the staff meeting of another NME facility. He coughs once; it is a muffled, nervous little sound. He stops tapping and rests his chin on the palm of one hand. He rubs his beard again and again. His face is completely devoid of expression.

Once the tape has finished, MacNamara has a few more questions for Agent Moses. Moses states that the federal investigation of Trojan and the Southwood facility remains ongoing and reads the stipulation that "Defendant Charles Trojan has admitted to writing and sending the letters while he was 'on his way to a turkey shoot in Arkansas.' "

Merry and Bob Scheck are deposed separately. Merry's voice becomes shaky only when she identifies the Trojan letter sent to her home. Bob Scheck says, in response to Lam's query about his reaction to the letter, that he felt "basically betrayed that someone would use what had been part of our daughter's treatment as a threat."

Alan Sidell is the next prosecution witness. He describes his work as a marketing executive at Southwood and identifies Charles Trojan as the defendant. He admits to his arrest for possession and sale of marijuana in 1993, and he identifies himself as the disguised person on *The Front Page.* When Lam asks Sidell to describe his reaction to the letter he received, he says he "took it very seriously" and that after speaking with Michael Pritchard he called the FBI and shortly thereafter relocated out of town.

"As a direct result of the letter?"

"Yes."

During the defense examination Sidell admits to being "armed while selling marijuana," denies any contact with the FBI after the two interviews already mentioned and the discussion of the letter from Charles Trojan. When Hughes asks Sidell if he knows another Southwood employee, a man named George Scolari, Sidell answers in the affirmative. He admits to having had lunch with Scolari after being fired from Southwood.

"During that lunch did you say, 'If it's the last thing I do, I'm going to get Charles Trojan'?"

"No, sir."

The government's case ends; the first defense witness is George Scolari. He identifies himself as a former Southwood employee and states that he left that facility in March 1993. When asked about the lunch with Alan Sidell and if Sidell had made any threats against Charles Trojan during the meal, Scolari stated that Sidell had said "he wasn't going to stop until he saw 'that man' behind bars." Scolari identifies "that man" as Charles Trojan.

Carol Lam gets to her feet. Scolari clears his throat softly; he is in his early to mid-thirties, and he is wearing a long-sleeved shirt and tie. Lam asks if Scolari said anything during the lunch with Alan Sidell. No. She asks if it was a one-sided conversation. Yes.

"Didn't Mr. Sidell ask if you would like to speak to the FBI during that lunch?"

"I think so. I don't remember a lot of things."

"Were you aware if other employees at Southwood were being interviewed?"

"I don't remember."

Scolari cannot recall if he told Charles Trojan what Sidell had said during the lunch, or if he told anyone at Southwood, including his immediate supervisor, that Alan Sidell had asked if Scolari wanted to speak to the FBI in reference to the investigation.

"Didn't you say that earlier?"

"I don't remember the whole lunch. I may have."

Now it is Charles Trojan's turn to take the stand in his own defense.

After a series of career-related questions and answers, Peter Hughes gets down to basics, asking why Trojan had requested a transfer from Southwood to Baywood Hospital in Texas.

"I left because we had to lay off over one hundred people because of media attention after Christy Scheck's death. I couldn't take it anymore. I was used to working *with* people. Now I was laying them off."

Trojan states that he had known of the government's investigation of NME facilities. "I heard of some problems in Texas, spreading through the system. I also heard that previous employees were talking to the FBI. When Baywood was sold, I quit."

Did Trojan see *The Front Page* when it was first broadcast?

"Yes." He explains that he was in the family room at his home in Houston, and he "received calls from a couple of employees at Southwood who were concerned about the negative media and people losing their jobs."

"Did you write two letters after the show?"

"Yes, I did."

Trojan testifies that the first letter was written to Alan Sidell but that he made no effort to disguise his handwriting. Nor, he stated, was he worried about the presence of fingerprints.

Hughes then asks why Trojan referred to details of Christy Scheck's medical records in his letter to her parents.

"Well, if the case went to court, her records would have to be brought out. Christy's counselors would be forced to testify in open court. The media would print things that should be confidential."

"Did you intend, by your letter, that you would go to the media?"

"Absolutely not."

"Were you at financial risk by the lawsuit?"

"Not really. I was listed, but we felt they were going after the company's deep pockets."

Trojan goes on to testify that the sight of Alan Sidell on television so angered him that he wrote the first letter. "I've never done anything like that," he explains. "It's the stupidest thing I've ever done, but I was so . . . mad." His voice quivers in what might be considered true outrage. He rips into Sidell for "counseling kids about drugs, then selling drugs at night.

"This is the stupidest thing I've ever done. I wrote the letters that night, but I didn't mail them until a month later. I tried to talk myself into throwing them away, but I was so mad. About Sidell. About the effects on the Southwood employees. I stuck the letters in my hunting gear, hoping I'd throw them away."

Hughes asks if Trojan mailed the letters from Houston.

"Not really."

Why were they mailed from Arkansas?

Trojan uncrosses his legs, crosses them again. "Well, I stopped for a hunting license and . . . I dropped them in the mail."

"Did you hope to impede the investigation?"

"*Absolutely* not."

It is now the prosecution's turn at bat. Carol Lam stands and moves around the counsel's table to face Charles Trojan.

"Why didn't you sign the letters, Mr. Trojan?"

"I didn't want to be caught."

"Where did you get Mr. and Mrs. Scheck's address?"

"I don't remember."

Trojan does say he remembers that the letters stayed in his hunting gear for one month before he mailed them. And he admits that even though writing the letters was "stupid," he did not call either Alan Sidell or the Schecks to tell them that he had written them.

"Have you sent any other unsigned letters, Mr. Trojan?"

Trojan sits up straight in the witness box. "Never." He snaps out the word.

"Was your letter to the Schecks sent to warn them of private details coming out? To warn them to settle?"

"They weren't realizing what could happen."

"So you were worried about them?"

"My concern was continued negative publicity." Then, in after-thought, "I was sorry about Christy."

"Do you usually not sign your letters?"

"No." Trojan is silent for a long moment. "That letter would never have been sent if I wasn't angry about Sidell."

Carol Lam has no further questions.

Peter Hughes's closing statement to the jury is an appeal to their collective common sense. He underlines his contention that the Scheck letter simply conveyed a factor that "they may not have been aware of, the thrust of which was 'no more confidentiality' and 'media frenzy.' He refers to Lam's question about why the letter wasn't signed. "That doesn't apply here. This letter is *only* critical of the lawyers. Common sense tells you, if a person is writing to someone and trashing their lawyer, they're not going to sign their name to it."

Hughes points to the blowup of the Scheck letter as he speaks. Trojan seems incapable of keeping his hands away from his beard: scratching, stroking, and rubbing it with stiffened fingers. "The testimony of Charles Trojan, and the content of the letter only show that he was *informing* the Schecks."

The closeup of the Sidell letter goes up again. Hughes points to the statement "You would be wise to leave San Diego."

"What's in San Diego and nowhere else? Southwood. But the FBI is *everywhere.*"

Hughes describes the "thrust" of the Sidell letter: "You trashed Southwood." He has been using a pointer. Now he places it on the counsel's table and faces the jurors. "Charles Trojan had to lay off fifty to one hundred people after the death of Christy Scheck." He turns to look at Trojan, turns back to face the jurors. "And he couldn't take it. He *had* to ask for a transfer." Now Hughes's tone changes. "Look at Alan Sidell: counseling kids, dealing drugs, then going on television and trashing Southwood."

Hughes winds up by reminding the jurors about the FBI search warrant executed at Baywood Hospital four days after the arrival of Charles Trojan. "That TV program was not news to my client. He knew about the FBI investigation. It had been going on for two years. He didn't disguise his writing; he made no attempt to hide his fingerprints. No way in the world could Charles Trojan have thought 'FBI' when he mailed those letters."

Hughes reminds the jury that Trojan has already admitted to count one of the charges: mailing a threatening communication. He asks them to find his client not guilty of the other two charges. The second charge was that of knowingly using the United States Postal Service to deliver any communication that contains a threat of injury to another person with intent to extort money, or anything of value, by depositing in a U.S. Post Office or Post Office box a communication that contains a threat of injury to another person. [Trojan, in mailing the letter to the Schecks, attempted to extort something from them, that is, their personal right to trial, or a lawsuit.] The third charge against Trojan was tampering with a witness: knowingly using intimidation or physical force with intent to injure, or with intent to delay investigation by the federal government or any future communication with federal law-enforcement officers.

Carol Lam makes the closing argument for the government. Her voice trembles with outrage as she talks about the "repulsive letter" that Charles Trojan wrote and mailed to Bob and Merry Scheck. "Out of concern? He writes a letter to the parents of the dead girl telling them that if they don't settle their lawsuit, he will trumpet their daughter's hospital medical records with allegations of molestation. You have learned that Charles Trojan will do anything not to draw attention to himself. He didn't say, in that letter, that *he* would call the media. Oh, no. The *case* would."

And, referring to Trojan's letter to Alan Sidell: "He threatens an ex-employee that 'his life will be stomped out.'"

"How could Charles Trojan *not* have known he was interfering with a federal investigation? He saw the trouble NME was in all over the country. It was all over San Diego that FBI agent Keith Moses was investigating Southwood. The defendant claims he wasn't worried about the Scheck lawsuit? Preposterous. Charles Trojan was CEO of Southwood, and as such he was at least partially liable for what went on there. If the Scheck suit went to trial, all the facts of all the events leading up to the death of Christy Scheck would come to light.

"Charles Trojan made a cold and calculated effort to mail those two letters. There was no moment of remorse: He waited until the FBI had his fingerprints before any admission was made. The evidence proves that Charles Trojan is guilty beyond a reasonable doubt. There is no reasonable excuse for his actions."

In his instructions to the jury, the judge emphasizes that the burden of proof rests with the government: "The government must prove that the defendant specifically intended to threaten. Even if he did not intend to carry out those threats. Your sole task is to seek the truth."

IT IS EARLY afternoon by the time the jurors file into the room where they will deliberate. Mike Pritchard, who has been sitting in the courtroom, joins me for a cup of coffee in a small cafeteria across the square. As Pritchard and I walk down the steps of the Federal Building, a knot of TV and print journalists crowd around Charles Trojan and Peter Hughes. Cameras click and flash and videotape rolls as questions are hurled at Trojan; he shakes his head, again and again: No comment. Hughes takes his upper arm and guides him through the crowd and down the steps.

Bob and Merry Scheck show up in the coffee shop a few minutes after Mike Pritchard and I arrive. They both greet us but neither of them sits down at the table. We are all edgy. Bob decides to take a walk around the square, and Merry moves off to another table. It's clear that she needs a moment to herself. Pritchard and I chat idly for a few minutes, and then he begins to talk about Charles Trojan.

"When I sat there listening to that cold bastard saying he wrote that letter to Sidell because he 'had to' "—Pritchard's voice assumes an operatic tone of overemphasis—" 'let all those good people go,' and that he just couldn't take the stress . . ." He pulls in a deep breath, then puffs it out. "I said to myself, at that moment, 'Trojan, you're an evil, evil man.' "

Charles Trojan was found guilty on count one, mailing a threatening communication. The jury could only agree on the single charge, to which Trojan had already admitted. He was ultimately sentenced to six months in a halfway house in Colorado (where the Trojan family had relocated), a $10,000 fine, and three years' probation.

CHAPTER FORTY-ONE

THE LOS ANGELES offices of Dummit, Faber & Briegleb (Brown is no longer with the firm) take up the fifteenth floor of a building that covers nearly a square block of prime Wilshire Boulevard real estate. One steps out of the elevator and into a reception area in which the murmur of wealth is nearly audible. Paneled walls and hardwood floors are waxed to a gleaming finish; chairs and sofas are upholstered in buttery leather. There are no showy floral arrangements, no magazines splayed out in careful array on tables. It is assumed, perhaps, that those who sit in this room are occupied with more pressing issues.

The windows in Craig Dummit's corner office look out over an impressive chunk of Brentwood. The room itself is less solemn than the reception area: The furnishings here bear the marks of handcraftsmanship, with desk and cabinets of rough-hewn wood sanded and smoothed to an unpolished finish. There are no family photographs in view; what appear to be eighteenth-century legal illustrations hang on the walls.

Dummit is a soft-spoken, sandy-haired man of medium height. His handshake is firm and warm, but the sensation is somehow more about fingers than palm. He gestures toward a chair opposite his, and we begin to chat. I had heard that Dummit sat with Vincent Bugliosi during the murder trial of Charles Manson and two of his disciples, and that Dummit and Manson engaged in staring matches across the courtroom. I ask about that now, and Dummit smiles slightly and nods.

"I clerked for Vincent Bugliosi during the summer before my senior year in law school at USC. In fact, I stayed on with him through late October, then I went back to school."

I mention the O. J. Simpson trial.

Dummit gestures toward the glass wall that separates his office from the main arteries of the firm. "We have an interesting relationship to the Simpson trial. The predecessor to this law firm was Kardashian, Dummit & Agajanian. Bob Kardashian† was our partner when we first started this firm, and he knew a lot of the people at NME. In fact, the predecessor to Kardashian, Dummit & Agajanian was Eamer, Bedrosian & Kardashian.

"When Bob Kardashian was with us in the first few months of the firm, O. J. Simpson was given, by us, a free office to use, next to my office. It was during that time, in fact, that he met Nicole Brown, because I remember seeing her, several times, coming to the office."

He points out a several-storied white building a few blocks to the south. Simpson still keeps an office there, he tells me. And the restaurant, Mezzaluna, where Nicole Brown Simpson ate her final meal, and where Ron Goldman worked as a waiter, is located just at the end of the street below us.

When I ask Dummit if he is comfortable with the way the Scheck case was resolved, he delivers a direct reply: "No."

Craig Dummit is, of course, mindful of the confidentiality terms binding both sides in the settlement, but his impression is that Bob and Merry Scheck were on a crusade after the death of their daughter Christy. "And I don't say that derogatorily, because I might feel the same way if I lost a son or a daughter. But they were definitely on a crusade, and that was one of the unfortunate things about it. The timing of that crusade wasn't real fair to our client.

"To sum up: The way I see the case is a tragic circumstance that did occur. An accidental tragic circumstance, obviously. But it was the result of a whole lifetime of activity that culminated in a tragic accident. And the case was prosecuted as if there was some corpo-

†Robert Kardashian later resurfaced as a member of the O. J. Simpson defense team in Simpson's trial for the murders of Nicole Brown Simpson and Ron Goldman in June 1994.

rate fraud or corporate wrongdoing, and that had absolutely nothing to do with the way the Scheck girl died. But that's where they thought their best evidence was. Where their inflammatory evidence was. And so I thought it was a shame that the case was developed—and publicized—as a case of corporate wrongdoing, when that was the furthest element of what caused [Christy Scheck's] untimely demise."

What about the cases against NME in Texas? In Florida?

"Most of those cases occurred in Texas, which obviously had nothing to do with what was going on in San Diego." Dummit pauses briefly before he speaks again. "For whatever perceived, or actual, or admitted shortfalls there may have been in other areas of the country—or even here in California—it was an interesting time. Because, and it is generally accepted, that NME just got caught doing what everyone was doing." He raps the desk for emphasis. "They got caught first. And they weren't doing anything—to the extent that they were doing *anything* wrong—that everyone else wasn't doing. And the irony was that NME was doing it better than the others. NME was providing better care than the other health care corporations that provided psychiatric care.

"And it's ironic, when you sit back and look at it, that this litigation—some say rightfully, some say wrongfully, so it's really irrelevant—but the litigation did drive NME out of the psych business. And I think the general consensus among the people in the psychiatric business is that it drove out the best providers of psychiatric services at that time. Because a lot of the allegations were based on things—contractual provisions for doctors, for example—that at the time were considered legal by the attorneys who put them together. Then two, three, four years later, there's some administrators and some court cases that cast legal doubt on those contracts. And that's essentially a big part of what National Medical got caught up in. And when the others saw what happened to National Medical, they started getting out real fast. Before they, too, got caught up in the allegations."

When Dummit asks if I have spoken with anyone connected with the San Diego Police Department, I tell him about my short exchange with Michael Duffy and Duffy's implacable belief that Christy Scheck had been molested by her father.

Dummit's lips twitch slightly. "When it was time for Duffy to be deposed, he got so angry at the Schecks' attorney that he stormed out of the deposition, and it was never completed."

I ask what could have triggered such an extravagant response.

"The line of questioning was about Duffy's conclusions to prosecute for child molestation. He got angry that his conclusions and motives were being questioned." Dummit's smile is chilly. "We were sorry to see him leave. He was helping our case." He becomes serious again.

"You know, I found something interesting in working on this case. And we're still working on it in Texas. But especially in [the Scheck] case, a lot of people were scattered all over California when Southwood changed owners. And it was real interesting that everyone who stayed in mental-health care would tell us—unsolicited—that 'You know, I had my problems and my quarrels based on personalities and things like that when I was working at Southwood, but I didn't realize just how high the quality of care was until I went to work for other corporations and companies in the psychiatric field.' "

Dummit pauses, and when he speaks again I cannot be sure if he is still quoting former Southwood staffers or expressing his own opinion. "There just won't be that quality of care again."

EPILOGUE

AT THE END, what we are left with is lawyers' words and phrases: Contractual provisions. Perceived shortfalls. Accidental tragic circumstance. Quality of care.

Bob and Merry Scheck are left with days and months: December, and Christmas. November, with Christy's birthday and Thanksgiving. Halloween, when both girls would put on the costumes Merry made for them and Bob would shepherd them, with other neighborhood kids, from house to house for trick or treat. June 1996, the month in which Christy would have graduated from high school. And, always, March, and the commemoration of Christy's death. A particularly bad day for Merry Scheck is November 12, the day she finally gave in and took Christy to Southwood. Merry still believes that she and Bob did the only thing they could, but the date is there every year as a reminder of the end of all that was balanced in their lives.

And for Bob Scheck, there is the sure, cold knowledge that there will always be someone who believes that he molested his daughter.

The Schecks travel more often now. Last year they took Molly to Florida to visit family, some of whom they had not seen since Christy's death. Both Bob and Merry remain active in parents' programs at Molly's school. Molly made the swimming team last year, and Bob is involved with that.

"But I'm no longer the aggressive, determined father—and person—that I once was," Bob says. "I've become more . . . sensitive, I think. And Molly isn't as strong-willed as Christy was. Molly's the mellow one. Her responses to directions are easier—

she thinks things through." There is a short silence, and when Bob speaks again, his voice is soft. "I'm no longer a positive person. But I know that I'm constantly changing, so I don't know what kind of person I'll become in the future. I only know that I've gone through a metamorphosis, and the final process isn't known yet."

Merry Scheck feels that life is pretty much the same, that everything moves on. "We're able to do a few more things for Molly now. The most noticeable change is how our family communicates. We used to have fun. It's only lately that we're able to communicate with each other with any of our old humor." She reflects for a moment. "But I still wake up in the middle of the night sometimes, with my heart pounding out of my chest. I still get that frightened. And my level of trust for other people is so shaken. It's hard for me to let Molly do even the normal things that kids do. I had such a hard time letting her go away to camp for a week last summer, and that's the kind of thing one normally wouldn't even think about." She sighs softly. "But to trust other people with my child again . . ." She hesitates. "Not that other people *can't* be trusted. I just have to take it one step at a time."

When Bob and Merry are asked if they would ever consider psychiatric hospitalization for Molly should it ever become necessary, Bob says that he would. "But only after an even more thorough investigation than we did before we placed Christy at Southwood. And I wouldn't even think about using any facility in or around San Diego."

Merry has a harder time with the question. "Knowing what I know now, it's a nearly impossible situation to even imagine. I'd have to do a lot of praying, and I'd have to place a lot of trust in God if that situation arose again. Just as I prayed when it was Christy who needed help." She pauses again, and when she speaks her voice is strong and clear.

"I would do everything possible not to have Molly hospitalized. If it came to that, she'd be in treatment every day if necessary, but she'd live here at home, with people I trust, twenty-four hours a day."

Would the Schecks have faith in treatment provided by their original family therapist, Gary Juleen?

Merry's reply is immediate. "Absolutely."

There is one more thought she wants to articulate: "Look, it's not that I'm against the mental-health profession. It's just that, for me, there's a stain on it. There are good people out there; I've seen them. And there are people with good intentions. But good intentions don't count unless they're backed up by knowledge."

BY 1995, UNDER the leadership of Jeffrey Barbakow, National Medical Enterprises had risen, phoenixlike, from its own ashes. In March of that year the company acquired American Medical Holdings (AMH), the parent corporation of American Medical International (AMI), for approximately $1.5 billion in cash and 33.2 million shares of stock. The newly combined company was named Tenet Healthcare Corporation.

The merger with AMI transformed Tenet Healthcare into the second-largest hospital company in the United States, with over $5 billion in revenue for 1995, 1.5 percent of the total hospital industry. Its earnings were surpassed only by those pulled in by Columbia-HCA Healthcare Corporation of Louisville, Kentucky, the leading company in hospital chains: $17.695 billion in revenue, 4.9 percent of the total hospital industry.

According to an independent survey performed by the firm of Donaldson, Lufkin & Jenrette, as of 1996 Tenet Healthcare wholly or partially owned 72 general hospitals with over 15,400 beds. The majority of the hospitals are located in the Southern states and in California. There have been several significant acquisitions, and as a result Tenet now holds a dominant position in key markets such as southern Florida, New Orleans, and El Paso. The company also owns 7 long-term facilities, 5 physical-rehab hospitals, 5 psychiatric facilities, and ancillary facilities that are connected with the general hospitals. A subsidiary, Medical Ambulatory Care, operates 36 kidney-dialysis centers.

Divestiture of foreign holdings seems to be part of the new order for the renamed company. In June 1995 Tenet sold off two hospitals and related health care businesses in Singapore for estimated proceeds of $242.3 million. In October of the same year, Tenet sold its 30 percent interest in Australian Medical Enterprises for $68.3 million. In the third fiscal quarter of 1996, Tenet's 40 percent interest in a hospital in Thailand was sold for $20.8 million, and investment bankers have been engaged to sell the company's 42 percent interest in Westminster Health Care, a chain of nursing homes in the United Kingdom.

Tenet Healthcare stock is currently going for $21.25 per share.

But the old NME battles in Texas are still ongoing. And they may prove to be costly. In a lengthy deposition taken in February 1996 in Dallas County, a former NME/PIA senior vice president testified to having attended operations meetings with other NME/PIA executives in which certain minutes, particularly those related to marketing issues, were "highly sanitized" for a number of years beginning in June 1990. The former executive further stated that certain NME/PIA facilities in Texas offered benefits such as jobs as well as payments to allied mental-health professionals (psychologists, social workers, et al.) in exchange for referrals. This practice, according to the Texas penal code, falls under the heading of commercial bribery and is, aside from being unethical, illegal.

The NME/PIA facilities in Texas accounted for more than 50 percent of the company's profits. According to the 1996 depositions, this was referred to, in corporate meetings, as "The Texas Gravy Train."

But, as attorney Craig Dummit was eager to point out, NME wasn't the only one taking the ride.

On March 2, 1994, the Columbia Hospital Corporation of Houston and several of its mental-health subsidiaries settled a suit brought by the state of Texas for alleged violations of marketing, admitting, and referral practices. The settlement stipulated that "the Defendants admit no fault, or liability, or the truth of any allegations or statements made in agreeing to this Agreed Permanent Injunction and Final Judgement." Nonetheless, a fee of $1.75 million was paid by the defendants to be "designated as attorney fees and/or investigative costs."

On November 30, 1995, attorneys for the Charter Medical Corporation signed an agreement with the state of Texas for a modified permanent injunction. One of the numerous orders in the agreement restrained the Charter Group (as well as its affiliated successors, officers, employees, et al.) from "engaging in any form of print, television, or radio media advertising with respect to the inpatient treatment of any Mental/Nervous Disease or Disorder without conspicuously disclosing that the diagnosis of a need for inpatient treatment can only be made by a licensed physician or psychiatrist."

Other stipulated orders referred to soliciting referral sources; offering the services of Charter employees to Texas public schools where referrals to Charter facilities might be provided without disclosing those employees' affiliation with the Charter Group; offering to renumerate any referral source "based upon the volume or value of referrals made by that referral source to Charter Group or any person associated with Charter Group."

Other orders referred to admitting procedures such as "misrepresenting to any person the availability or amount of insurance coverage or the amount and percentage of any charges for which the patient shall be responsible for purposes of inducing an admission." And "representing to any person who requests to leave a Charter facility against medical advice that if the patient leaves the facility against medical advice, the patient's insurance company will refuse to pay all or any portion of the medical expenses previously incurred." And "admitting any minor under the age of twelve (12) years to a facility for inpatient treatment . . . who has not been evaluated face to face by a psychiatrist who is board certified or board eligible in child and adolescent psychiatry within twenty-four (24) hours prior to the admission."

Added provisions in the permanent injunction included: "Requiring or permitting any employee who is not a licensed mental health professional or a member of the patient's interdisciplinary treatment team to advise, instruct, suggest or induce any physician to order additional treatment procedures or therapies or to refrain from discharging a patient." And "misrepresenting the need for psychiatric treatment of children and adolescents to the State of Texas, and any of its agencies or political subdivisions."

There was a stipulation stating that "this agreement and the consideration transferred pursuant to this agreement shall not be construed as an admission of liability by the Charter Group, but are made to avoid litigation."

Nonetheless, it was further ordered that the Charter Group pay, to the state of Texas, "assessed fees of $1,500,000 in settlement of all its claims relating to any alleged violations" and that "these assessed fees will be designated as attorney fees and/or investigative costs."

As part of the Second Agreed Order Amending Agreed Permanent Injunction, the Charter Group was ordered to provide the following services for children and adolescents in Texas through a service program administered by the Texas state mental health department (TXMHMR): 1,400 bed days of inpatient psychiatric care and treatment based on bed days actually utilized at the discretion of TXMHMR during the period beginning December 1, 1995, and ending November 30, 1996, as well as the period beginning December 1, 1996, and ending November 30, 1997. The bed days were to be provided by eight Charter facilities located in Texas, all of which had been listed as defendants in the injunction. The provision stated, "There will be no distinction in the quality of care that Charter provides to children who participate in this program and those who do not. Charter will provide these services at no cost to the State of Texas."

The Charter Group further agreed "to reimburse TXMHMR

for actual costs of a TXMHMR employee to administer this program up to $73,690 for the two years."

This was not Charter's first brush with trouble. Lawsuits for false imprisonment were filed against two of Charter's Florida facilities at the beginning of the nineties, and in Arizona a Charter admissions counselor filed suit with allegations that she had been fired for failing to admit a patient with 100 percent insurance because the hospital was, according to the files, "filled beyond capacity." The same admissions counselor also alleged that she had been paid a $200 bonus for keeping the hospital filled.

Charter Medical filed suit for Chapter 11 (corporate reorganization) bankruptcy in 1991 after failing to make over $150 million in payments toward a $1.6 billion debt. By 1992 the company was back in business with a first annual report that was vaguely penitent in its sworn fervor for future ethical practices.

And the beat goes on:

On March 29, 1997, an Associated Press item in the *Los Angeles Times* stated that the Columbia-HCA Healthcare Corporation (as it is called, post-merger) faces a federal criminal investigation for possible Medicare fraud. Columbia-HCA is the nation's largest health care company, with 350 hospitals across the country; it must now confront questions about whether it sent out padded bills to the government. Queries will also be raised about suspicions that the company violated a 1992 law barring doctors from investing in medical facilities to which those doctors refer patients. One possible issue is whether Columbia asked its doctors to invest in the hospitals at which they worked when those same hospitals sponsored new home-care and rehabilitation services.

On March 27, two days before the AP report, a "Column One" article by David Olmos appeared on the front page of the *Los Angeles Times*. The piece placed Tenet Healthcare (formerly National Medical Enterprises) at the center of a growing controversy involving two physicians—a urologist and a neurosurgeon—who practiced out of a pelvic-pain treatment center in an obscure little hospital located in a working-class neighborhood in Montclair,

California. The hospital was owned, until 1994, by NME/Tenet. Both urologist Larrian M. Gillespie and neurosurgeon Kenneth P. Burres played leading roles in a highly lucrative marketing scheme that served up large numbers of surgical patients with "generous medical insurance plans" to the pain center. A good part of the marketing strategy involved airline tickets, hotel suites, and chauffeur-driven limousines, all provided and paid for by the hospital. The great majority of the patients were women suffering from pelvic and bladder pain caused by interstitial cystitis and/or vulvodynia, disorders that are difficult to treat. Gillespie's contention was that the disorders were often caused by back and spinal problems stemming from pressure on nerves in the lower back that lead to the bladder and pelvic region. According to leading authorities in the field, Gillespie presented and acted upon this theory without the benefit of credible research.

Nevertheless, patients who had perceived their conditions as hopeless swarmed from all over the country to the Pelvic Pain Treatment Center at Doctors Hospital in Montclair. The surgeries were performed by Kenneth Burres, whose professional history was decidedly checkered. In 1987, fleeing a medical board investigation of several malpractice suits against him in Denver, Burres literally abandoned his practice, medical partner, staff, and patients and went to California. Two weeks later he began work at a Kaiser-Permanente Hospital in Fontana, a job he secured eleven days before he deserted the Denver practice. By 1989, after leaving Kaiser when that company became aware of the charges against him in Denver, Burres went to work at NME's Doctors Hospital of Montclair, lured by a guarantee of "nearly $350,000 a year, including a $96,000 'directorship fee,' and other perks." This in spite of the technical revocation of Burres's medical license for abandoning his practice in Denver and a subsequent suspension of that action for five years' probation. The probation was lifted by the California board in 1994, eighteen months ahead of schedule, by which time Burres was performing spinal surgery with Larrian Gillespie at Doctors Hospital.

According to Olmos's article, Gillespie was recruited to set up the pelvic-pain clinic at the Montclair facility, one of thirty-five general hospitals in the NME chain, in 1991. The hope was that Gillespie could deliver patients and revenue to the hundred-bed hospital and its corporate parent. She was promised that the hospital would spend at least $50,000 to help market her program, pick up the tab for her clinic's operating expenses, and, finally, provide a toll-free number for patients. Gillespie would also receive a $7,500-per-month hospital directorship fee. Gillespie, Burres, and the hospital shared the income from patients' bills, which, aside from an approximate $5,000 for diagnostic tests such as bloodwork and MRIs and a $4,500 hospital fee, could soar as high as $60,000 for each patient undergoing spinal surgery.

Gillespie, who kept another office going in Beverly Hills, presented a rather flamboyant image, arriving daily at the grim little Doctors Hospital in a chauffeur-driven limousine. She once signed a memo to one of the hospital administrators "Your Megabucks Baby, Larrian."

A downward spiral began in 1995 when, after being served with a series of malpractice suits, Gillespie closed her practice. In November 1996, the California Medical Board suspended her license for "repeated negligent acts." Olmos's research showed that "among the board's findings were that in her treatment of four urology patients in 1993 and 1994, Gillespie ordered excessive and unnecessary lab tests, made diagnoses with insufficient evidence and failed to perform routine physical exams."

In February 1997, Gillespie agreed to pay $2.6 million in settlement of the claims against her. But ten other lawsuits in Los Angeles continue against Kenneth Burres and Tenet Healthcare. Burres, at the time of the "Column One" feature, was practicing surgery at Columbia Chino Valley Medical Center in California.

On April 3, 1997, another article by David Olmos appeared on the front page of the *Los Angeles Times* business section, this one about nonprofit health care giant Kaiser-Permanente, "whose success," Olmos wrote, "is closely tied to its reputation for quality health care." However, according to the article, Kaiser's operations in Texas may be shut down due to problems with the quality of patient care as well as a shaky financial status. And in Northern California (the Bay Area in particular), federal and state health authorities are reviewing complaints concerning the deaths of several patients who were treated at Kaiser facilities. Olmos's research showed that "investigators from the California Department of Mental Health Services are reviewing allegations of long delays in patient transfers from a Kaiser hospital in Richmond and inadequate staffing levels at two area hospitals."

Although Kaiser officials have insisted that the wrongful-death cases "have no relationship to quality of care," the California Nurses Association, a labor union, has complained repeatedly that Kaiser's efforts toward cost-cutting have "eroded the quality of patient care."

At a state court hearing on April 1, a Texas Department of Insurance attorney testified that the investigation began as early as January 1996. Approximately twenty wrongful-death lawsuits filed against Kaiser and its doctors over the past several years, which are still pending, were included.

Court papers show that there have been allegations by Texas state regulators that Kaiser "discouraged emergency care and denied payment for services in some cases." The report also stated that Kaiser "violated state law in 13 cases related to 'quality assurance issues,' and that the HMO had inadequate medical oversight, or 'peer review.' "

Kaiser has won a court order blocking the release of the state's investigative report; the company is asking that the report be permanently sealed and that the still-unspecified sanctions be thrown out.

HEALTH CARE FRAUD is estimated to cost American taxpayers upwards of $80 billion a year.

Things are changing in the $400 billion hospital industry. Growing demands for health care reform and an increased sense of cost-consciousness, of just how pricy it is to get sick in America, are concerns that are not about to go away. Hospital care is a rapidly expanding slice of the health care dollar, and the bulk of that burden falls to the federal government. Occupancy rates are dropping, while staffing rates have gone up, creating a scramble among hospital CEOs to rethink strategies. As a result, staffing and services have been reduced. The wave of the future is in mergers and consolidations, and they are increasing at a rapid rate, with minimal interference from regulators.

In April 1994, Aetna Life and Casualty, Inc., announced that it would acquire a Pennsylvania-based HMO, U.S. Healthcare, for $8.6 billion. The new enterprise would provide health care coverage for one in twelve Americans. But many experts agree that the merger will spawn a new generation of for-profit health care leviathans that will ultimately achieve market dominance and lead to an eventual rise in prices. Not even the experts can hazard a guess as to what the quality of care will be. But it is difficult not to think about what Craig Dummit said four years after Christy Scheck hanged herself while on a suicide watch at Southwood Psychiatric Center: "There just won't be that quality of care again."

What if he's right?

NOTES

page 52   "It must be noted that between 1980 and 1985, increases in . . .": The Congressional Hearing before the Select Committee on Children, Youth and Families, April 28, 1992.

page 54   "The case in Texas involved . . .": *Newsweek,* November 4, 1991.

page 55   "There were similar incidents at other PIA facilities . . .": NME Shareholders' Derivative Action No. BC039354 brought by Plaintiffs Harry Polikoff, Harry Ackerman, and Bette Rita Grayson, Derivately on Behalf of Nominal Defendant National Medical Enterprises, Inc., v. Richard K. Eamer; Leonard Cohen; John C. Bedrosian; William S. Banowsky, Ph.D.; Jeffrey C. Barbakow; Bernice B. Bratter; Maurice J. Dewald; Peter de Wetter; Edward Egbert, M.D.; Michael H. Focht, Sr.; Raymond A. Hay; Nita P. Heckendorn; Taylor R. Jenson; Lloyd R. Johnson; James P. Livingston; A. J. Martinson, M.D.; Howard F. Nachtman, M.D.; Richard S. Schweiker; Richard L. Stever; Norman A. Zober; Scott M. Brown; Maris Andersons; Marcus E. Powers; Bruce L. Busby; and Raymond L. Mathiasen, defendants, and National Medical Enterprises, Inc., a Nevada corporation, Nominal Defendant, December 22, 1992.

page 63   "They could see, for example . . .": R. S. Barack, "Hospitalization of Emotionally Disturbed Children: Who Gets Hospitalized and Why," *American Journal of Ortho-Psychiatry,* April 1986; also L. J. Milazzo-Sayre; P. R. Benson; M. J. Rosenstein; and R. W. Mauderscheid, "Use of Inpatient Psychiatric Services by Children and Youth Under Age 18," National Institute of Mental Health (Division of Biometry and Applied Sciences), Mental Health Statistical Note #175 (1986).

page 71   "NME's psychiatric division was bringing in . . .": *The Wall Street Journal,* January 8, 1993.

page 85   "Tricyclic antidepressants have been . . .": Peter R. Breggin, M.D. *Toxic Psychiatry,* St. Martin's Press, 1991; also *Drug Facts and Comparisons* (pharmacists' manual), J. P. Lippincott 1996 (updated monthly).

page 94   "Walker had been employed at Southwood . . .": Deposition transcripts of Brenda Willis-Hughes,* *Scheck* v. *Southwood,* March 26, 1994.

page 95   "Another ethics-compromising practice at Southwood Psychiatric Center involved altering documentation of patients' medical records. . . ." Deposition transcripts of Brenda Willis-Hughes, *Scheck* v. *Southwood,* March 26, 1994. (This information was also included in the testimonies made by Southwood employees to a federal grand jury.)

page 116   "Stuckey stated, in a letter to Jaffe dated September 25, 1991 . . .": Congressional Hearing before the Select Committee on Children, Youth and Families, April 28, 1992.

page 141   "The evaluation stated, among other observations . . .": Deposition transcripts of Bria Altshult,* *Scheck* v. *Southwood,* February 23, 1994. (It was stated, by various staff workers, during their individual depositions, that the psychological evaluation done on Christy Scheck at the time of her admittance to Southwood was not referred to in the course of her treatment.)

page 150   "Although Merry has been able to provide . . . ": Barbara Korda* was unavailable for comment. She is no longer employed as a caseworker by Child Protective Services and they had no forwarding address for her.

page 159   "Shortly after Altshult began her duties on the early-adolescent unit . . .": Deposition transcripts of Brenda Willis-Hughes, *Scheck* v. *Southwood,* March 26, 1994.

page 161   "In response to HMS's attempt to decertify the RTC for CHAMPUS benefits . . .": Southwood/NME memos provided to the author by Michael Pritchard.

page 164   "A 'significant event' was written up by Brenda Willis-Hughes . . .": Chart notations acquired by Bob and Merry Scheck after the death of Christy Scheck.

page 165   "Rebecca Boyle suggested that Christy begin to document her memories of the incidents . . .": Deposition transcripts of Rebecca Boyle,* June 21, 1994.

page 168   "During this time, Bria Altshult wrote up a 'significant event' in Christy's chart . . .": Copies of chart entries acquired by Bob and Merry Scheck after the death of Christy Scheck.

page 204   "On the morning of April 28, 1992 . . ." Congressional Hearing before the Select Committee on Children, Youth and Families, April 28, 1992.

page 217   "In June 1992, less than two months after the congressional hearings . . .": Michael Jonathan Grinfeld, "Damage Control," *California Lawyer,* January 1995.

page 218   "The allegations made against the corporation and the defendants listed in the suit . . .": NME Shareholders' Derivative Action No. BC039354 brought by Plaintiffs Harry Polikoff, Harry Ackerman, and Bette Rita Grayson, Derivately on Behalf of Nominal Defendant National Medical Enterprises, Inc., v. Richard K. Eamer; Leonard Cohen; John C. Bedrosian; William S. Banowsky, Ph.D.; Jeffrey C. Barbakow; Bernice B. Bratter; Maurice J. Dewald; Peter de Wetter; Edward Egbert, M.D.; Michael H. Focht, Sr.; Raymond A. Hay; Nita P. Heckendorn; Taylor R. Jenson; Lloyd R. Johnson; James P. Livingston; A. J. Martinson, M.D.; Howard F. Nachtman, M.D.; Richard S. Schweiker; Richard L. Stever; Norman A. Zober; Scott M. Brown; Maris Andersons; Marcus E. Powers; Bruce L. Busby; and Raymond L. Mathiasen, defendants, and National Medical Enterprises, Inc., a Nevada corporation, Nominal Defendant, December 22, 1992.

page 228   "For the year ending on May 31, 1993, Eamer's total compensation . . .": *The Wall Street Journal,* September 27, 1993.

page 228   "On August 26 more than six hundred federal agents raided . . .": Michael Jonathan Grinfeld, "Damage Control," *California Lawyer,* January 1995.

page 275 "The NME/PIA facilities in Texas accounted for more than 50 percent of the company's profits. . . .": Deposition transcripts of Harvey Friedman (former NME/PIA senior vice president), in *Dorothy A. et al.* v. *National Medical Enterprises, Inc., et al.,* February 13, 1996.

page 275 "On March 2, 1994, the Columbia Hospital Corporation of Houston . . .": Agreed Permanent Injunction and Final Judgement, #94-02407, *State of Texas* v. *Columbia Hospital Corporation; West Houston Health-Care Group, Ltd.; Orlando Depression Center, Inc.;* et al., March 2, 1994.

ABOUT THE AUTHOR

LÉON BING is the author of two
previous books, *Do or Die* and
Smoked. She has a daughter, Lisa, and
lives in Pasadena, California.